German Blitzkrieg Fortificacions in the West and East

Esquina de la Historia Atenas Editores Asociados

La Esquina de la Historia
Atenas Editores Asociados 1998-2017

www.thegermanarmy.org

Tittle:
German Blitzkrieg Fortifications in the West and East
© Atenas Editores Asociados 1998-2017
© Gustavo Urueña A
© Photos Bundesarchiv and others internet sites
More information:
http://www.thegermanarmy.org
First Published: July 2010

Design: Atenas Editores Asociados 1998-2017

© Atenas Editores Asociados 1998-2017
The Editors welcome all comments and observations:
1939europa@gmail.com

This is an editorial project of Athens Editors Asociated based on 20 years of studies and works related to Economy-Politics, GeoPolitics, Social Sciences and the development of Military Science from its beginnings with the Battle of Cannas where under Anibal took place The first blitzkrieg-style confrontation to its use in the Desert Storm Campaign and all the political, economic, and military consequences these events have had on the development of Humanity. The Editor of the same came to the conclusion that to locate in the context of any era of History is necessary to have read about the political, economic and military events of the time under study, in order to draw the appropriate conclusions, thus, if we want to locate ourselves in the history of Greece, Egypt, Russia, Germany, Colombia at any time, we can not judge those events under the magnifying glass of the context of the XXI Century, because that will only give us a distorted view of why events happened as they did.

The editor

Introduction

The Origins of Second World War

BY now there is some degree of agreement among historians as to the sequence of events leading up to the World War of 1914-18. This agreement has been made possible by the vast compilations of diplomatic documents published by the various Powers since the close of that war. Concerning the origins of the present war, however, the belligerent governments have not yet been able to publish such extensive documentary collections. They have, however, issued books of various "colors," in which they seek to present their respective cases by making public the texts of documents taken from their archives.[i] This article attempts to weigh and interpret these documents, with particular attention to the German case.

German Polish Relations before 1933

On November 5, 1916, in the midst of the First World War, Poland was made an autonomous state by Germany and Austria-Hungary. After the collapse of the German Empire in November 1918, Poland became independent and at Versailles received new boundaries which included a considerable amount of formerly German territory. By cutting off East Prussia from the rest of the Reich and by setting up the Free City of Danzig as an independent political organism, a source of conflict was created which, together with the minorities question, eventually made German-Polish relations intolerable and helped cause this war.

The Versailles Treaty also sought to assure just treatment for the German minorities in Poland; but the Poles did not live up to these obligations. Complaints by the German Government, which began in November 1921 and were continually repeated, led to no improvement in the conditions under which the German communities lived. Arbitrary arrests were frequent; Germans were assassinated and the culprits often left unpunished; and German-owned lands were expropriated. As a result of all this there was a large German emigration. But the Weimar Republic, deprived of military force by the Versailles Treaty, was unable to defend German rights against Polish arrogance.

Germany' search for and understanding with Poland 1933-1939

At the beginning of May 1933, the new National Socialist Government made its first attempt to come to an understanding with Poland. But from the very outset it left no doubt that the permanent preservation of peace between the two nations was unthinkable as long as the Versailles boundaries were retained. Also, it refused to recognize that Poland had a special right to Danzig. Nevertheless, in spite of all this, negotiations between the two countries led, on January 26, 1934, to a declaration that in the future they would under no circumstances use force for the settlement of any future disputes (G 37). However, in spite of this agreement, German-Polish relations remained more or less the same as before. On November 5, 1937, Germany and Poland concluded a new agreement for the mutual protection of minorities. But the expected improvement in the condition of the German communities in Poland still failed to take place, and unemployment, especially among the youth, steadily increased. The Germans felt this to be especially hard, since in the Reich Hitler had managed within a few years to put an end to unemployment.

The situation in Danzig demands special consideration. Under the Versailles Treaty, Danzig and its immediate vicinity had been separated from Germany and made into a "Free City" and its external political relations placed under a League of Nations Commissioner. Poland was given certain special economic and transport privileges, while on the Westerplatte, an island at the mouth of the Vistula, she had the right to maintain a fixed number of troops for the protection of a munitions depot. An economic agreement between Danzig and Poland, signed in August 1933, if loyally carried out, might have brought about a lessening of the friction. But the Polish Government, besides building up the purely Polish port of Gdynia, held fast to its expansionist policy toward Danzig, and tried by unjustified tariff policies to deflect commerce from the Free City. Polish propaganda even demanded the annexation of Danzig.

In spite of Poland's intransigent attitude, Germany continued to seek an understanding concerning Danzig and the Corridor. Towards this end the German Foreign Office made certain concrete proposals at the end of 1938. In these, Poland was asked to agree to the return of Danzig and to the establishment of an extraterritorial highway and railway connection across the Corridor to East Prussia. In return, Germany was to give Poland a similar connection with Danzig, and, when the agreement came into effect, definitely to recognize Poland's boundaries.

In the course of these negotiations a meeting took place at Berchtesgaden (January 5, 1939) between the Führer and Foreign Minister Beck of Poland. In friendly terms Hitler explained how German-Polish relations, and in particular the Danzig and Corridor questions, should in his view be regulated. Concerning Danzig, he had in mind a formula "according to which Danzig should become a part of the German body politic but in economic matters should remain with Poland" (G 200). The Polish Foreign Minister promised to think the matter over.

However, Poland's dilatory tactics continued. But before pursuing the German-Polish question, we must turn to relations between Germany and Britain after Munich.

Anglo-German Relations from Munich to Prague

Upon his return from the Munich Conference, Mr. Chamberlain, the British Prime Minister, no doubt fully intended to carry out a policy of peace. But the Conservative Opposition was of a different mind, and Chamberlain was therefore unable to put the Anglo-German rapprochement on a firm basis. Munich was a bud which failed to blossom. The tension created by Italy's claims in the Mediterranean compelled Chamberlain to speed up the pace and volume of the British rearmament program. Furthermore, as early as October 1938, Hitler found himself obliged, as a result of statements by British politicians about the fate of German citizens inside the Reich, to protest against London's attitude of "governess-like guardianship." The Reich, he said, did not bother itself about similar matters in the British Empire -- referring to events in Palestine (G 219).

On January 30, 1939, Hitler emphasized in a speech to the Reichstag that National Socialist Germany and Fascist Italy were strong enough to win any conflict frivolously caused by irresponsible persons. Germany, he said, had no territorial demands to make on England and France, except the return of her colonies. There was not a single German, especially no National Socialist, "who had any thought of making difficulties for the British Empire" (G 241). In February and March he delivered other speeches of a similar import.

To sum up, the causes for the growing tension between the Axis Powers on one hand and Britain and France on the other were: the rivalry between Italy and France in the Mediterranean, which indirectly made Anglo-German relations worse; the exaggerated notions about Germany's expansionist aims in Southeastern Europe; and the difference in *Weltanschauung* represented by the British and the National Socialist Governments.

Prague

The tension was sharply intensified when, in the middle of March, Czechoslovakia fell to pieces after the declaration of independence by the Slovak legislature. Hitler therefore

put an end to the untenable situation in Bohemia and Moravia by joining them to the Reich under a Protectorate.
The Czechoslovak President, Dr. Hacha, "in order to assure quiet, order and peace," trustfully laid the fate of the
Czech people in the hands of the Führer. The Czechs were
promised "an autonomous development of their national
life in accordance with their character" (G 260). The text
of the agreement of March 15, establishing the new relationship between Berlin and Prague, was at once forwar-
ded with explanations to England and France (F 69). Britain thereupon suspended negotiations for a trade pact
and the British Ambassador, Sir Nevile Henderson, was called to London to report. The English and French Governments also entered formal protests against Germany's action in Czechoslovakia as being illegal and contrary to the
Munich Agreement (F 70, 76; B 10). The Germans rejected
these protests with the observation that they lacked "all
political, legal and moral foundation" (G 262). In this connection it might be pointed out that, in answer to a question in the House of Commons, the Undersecretary of State for Foreign Affairs declared that according to his knowledge the Communiqué of Munich "contained no such declaration" that Hitler had promised, with reference to the
Czechoslovak State, to negotiate with the British Government (G 259, 264).

The significance of the German occupation of Prague lies
not so much in any pretended disregard of the Munich
Agreement or in an abandonment of political principles on
Hitler's part as in the fact that Chamberlain took it as an
occasion for making a fundamental change in his policy --
by actively interfering in the German-Polish affair through
the granting of a British guarantee to Poland. Chamberlain
revealed his thoughts in a comprehensive speech at Bir-
mingham on March 17. In this he made a detailed defense
of his Munich policy, which he said had saved peace in Europe. He remarked very aptly that even if England, instead

of signing the Munich Agreement, had gone to war and after frightful losses had been victorious in the end, "never
could we have reconstructed Czecho-Slovakia as she was
framed by the Treaty of Versailles" (B 9). (If one applies
these phrases to the Polish question, one perceives the futility of the present war.) He went on to say, however, that
the annexation of Czechoslovakia belonged in a different
category and that it raised several questions: "Is this the
end of an old adventure or is it the beginning of a new"
one, was it not in fact only another step in Germany's attempt "to dominate the world by force?"
Now the proceedings in Prague constituted neither an old
nor a new adventure, but merely a further revision of the
Versailles and St. Germain Treaties -- a revision which,
despite Hitler's previously expressed opinion to the contrary, had now proved to be necessary. To try to construe
from this a breach of promise on Hitler's part would justify
making the same reproach of Chamberlain, made in the
"German White Book," for his declaration of war on Germany on September 3, 1939. Chamberlain's words about
Germany's attempt to dominate the world by force gave expression to an old fear of Conservative circles in England
that "a consolidated territory in the East under German he-
gemony would, after consolidation, throw itself with its
whole strength against England" (G 275). Here was the same English fright at spectres that had found expression in
Arthur Nicolson's report to Sir Edward Grey in March
1909, during the first Balkan crisis.[ii] This notion, absurd
as it is, was deeply rooted in the Foreign Office at London
and in it lay the precise cause of the wars of 1914 and 1939.

The Negotiations with Poland March 1939
After Prague, English diplomacy began feverishly to meet
Germany's imagined plans for world domination by exten-
ding the British system of alliances -- the old method of en-

circlement. London wanted a Four Powe

England, France, Poland and Russia (G 2)
Hitler, on the contrary, sought to come tu ...
land by negotiation. On March 21, Ribbentrop tried to convince Mr. Lipski, the Polish Ambassador in Berlin, that
Germany and Poland should conclude an agreement on
the basis of Germany's well-known terms: the return of
Danzig to the Reich, an extraterritorial railway and highway connecting the Reich and East Prussia, and a German
guarantee that the Corridor should remain Polish. In order
to make clear to Lipski the urgency of the affair, Ribbentrop proposed that the Ambassador make a trip to Warsaw; otherwise, he said, Hitler would get the impression
"that Poland simply was not willing" (G 203).
But the Polish Government had little intention of negotia-
ting on this basis, as was indicated on March 24 when it
called up reservists (G 204). In order to understand Poland's intransigent attitude, one must keep in mind that
England was then seeking to create a Four Power Pact in
which Poland was to join. Instead of following up the German proposals, Lipski, at another interview with Ribbentrop on March 26, delivered a memorandum from his Government in which it refused to consider the proposal by
which extraterritoriality was to be granted to German
transportation lines across the Corridor, though it offered
them certain traffic facilities (G 214). As for Danzig, the
Polish memorandum proposed a joint Polish-German guarantee. After taking note of this communication, Ribbentrop declared that since the position taken by the Polish
Government "could offer no basis for a German-Polish solution," the Führer could not regard its proposals as satisfactory. "Only a clear reunion of Danzig, an extraterritorial
connection with East Prussia, and a 25-year non-aggression pact with boundary guarantees" could, he declared,
lead to a definite and clear understanding (G 208).

On the same day, in the formerly German town of Bromberg in the Corridor, outbreaks occurred which were organized by the Polish West Association and in which cries of
"Down with Hitler," "We want Danzig," "We want Koenigs-
berg" were heard. Ribbentrop therefore on the following
day declared to the Polish Ambassador that these new in-
sults had made a catastrophic impression in Germany.
Further, he added that he could not understand why the
Polish Government had rejected Germany's generous proposal and that a Polish *coup de force* against Danzig would
be a *casus belli*. Lipski replied that he was willing to do
everything in his power to overcome the difficulties (G
209).

On March 29 Beck told Moltke, the German Ambassador
in Warsaw, that a unilateral attempt by Germany to change the Statute of the Free City, or an independent action by
the Danzig Senate, would be regarded by Poland as a *casus
belli* (G 211). Beck sought to justify Poland's mobilization
measures by pointing out that, after what had happened to
Czechoslovakia and Memel, the Poles had come to regard
Germany's Danzig demands as an alarm signal. Moltke re-
minded Beck of the proposals made by the Führer in January at Berchtesgaden, and pointed out that the present
ones merely aimed at putting German-Polish relations on
a sound basis (G 211). With this interview German-Polish
negotiations came to a temporary halt.

On March 31, Chamberlain came forward openly as Poland's protector. He declared in the House of Commons
that his Government had no confirmation for the rumors
that Germany was planning an attack on Poland, but that
in the event of any action which threatened Polish independence and which the Polish Government considered it
necessary to resist with its national forces, the British Government would feel bound "to lend the Polish Government all the support in their power" (B 17). The French Government undertook the same commitment. This, of cour-

se, meant the definite end of Munich, for England had become Poland's partisan. As was to be expected, Britain's action only increased Poland's intransigence.

On April 6, a communiqué issued by the British and Polish Governments announced that they had decided to replace their existing unilateral assurances with a reciprocal agreement. Pending the conclusion of this agreement, Poland promised to render assistance to England under the same conditions as those contained in the assurance already given by London to Warsaw (B 18). On the same day, Lipski informed Secretary of State von Weizsaecker that Poland wished to preserve the 1934 agreement with Germany. The Anglo-Polish accord, he said, was a bilateral, purely defensive arrangement; there was no question of Poland's joining a bloc (G 212). Weizsaecker expressed his astonishment that Poland had not taken up Hitler's generous offer, and pointed out that the Anglo-Polish accord, the terms of which to be sure were not yet known, was incompatible with the German-Polish Agreement of 1934. To this Lipski replied that the Franco-Polish Alliance, dating from 1921, had not been regarded as incompatible with that Agreement (G 213).

April 28, 1939

Britain's guarantee to Poland, and the failure of German-Polish negotiations over Danzig and the Corridor led the German Government to draw up two memoranda. These were handed to the Polish and British Governments on April 28 at the same time that their contents were being made public by Hitler in a speech to the Reichstag. The memorandum to Poland, after reviewing the efforts of the National Socialist Government to come to terms with its eastern neighbor, stated that the Polish Government, having rejected the opportunity to settle the Danzig question and having undertaken obligations towards another state (England) incompatible with the German-Polish Agreement of 1934, had thereby deliberately and unilaterally voided that document. Nevertheless, it continued, the German Government was ready to enter a new agreement provided it were based on a clear obligation binding on both parties (G 213, 214, 294, 295; B 21, 22).

In its memorandum to the British Government, the Reich declared that Britain had shown, by her recent policy and by the attitude of her press, that she regarded preparation for a war on Germany as the principal problem of her foreign policy; and that by pursuing this "encirclement policy" the British Government had removed the basis for the Naval Agreement of June 18, 1935, which was therefore no longer in force (B 22).

As for Hitler's speech, insofar as it dealt with England it expressed deep resignation. During his whole political career, he said, he had always expounded the idea of Anglo-German friendship, an idea founded on the belief that the continued existence of the British Empire was in the interest of mankind. He had never made any mystery of the fact that he regarded England as an invaluable element in the world's cultural and economic life, and that the colonizing work of the Anglo-Saxon people aroused his "sincere admiration." However, his respect for this achievement could not obscure his duty to protect the interests and aspirations of his own people. Nor did he fail to recall that Germany herself had once been a great empire. In concluding, he expressed his regret that the English people were of the opinion that, no matter in what conflict the Reich might be involved, "Great Britain would always have to take her stand against Germany." He deeply deplored this because, after all, his only demand on England was the return of the former German colonies--and this, he declared, could never become a cause for Germany's going to war with England (G 295; B 21).

Germany, England and Poland: August 25

In a speech delivered on May 5, Beck rejected Hitler's proposals of April 28. At about the same time anti-German demonstrations took place in Thorn, Katowitz, Lodz and Posen (G 349-417). On May 12 the German community in Poland presented a respectful petition to President Moscicki reviewing the old complaints concerning church and school questions as well as the dismissal of German factory workers -- again with no result. A few days later the German Consul in Lodz reported that German workers had been driven out of certain factories by a Polish mob, that all German places of business and private dwellings had been systematically demolished, and that the police had done nothing to prevent it. Reports from the German Ambassador in Warsaw also revealed that the "German Houses" in Bromberg, Lodz and Tarnowitz had been expropriated and that in seventeen cases the German clergy had been mistreated or their church property destroyed.

These outbreaks were the result not only of racial hatred but of Polish propaganda. It was, for instance, widely believed in Poland that crowds of famished German soldiers were daily deserting across the border, that the German war *matériel* was of doubtful value, and that German foreign policy had suffered one defeat after another. Even among the Polish intelligentsia the relative strength of Germany *vis-à-vis* Poland was completely misjudged. Nor did the failure of the Anglo-Polish loan negotiations dampen the bellicose ardor of Polish opinion.

In July, a slight lessening of the tension in Danzig seemed possible, but by the beginning of August the situation had become extremely critical. In particular, conflicts arose between Warsaw and the Danzig Senate over the question of customs administration (B 42). The Polish Government had notified the Danzig Senate, in a communication which took the form of an ultimatum, that the Danzig authorities must not interfere with Polish customs officials in the execution of their duties (B 43, 46; F 181, 193). When the Reich Government learned of this, it informed Warsaw that a repetition of such peremptory demands on the Danzig Senate, coupled with the threat to use force, would only aggravate German-Polish relations (G 445). Poland sharply rejected this intervention as without legal justification, and informed the Reich that she would regard any interference by it in Danzig "as an aggressive action" (G 446). This statement, made on August 10 by the Polish Undersecretary for Foreign Affairs to the German Chargé d'Affaires in Warsaw, created a very serious situation (G 447; B 47).[iv]

On the evening of August 15, a hectic conversation took place in Berlin between Weizsaecker and Sir Nevile Henderson, in which they were unable to reconcile their widely divergent points of view in regard to the Polish situation. In a later conversation Henderson declared that if Germany used force, England would do likewise. Weizsaecker tried to impress upon him the German view that Poland's attitude was such that the British Government was freed from any obligation "to follow blindly every eccentric step on the part of a lunatic" (B 48). He went on to say that Beck, in his last parliamentary speech, after having "sat himself like a Pasha on the divan," had announced that if Germany accepted the Polish thesis he was ready within these limitations graciously to receive proposals (G 450). Weizsaecker expressed his confidence that Russia would join in sharing the Polish spoils. In reply, Henderson again reiterated that British intervention was inevitable if Poland were attacked (B 48). This conversation showed that England was no longer master of the situation.

The action which the British Government undertook in Warsaw to postpone or prevent the conflict between Germany and Poland consisted in having Lord Halifax, Secretary of State for Foreign Affairs, instruct its Ambassador to

Poland, Sir Howard Kennard, to beg the Poles to avoid giving Hitler a pretext, to moderate their press campaign against Germany, "to intensify their efforts to prevent attacks on their German minority," and in the future to deal with Danzig questions through the mediation of the High Commissioner. Halifax further stated in these instructions that the Polish Government, "provided essentials can be secured," would do well to declare its readiness "to examine the possibility of negotiation over Danzig if there is a prospect of success." The British Ambassador was instructed to consult with his French colleague before talking to Beck (B 50).

In view of the state which affairs had reached by this time, such a cautious *démarche* on the part of Britain could not cause Poland to change its policy toward Germany. The Poles must have been aware that the Allies' negotiations with Russia would fail and that Poland, as their only reliable ally in Eastern Europe, could therefore command a high price. At this stage tension might have been relaxed only if England had come to a general political understanding with Germany. But this would have meant Britain's dropping Poland so that Germany could have revised the Versailles Treaty by direct negotiations with Warsaw.

On August 15, Weizsaecker also talked about Poland with the French Ambassador, M. Coulondre. The State Secretary said he could not understand why France should regard her aid to Poland as "automatic and a matter of course." Coulondre sought to explain that French policy was identical with the maintenance of the balance of power in Europe. If Poland were to be overrun by Germany, he said, one could foresee that France's turn would come next. France, therefore, could not agree to put pressure on Warsaw (G 449; F 194).

Exchange of letters between Chamberlain and Hitler

After the announcement of the non-aggression pact between Germany and Russia, the English Cabinet decided on August 22 to pass the Emergency Powers [Defense] Bill. On the same day Chamberlain sent a letter to Hitler in which he spoke of the approach of war and suggested postponing the discussion of the German-Polish problem until a better atmosphere could be created. He also declared himself ready to examine with Germany the larger international problems of the future and to stop the press polemics. But he stressed Britain's determination to fulfill her obligations to Poland. He did this, he said, in order that the tragic misunderstanding of 1914 would not occur again (G 453, 454; B 56). This letter was discussed the following day at a conference between Hitler and Henderson at Berchtesgaden. The British Ambassador observed that in England it was recognized that Anglo-German coöperation was necessary for the wellbeing of Europe. Hitler replied that this ought to have been recognized sooner. Henderson declared that England must stand by her guarantee to the Poles and that she was only opposing the principle of force. Hitler's rejoinder was merely to remind Sir Nevile of Versailles (G 455).

In his answer to Chamberlain, Hitler, after once more stating his views without adding any essentially new points, concluded by remarking that throughout his life he had always fought for Anglo-German friendship, but that British diplomacy had convinced him of the futility of such a policy. Should the future bring any change in this respect, nobody, he said, would be happier than he (G 456; B 60).

On August 25, Hitler saw Henderson again and told him: that the Polish provocations had become intolerable; that Germany was determined to put an end to the "Macedonian conditions" on her eastern frontier; and that the problem of Danzig and the Corridor must be solved. After this had been done, he said, he was determined once more to approach England with a comprehensive offer. He accepted the British Empire and "pledged himself personally for its continued existence" if his colonial demands, which could be negotiated by peaceful methods, were fulfilled. He did not ask that England give up her obligations toward France, any more than he intended to give up his toward Italy. He also emphasized Germany's determination never again to enter into conflict with Russia. And he declared that he was ready to accept a reasonable limitation of armaments which would correspond to the new political situation (G 457; B 68).

On this same day the assurances which had already been exchanged between England and Poland in March were signed in a mutual assistance treaty (B 19; G 459).

Exchange of letters between Hitler and Daladier

On August 25, Hitler begged the French Ambassador to tell Daladier that he would very much regret a war between Germany and France. He felt no hostility toward France, he said. He had renounced Alsace-Lorraine and had recognized the Franco-German border; but, he said, he would "reply by force to any further provocations." Coulondre assured him that Poland would be given reasonable advice, but that in case the Germans attacked that country, France would be found on Poland's side (F 242). On August 26, Daladier sent Hitler a personally-signed telegram, in which he emphasized that France would live up to her obligation to Poland; at the same time he promised to make every effort to bring about a peaceful solution (F 253; G 460).

In his answer of August 27, Hitler recalled how he had succeeded in getting rid of the most intolerable provisions of the Versailles Treaty without shedding blood. He then sought to clarify Germany's position in the Corridor question by comparing Danzig with Marseilles, and concluded with the observation that a war of destruction between

Germany and France would be very painful to him. But, he said, he saw no peaceful means by which he could persuade Poland to pursue a course acceptable to Germany (F 267; G 461).

Climax of the Crisis

Hitler's reply to Chamberlain's letter and his statements to Henderson were answered in a memorandum which the latter handed the Führer late on August 28 (B 74; F 277; G 463; H 39). The British Government declared in this memorandum that it could enter into discussions for an Anglo-German understanding only after the differences between Germany and Poland had been settled. It once again stressed England's obligations to Poland and asserted that any German-Polish agreement must be guaranteed by the other Powers. The British Government stated that it had already received "a definite assurance" from Poland that she would negotiate upon the basis of such a guarantee, provided that "Poland's essential interests" were safeguarded. But this was not true, for in reality there was only an "intimation by the Polish Government" that it was ready to hold conversations (G page xv; B 73, 74).

In his interview with Henderson on the twenty-eighth, Hitler declared himself ready to negotiate with any Polish Government that really had the country under control and was reasonable. But he could not, he said, repeat his generous offer of March, for now he desired the return of Danzig and the Corridor, together with the rectification of the frontier in Silesia. The British envoy maintained that Hitler must choose between Britain's offered friendship and his own excessive demands on Poland. When Henderson remarked anew that it was not merely a question of Danzig and the Corridor but of Britain's determination to meet force with force, Hitler excitedly insisted that in the Rhineland, Austria and Sudetenland he had succeeded in finding a peaceful solution without using force and intimated that the Polish problem could likewise be settled pacifically if only Poland were not given encouragement by outside Powers. With this observation Hitler struck to the very core of the problem. In response to Henderson's question as to whether he was willing to negotiate directly with the Poles, Hitler declared that he could reply only after a careful examination of the British note, and that he would at once talk with Göring about it (B 75).

On August 29, Chamberlain delivered an important speech in the House of Commons, in which he said that Berlin had been given clearly to understand that England would fulfill her obligations to Poland (B 77). At about 7 p.m. on the same day, the Führer handed to Henderson his answer to the British memorandum. In this he called attention once again to Poland's negative attitude toward the March proposals, as well as to the maltreatment and persecution of the Germans living in Poland. The German Government therefore demanded the return of Danzig and the Corridor, and the safeguarding of the existence of the German national groups in the territories remaining to Poland. It declared that the British proposal that Germany's differences with Poland be settled by negotiation unfortunately could not be accepted unconditionally. It had attempted to negotiate, but had received no encouragement from Warsaw. Nevertheless, impressed by the prospect of a treaty of friendship with England, Germany would accept the proposal that direct conversations be initiated with Poland, on the understanding that the Soviet Union, with which Germany had signed a non-aggression pact on August 23, should participate in any rearrangement of Polish territory. The German Government disclaimed any intention of touching Poland's vital interests and was ready "to accept the British Government's offer of their good offices in securing the despatch to Berlin of a Polish Emissary with full powers. They count on the arrival of this Emissary on Wednesday, the 30th August 1939." Corresponding proposals would be immediately worked out for an acceptable solution, and, if possible, placed at the disposal of the British Government before the arrival of the Polish negotiator (G 463, 464; B 78).

In his interview with Hitler, Henderson had got the impression that the Führer's desire for good relations with England "was undoubtedly a sincere conviction" (H 44). When Henderson remarked that the demand for the arrival of a Polish plenipotentiary by August 30 sounded like an "ultimatum," he was told that this stipulation had been made only in order to emphasize the urgency of the matter. The plenipotentiary would "naturally" be received in a friendly manner, and the discussion would be conducted on a footing of complete equality (B 79, 80; F 291, 293). When Henderson tried to indicate the difficulty of getting a Polish negotiator to Berlin by the thirtieth, Hitler declared that "one could fly from Warsaw to Berlin in one and a half hours" (B 82). During the night of the thirtieth Halifax informed Henderson that the German note would be carefully considered, but that it would be unreasonable to expect England to produce a Polish representative in Berlin on that very day (B 81). The British Ambassador conveyed this message to Ribbentrop about 4 a.m. In a despatch to Halifax, Sir Nevile nevertheless recommended "that the Polish Government should swallow this eleventh-hour effort to establish direct contact with Hitler" (B 82).

In Warsaw, however, the German proposal was held to be impossible. The Poles declared they would sooner fight and perish than submit to such humiliation. The British Ambassador in Warsaw remarked very correctly that Poland would not agree to the present proposals, which went beyond the March terms, because she could now rely on the support of Great Britain and France (B 84).

At about 5:30 p.m. it was reported from Warsaw by telephone that general mobilization had been ordered. This made Poland's attitude quite clear (G 465). Halifax informed Henderson about 7 p.m. that, though he assumed the German Government was insisting on the despatch of a Polish representative to Berlin with full powers, he could not advise the Polish Government to comply with this procedure. He therefore recommended inviting the Polish Ambassador in Berlin to accept the German proposals for transmission to Warsaw (B 88).

On August 30 about midnight, Henderson was in a position to give Ribbentrop the full text of the British reply, in which a futile attempt was once more made to spin out the business heedless of the acute tension then prevailing (G 466, Appendix 1; B 89). In the discussion which followed the delivery of this note, Henderson once more recommended that Germany open negotiations with Poland in the normal diplomatic way. In reply Ribbentrop confined himself to complaining that the only result produced so far by British mediation had been that Poland had ordered general mobilization. Since a Polish negotiator had not arrived in Berlin, he said, the German proposals were no longer relevant. However, in order to show Henderson what Germany had intended to propose to the Polish representative, Ribbentrop read him, in the German language and somewhat more rapidly than Henderson would have wished, the comprehensive German proposals. Henderson's request that he be given a copy of the document was refused, because it was "now too late," no Polish emissary having arrived at Berlin by midnight. A final suggestion by the British Ambassador that Ribbentrop should give the proposals to the Polish Ambassador was likewise rejected. These proposals, consisting of 16 points, included: the return of Danzig to the Reich, a plebiscite in the Corridor, the establishment of provisional transit facilities to East Prussia across the Corridor, an exchange of populations in case after the plebiscite the Corridor should return to the Reich, the arrangement of special rights for Danzig and Gdynia, and the regulation of the rights of minorities. Acceptance of these proposals was to be immediately followed by de-mobilization (G 466, Appendix 2; B 92, 98; F 336).

Henderson at once informed Lipski concerning the princi-pal German points and explained that so far as he had co-rrectly grasped them "they were not on the whole too un-reasonable." Lipski promised to transmit the proposals to his Government (H 55, 56). Coulondre, with whom Hen-derson had communicated during the night before seeing Ribbentrop, was also of the opinion that the Polish Go-vernment should consent to send a plenipotentiary. He thought, however, that a place near the frontier ought to be chosen for the negotiations.

Poland's attitude toward Germany's demands and Britain's mediation suggestions is indicated only indirectly in the British and French documents. During the night of August 30, Lord Halifax directed the British Ambassador in War-saw to transmit the above-mentioned British note to the Polish Government. Halifax characterized as unreasonable the most essential point of the German demands -- i.e., that a Polish representative should arrive in Berlin that sa-me day. He also informed the Polish Government that the Germans were now working out proposals on the basis of which a decision must be taken (B 90). This information, however, conflicted with Ribbentrop's position, made known later, that these proposals had been withdrawn sin-ce no Polish representative had appeared within the stipu-lated time (G 466; B 92). Beck promised a comprehensive reply to this British communication by noon of the next day.

But at that hour a further message from Lord Halifax rea-ched Warsaw directing Kennard to propose, along with his French colleague, that the Polish Government accept the principle of direct negotiations. In a subsequent telegram Halifax requested that the Polish Government inform the German Government through its Ambassador in Berlin that the latter was ready to transmit any proposals to the

Polish Government for examination and to make suggestions regarding early discussions (B 95). On the afternoon of August 31, Beck handed Kennard a note containing the views of the Polish Government. This communication, however, limited itself to outlining a *modus procedendi* for an immediate exchange of views with the German Government, and therefore came too late (B 97). The British Ambassador urgently advised Beck to direct Lipski immediately to put himself in touch with Ribbentrop or Weizsaecker (B 96). Late in the evening of August 31, Henderson was directed by Halifax to inform the German Government that the Polish Government was taking steps through its Ambassador in Berlin "to establish contact" with the German Government (B 99).

Halifax telegraphed to Warsaw that he did not see why the Polish Government should feel any hesitancy about authorizing its Ambassador to accept a document from the German Government, and that he earnestly hoped that it would modify its instructions to him. A refusal to receive proposals "would be gravely misunderstood by outside opinion," he asserted (B 100). Lipski meanwhile called on the German Foreign Minister about 6:30 p.m., but this visit did not diminish the tension because, not being empowered to negotiate, he could only declare that Poland was giving the British suggestions favorable consideration (G 468).

War with Poland

In the last days of August countless small fights, principally around customs houses, occurred along the German-Polish border. Because of these incidents and because of Poland's unreadiness to negotiate, the German Army invaded Poland early in the morning of September 1. On that same day, Hitler delivered a detailed speech to the Reichstag in which, after tracing the origins of the conflict, he specified Germany's aims and declared that he would not wage war on women and children (G 471).

Entrance of England and France in War

On September 1, Henderson handed Ribbentrop a note stating that the British Government would fulfill its obligation to assist Poland if Germany did not immediately withdraw her troops from Polish territory. In reply, Ribbentrop pointed out that regular and irregular bands of Polish troops had raided German territory, that Poland had been acting provocatively toward Germany for months, and that he had waited in vain for a Polish negotiator even for a whole day beyond the limit originally set (B 110, 111; G 472). An hour later the French Ambassador handed a similar note to the German Foreign Minister (F 345; G 473). Meanwhile the German Army continued its invasion of Poland.

After two days, at 9 a.m. on September 3, Henderson presented a British ultimatum, declaring that no reply had yet been received to Britain's demand that Germany should immediately withdraw her troops from Polish territory. Unless a satisfactory assurance to the above effect were given by the German Government not later than 11 a.m. -- that is, within two hours -- a state of war would exist between the two countries as from that moment (B 118; G 477).

Since no reply was forthcoming within the time set, at about 11:15 a.m. the German Chargé d'Affaires in London was handed a note of which the last paragraph contained Great Britain's declaration of war on Germany (B 118; G 478). Fifteen minutes later Ribbentrop handed Henderson a note declaring that the German Government and people refused "to receive, accept or indeed fulfill ultimatum-like demands from the British Government." It further stated that without the interference of Britain, Germany and Poland would certainly have found a reasonable solution in which the rights of both parties would have been respected. It also gave the reasons why the British Government must bear the responsibility for the calamity which had now overtaken so many peoples (G 479). At 12:30 p.m. the French Ambassador had a short interview with Ribbentrop in which, after discussing Mussolini's mediation proposal,[v] Coulondre handed over a note stating that France would, as from 5 p.m. on that day, fulfill her treaty obligations to Poland (G 481; F 367).

Conclusion

The incidents that led to the outbreak of the war arose from the unfortunate form given to Poland's frontiers at Versailles. It was only natural that after Germany had again grown strong, she should seek to remedy the intolerable conditions along her eastern border. The right course would have been for the Western Powers themselves to have sponsored a just settlement of German-Polish problems. Instead of that, however, they fortified Poland in her opposition to change, and made it impossible for Germany to secure her aims by negotiation.

The antagonism between England and Germany was only a secondary cause of the war. The primary causes were the exaggerated notions that prevailed in various countries concerning Germany's policy of economic expansion towards the Southeast and the tension between France and Italy over Mediterranean questions. This latter factor must not be neglected, merely because the relevant documents have not as yet been published. Up to Munich, Chamberlain was on the right path, and had found in Henderson an excellent second. But after Munich, the British Prime Minister fell under evil influences which again brought England, and France with her, into conflict with Germany. In the late winter of 1939, just as Franco-Italian tension was relaxing, came the German occupation of Prague. This event gave English policy a new orientation that made a

European war inevitable.

One cannot escape the conclusion that Germany's annexation of Czechoslovakia and the settlement of the Danzig and Corridor questions in the way intended by Hitler, need not have caused Britain and France to involve Europe anew in a general war. Just as the Austro-Serbian hostilities might have been localized in 1914, so in 1939 it should have been possible for Germany and Poland to settle their difficulties by themselves. Only as a result of the interference of the Allies did a relatively unimportant conflict in Eastern Europe develop again into a great war.

Notes

[i] In this article the relevant documents will be indicated parenthetically in the text by the following symbols: G, for the Second German White Book; B, for the British Blue Book; and F, for the French Yellow Book. The figures refer to the document numbers. The symbol H refers to the "Final Report of Sir Nevile Henderson" of September 20, 1939 (London, His Majesty's Stationery Office, 1939) Cmd. 6115.

[ii] Alfred von Wegerer, "Der Ausbruch des Weltkrieges, 1914." (Hamburg: Hanseatische Verlagsanstalt, 1939) v. I, p. 49.

[iii] See also the report of Lukasiewicz to Beck of March 24, 1939 (*The New York Times*, March 30, 1940), from which it appears that Poland had little inclination to adhere to this pact, because she did not have sufficient confidence that English assistance would be forthcoming in a crisis. This document was among those reportedly found by the German authorities in the Polish archives after the capture of Warsaw.

[iv] In 1909 the Serbs had sent the Vienna Government a similar note, which Sir Edward Grey characterized as "sha-

meless" and which caused England to withdraw her support from Serbia, thereby putting an end to a crisis which had brought Europe to the brink of war. *Cf.* Wegerer, *op. cit.* v. I, p. 48.

[v] This mediation proposal failed because England insisted that Germany must withdraw her troops from Poland before the conference suggested by Mussolini could take place.

German Blitzkrieg Fortificacions in the West and East

France's World War II era fortifications date back to the close of the Franco-Prussian War in 1871. After the humiliating defeat and harsh peace terms that resulted in the loss of the province of Alsace and a large part of Lorraine, the French government and military establishment resolved to fight to restore the lost territories and national honor. Until the time for "revenge" came to pass, the French High Command decided to erect a strong defensive barrier to prevent any further intrusions that might lead to another embarrassing episode.

While the French statesmen busied themselves forging alliances, the military rebuilt the army and began establishing a series of fortifications to protect vulnerable areas and major economic centers. General Raymond-Adolphe Sere de Rivieres was charged with the creation of a series of fortified rings linked together by a line of isolated forts. The most important of these rings were those of Verdun and Toul, and Epinal and Belfort. Others went up at Lille, Maubeuge, Langres, Dijon, Besangon, Grenoble, Briancon, and Nice. In addition, a number of isolated positions were established between most of these fortress rings. In most cases, Sere de Rivieres positioned the guns in open positions but placed the supporting facilities, such as the magazines, in protected locales. He used narrow and/or rear facing courtyards to reduce the vulnerability of the exposed facade to high-angled fire and surrounded his forts with dry moats or fosses with coffres at the corners of counter scarps, covering them with infantry weapons.

By the mid-1880s, Sere de Rivieres' forts-many far from being finished-became virtually obsolete, like most of the European fortifications of the period. This sudden disaster, called the "Crisis of the torpedo shell" by French historians, was caused by a new high explosive that triggered the development of more effective and destructive artillery shells. Beginning in 1881, the new chrome-tungsten steel shells were able to crack cast-iron armor.

As a result, between 1889 and 1914, profound changes took place in the field of military architecture. Many forts had to be redesigned and those in the final stages of construction had to be altered. After 1889 the French perfected a nickel-steel armor that could stand up to the new ammunition. They also reinforced their concrete with steel, producing a ferro-concrete that could withstand bombardment from the new shells. Other nations responded with similar developments, although methods for pouring concrete and the use of reinforcement varied from country to country. The French used metal rods near the interior and exterior edges of their concrete to prevent it from cracking badly.

In the key Sere de Rivieres forts, the vulnerable open gun positions were replaced with artillery turrets. Machine-gun turrets supplanted the vulnerable infantry positions on top of the forts. The *Casemate de Bourges,* usually containing two gun rooms for 75-mm guns, was developed to protect the forts' flanks. Some of the older forts received and maintained cast-iron Mougin turrets for 155-mm guns. Only the key forts between Belfort and Verdun were equipped with the new steel 75-mm gun turrets. Fixed steel turrets or *cloches* meant primarily as observation posts were installed in many forts. Many of the features of these defenses would persist in the period between World Wars.

Before the end of 1914 the French lost confidence in the ability of their forts to resist the new heavy German artillery that had devastated Fort Manonviller and the Belgian forts.. Manonviller, an old fort built in the late 1870s and modernized several times, was equipped with a variety of gun turrets. It served as an isolated French border fort, becoming an easy target for the new German heavy artillery in August 1914. When the Germans turned their attention towards Verdun in 1916, launching a massive offensive, they found a fortress ring that had been largely disarmed.

Three factors of this campaign would play a key role in shaping the future French fortifications. The first was the fall of Fort Douaumont to a few bold German soldiers, who quickly overpowered the skeleton garrison. It took the French army several months to recapture its own fort, after it had endured heavy bombardment and bloody close fighting before surrendering with most of its components still functional. The second factor was Fort Vaux's spirited resistance, despite the loss of its only 75-mm gun artillery turret before the battle, and eventual surrender, caused by weaknesses in its design. The third factor was the successful performance of the intermediate work of Froideterre. Its new design, consisting of dispersed positions, reduced its vulnerability to enemy artillery and assured its effectiveness. After the Great War, France was left with a large air force and tank force that foreshadowed the future in warfare. [1]

However, aircraft and tanks, which were offensive arms, lost their popularity in the post-war peace, a period of military retrenchment for the France. Having lost a \s~hole generation to the war, France was disenchanted with all things military. Thus France began to reduce the size of its armed forces and its High Command concluded that its best course would be to take a strong defensive stance. The crippling effects of the Versailles Treaty on their enemies notwithstanding, the French military leaders feared a resurgence of German military power. France's occupation

---

[1] The fort had the following armament: 2 old cast iron Mougin turrets with 2 x 155-mm guns each; 2 new disappearing steel turrets with 2 x 155-mm guns each; 2 new disappearing steel turrets with 2 x 57-mm guns; 1 new disappearing steel turrets with a machine gun; two 80-mm guns in open position; six 220-mm mortars; four 150-mm mortars; 12 machine guns

of the Rhineland could only be expected to keep the Germans in check until the end of the 1920s. The main object was to create a barrier to protect the recovered provinces from a future German invasion. The design and layout of these new works was the subject of much discussion among the military planners in the early 1920s.

The outcome was that the government approved the creation of the Maginot Line, which would later be erroneously described as a giant "concrete trench".

The Maginot Line

When completed the Maginot Line consisted of three major sections: The Maginot Line Proper, the Maginot Extension, and the Little Maginot Line. [2] The original Maginot Line on the Northeastern Front included the Maginot Line Proper and the Rhine Defenses. The Maginot Line Proper was divided into two Fortified Regions (Regions Fortifiees or RF) that included the RF of Metz and the RF of La Lauter. Between the two RFs the Sarre Gap, devoid of heavy defenses, relied on a system of inundations. Along the Rhine, from the vicinity of Haguenau and Seltz, a system of light fortifications known as the Rhine Defenses extended up the river to the Swiss border.

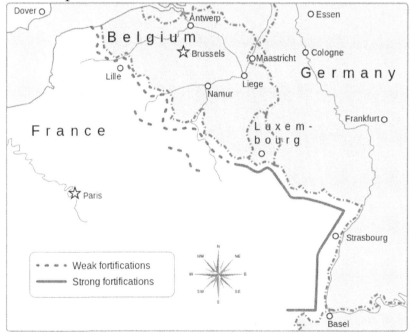

The Maginot Line Proper spanned a variety of terrain. The RF of Metz began near Longuyon in a hilly mining region

---

[2] These names were not applied to these sections before the war, but were adopted after the war for convenience's sake.

of Lorraine, made a semi-circle around the previously German-fortified industrial town of Thionville, and continued on to the edge of the Sarre Gap near St. Avoid. This RF covering Lorraine occupied a largely wooded plateau region. The Moselle River cut through it as it meandered from Metz to Thionville and on to the German border. These defenses covered about 75 km.

At a lower elevation than the RF of Metz, a number of small lakes and ponds occupied the Sarre Gap. This sector spanned about 25 kilometers from the vicinity of St. Avoid to the east bank of the Sarre River near Sarralbe. Although this region is seldom marked on maps because of its small size, it has served as a major invasion route throughout history. The Germans had passed through it in the Franco-Prussian War in 1870. Since the terrain was not favorable for the building of subterranean fortifications, the French opted to create a defended water barrier here. The RF of La Lauter ran from the east end of the Sarre Gap to a point near the Rhine. On a simple map of the region this RF appears to be similar to the RF of Metz. However, it contained a smaller number of fortifications and it did not constitute a continuous line because of the terrain. The Vosges creates a major natural barrier and is more heavily wooded and dissected than the plateau of Lorraine. This RF was divided into two large fortified sectors. [3]

----

[3] Surface block 3 of the gros ouvrage of Rochonvillers. Maginor Line, France

One of the major sections of the RF extended between the Sarre Gap and a point east of Bitche, where the Vosges becomes heavily wooded. At the other end of the difficult sector of the Vosges, which was about 20 km wide, began the next set of heavy fortifications that continued to a point where the mountainous terrain met the Rhine Valley. The plain created by the Rhine was covered by lighter defenses that extended up to the river itself.

The Rhine defenses, which stretched from a point down river from Strasbourg all the way to the Swiss border, were over 120 km long. They were not part of the Maginot Line Proper and included no large fortifications except older pre-twentieth century forts. The defenses covered the low terrain of the Rhine valley, the river bank, and the line of villages behind it. To the rear, the Vosges afforded a formidable barrier. The Rhine-Rhone Canal also formed an obstacle to the rear of the river line. A gap in the Vosges, to the northwest of Strasbourg, between Saverne and Sarrebourg, afforded easy passage. There was another gap near the end of the Rhine Defenses, the Belfort gap, between the Vosges and Jura Mountains. Plans were made to build a third RF and further fortifications in this area but did not materialize.

Maubeuge and the Maginot Extension

A limited number of fortifications along the Northeastern Front, on the Belgian border, were also set up. However, no continuous line of major defensive positions existed between Longuyon and the North Sea. The industrial city of Lille sat astride the border, making the defense of the area around it rather difficult, especially since the low terrain of Flanders was not favorable for underground works. The old forts of Maubeuge, which defended a major invasion route that passed through Liege and Namur in Belgium, were modernized. The Maginot Extension, about 20 kilometers long, was linked to the main line by a small, 30 km-long area defended by smaller works. Part of a newer building program, it was designed to expand the line of defenses towards Sedan to block a possible German invasion through southern Belgium, via Luxembourg. It was separated from the Maginot Line Proper by a small defensive sector that relied mainly on the rough terrain for its defense.

The Little Maginot Line (The Alpine Defenses)

The Little Maginot Line spanned an area greater than the Maginot Line Proper, but its fortified lines actually occupied slightly less territory. In fact, almost half of the Alpine line had no fortifications, due to the forbidding nature of the terrain. This line included four major fortified positions: the first covered the city of Modane and the valley leading to the Mount Cenis Pass, the second guarded Briancon and the pass of Montgenevre, the third protected Barcelonnette, and the fourth shielded the Larche, Pourriac, and Per passes. Finally, an almost continuous line of fortifications defended the Maritime Alps and ended on the Mediterranean, spanning about 60 to 70 kilometers. In addition, a smaller position covered the Little St. Bernard Pass, near Bourg St. Maurice, at the northern end of the Alpine sector. [4]

Coast Defenses

The most important of France's inter-war coastal defenses were built on the southern tip of Corsica to defend against an Italian invasion force crossing over from Sardinia. France also created other coastal batteries in the 1920s and 1930s at key ports and had completed some modern works by 1939. The major coastal defenses guarded French harbors such as Toulon, Marseilles, Brest, and Cherbourg. Most were designed to cover the approaches to the harbors and included forts on dominating terrain overlooking the area and on islands controlling the approaches. Many of

[4] Casemate de Dambach Nord – The frontage

the French coastal batteries, some dating back to the eighteenth and nineteenth centuries, were later incorporated into the German Atlantic Wall.

History

After the Great War, the French High Command took a closer look at the forts of the Verdun ring, finding a number of disquieting flaws such as a lack of gas protection and proper ventilation under heavy fire. On the other hand, the old forts also had some strong points in their favor, such as the retracting turrets and the Casemates de Bourges, which had proved their worth in combat. Forts Douaumont and Vaux had demonstrated that the forts needed better infantry positions and interior defenses. Despite emphatic disclaimers on the part of the French, it appears that the German Feste, acquired with the return of Metz and Thionville, had a decided influence on the architects of the Maginot Line.

Before the Ministry of War finally made a decision regarding the type of fortifications to build, a disagreement arose between Marshal Philippe Petain and Marshal Joseph Joffre. In March 1920, the Minister of War, Andre Lefevre, directed the *Conseil Superieur de la Guerre* to make a study of the defensive needs of the new eastern frontier. In 1922, the War Ministry formed the *Commission de Defense du Territoire* (Commission of Territorial Defense) under the leadership of Joffre to further examine the problem. Joffre suggested building strong fortified positions like the ring of Verdun, but Petain insisted on lighter defenses supported by a *pare mobile de fortifications* (mobile park of fortifications), which could reinforce any sector and give depth to the defenses. Other commission members such as General Louis Guillaumat, Marshal Ferdinand Foch, and General Marie Debeney, who replaced a member of Petain's faction who had died in 1923, finally opted for two heavily fortified regions. In deference to Petain, a compromise solution was suggested; the defenses would form a continuous line.

In 1926, the War Ministry created the *Commission de Defense des Frontieres* (Border Defense Commission) under General Guillaumat, which prepared the plans for the new defensive system. At the end of the year the commission recommended three RFs on the Northeastern Front, but the third, the RF of Belfort, was soon eliminated. The commission recommended the creation of several Fortified Sectors (SFs) on the Southeastern Front to defend the likely invasion routes through the Alps. Most of the initial work for the new fortified line was undertaken by Minister of War Paul Painleve and his administration. When Andre Maginot replaced Painleve in 1929, the work was finally set into motion. The new defenses were given the name of the hero of Verdun, who was then in charge and had vigorously endorsed their creation. The Maginot Line was first planned and designed to act as a temporary shield that would hold the enemy at bay for several weeks, giving the army time to mobilize. However, early in the 1930s the original concept underwent a significant modification. The new fortifications would no longer serve as a temporary front, but would stop the enemy from advancing.

Maginot urged that the new line be completed before the French army was scheduled to withdraw from the Rhineland in 1935. By the time he became War Minister, the government had moved the pull-out date to 1930. The legislature appropriated a huge sum for the construction work in January 1930. However, by the time the line was completed the cost had soared to more than double the amount originally appropriated.

In *1927,* the *Commission de Defense des Frontieres* set up the *Commission d'Organisation des Regions Fortifiees* (Commission for the Organization of the Fortified Regions or CORF) to prepare the designs for various types of fortifications. General Fillonneau, the Inspector General of Engineers, was nominated president of CORF. He appointed other officers to the commission, including representatives of the artillery and the infantry. General Belhauge replaced Fillonneau in 1929, before the actual construction began, and directed CORF until its dissolution in 1935.

In 1928 work began on Rimplas in the Alps, the first fort to be built. This led to CORF making many design changes. Full scale construction work on the Maginot Line's CORF-designed installations began in early 1930. The main priority work was on the Maginot Line Proper and the Rhine Defenses, which later were designated as the "Old Fronts" after plans were drawn up for "New Fronts." As Hitler ascended to power in 1934, a new sense of urgency arose in France for the completion and expansion of the fortifications. Unfortunately, Marshal Petain, who was the Minister of War at the time, did little to help their cause when he declared that the Ardennes were "impenetrable." In 1935, his successor began to work on the "New Fronts." By 1936, the government authorized new funds to improve the Southeastern Front when Mussolini's war with Ethiopia led to the creation of the Berlin-Rome Axis.

The military considered using new 145-mm guns with a range of about 29 km in turrets and the 340-mm naval guns from the *Normandie* Class battleships. However, these plans were indefinitely postponed, making the 75-mm gun the largest gun to be used.

The Maginot Line went on active duty in 1936, when the Germans reoccupied the Rrdneland. After this crisis a number of problems, such as the organization of the garrisons and defects of design, became apparent. Since the New Fronts had not been completed by the time, and much work still needed to be done on the Maginot Line Proper and the Southeastern Front, it was possible to resolve most of these problems during the last years of the decade.

Nonetheless, a planned stop line behind the main line was never adequately completed and the linkage between the forts and the outside electrical power grid remained unfinished. Some of the weapons for the ouvrages, such as the 25-mm guns for machine gun turrets and 60-mm mortars for special bomb throwing cloches, were also not ready for installation either when the war began. Despite these shortcomings, both the Northeastern and Southeastern Fronts of the Maginot Line and their forts were practically ready for action by September 1939.

The task of protecting France's coast was turned over to the navy in 1917. However, a plan for the reorganization of the coastal gun batteries was not formulated until 1922 and was revised in 1926. The program called for the installation in concrete emplacements of artillery from warships headed for the scrap heap. These weapons included the mostly obsolete 75-mm, 138-mm (Mle 1910), 164-mm (Mle 93-96), and 194-mm guns as well as the old 220-mm cannons. Many, especially the light weapons under 138-mm caliber, were placed in open positions with light armored shields and 360 degrees of fire.

The navy also intended to use the 305-mm guns from two older classes of battleship slated for the scrap heap, but their equipment turned out to be unsuitable. Instead it ordered the newly-designed twin gun turrets from Schneider, Mle 1924, for mounting the 340-mm guns in coastal positions since the quadruple turrets of the *Normandie* Class battleships were not practical for land installations. Key ports received these new batteries during the 1930s.

Characteristics

The Maginot Line

The Maginot Line included two Fortified Regions (RFs): the RF of Metz and the RF of La Lauter. Each RF had several Fortified Sectors (SFs).

The RF of Metz consisted of:

SF of La Crusnes   3 gros ouvrages, 4 petits ouvrages, 36 casemates, 5 observatories, and1 abris

(4th Brigade)

SF of Thionville   7 gros ouvrages, 4 petits ouvrages, 17 casemates, 4 observatories, and 18abris.

(3rd Brigade)

SF of Boulay   4 gros ouvrages, 8 petits ouvrages, 14 casemates (including 2 artillery), [5] 2 observatories and 14 abris.

(2nd Brigade)

SF of Faulquemont   8 petits ouvrages and 16 casemates (including 3 artillery)*.

(1 st Brigade)

The RF of La Lauter consisted of:

SF of Rohrbach 1 gros ouvrages, 4 petits ouvrages, 18casemates and 3 abris.

(7th Brigade)

SFoftheVosges 3 gros ouvrages, 1 petit ouvrage, 35casemates (including 3 artillery),* 19 blockhouses, observatory, and 7 abris.

(5th Brigade)

SF of Haguenau   2 gros ouvrages, 37 casemates, 2 observatories, and 15 abris.

(6th Brigade)

The Defensive Sector (SD) of the Sarre, which occupied the gap between these two RFs, did not include any of the standard types of positions found in the RFs, except for four small artillery casemates. The sub-sectors of Kalhouse and Bining, which were part of the New Fronts built after 1935, joined the older sub- sector of Legeret to form the SF

---

[5] The artillery casemates noted above were built shortly before the 1940 campaign and were not part of CORF's original plans. They mounted either one or two 75-mm guns. Some of these were also found on the New Fronts.

of Rohrbach, of the RF of Lauter.

Each SF was organized as a fortress brigade consisting of one active fortress infantry regiment and one artillery regiment. The SFs consisted of three or four sub-sectors. On mobilization the regiments quickly expanded into three regiments with the addition of reservists. At that time, a whole fortress infantry regiment would occupy each sub-sector. During mobilization, as the brigade expanded, an additional artillery regiment was formed, one or two battalions of which was assigned to each sub-sector. After September 1939, the SFs were dissolved. Some, mainly those outside of the Maginot Line Proper, were formed into fortress divisions.

The Maginot Line Proper consisted of a thin line of blockhouses and casemate positions with barbed wire and anti-tank obstacles. The ouvrages, which formed the backbone of its defenses, were far better built than the forts of Verdun, but their fire-power was not much different. The French classified the larger works as *ouvrages d'artillerie* (artillery ouvrages) or *gros ouvrages* (big ouvrages) and the smaller as *petits ouvrages* (small ouvrages). The former wielded the firepower of the Maginot Line while the latter, usually lacking artillery, were supplied with infantry-type support weapons.

The RFs consisted of an almost continuous line of ouvrages that covered each other with fire. The ouvrages also received support from, and in turn gave support to, the interval casemates and observatories. The abris, or infantry shelters, acted as command posts and service positions for the regiments occupying the sectors. In many cases the petits ouvrages were placed between gros ouvrages to cover gaps. In a number of places there were no artillery forts because they were not completed as originally planned and were transformed into petits ouvrages instead. This happened especially in the SFs on either side of the Sarre Gap and the SF of Haguenau on the right flank of the RF of La

Lauter. The Sarre Gap was defended by positions that were mostly not designed as part of the permanent fortifications. The distinctive feature of the SD of the Sarre was its network of dams designed to create and maintain water reservoirs whose water would be released to flood the surrounding area. Most of these dams had their own defenses. In front of the main line of defenses was an advanced line of light positions whose mission was to give early warning and delay an enemy advance. This line of *avant-postes* (advanced positions) usually consisted of small concrete structures for automatic weapons that, in many cases, also included road barriers and other obstacles. Fortified houses were located in this forward line, or probably even closer to the border. They usually stood in towns along the routes of advance from Germany. These houses varied in style, often consisting of a concrete bunker surmounted by a residential-like structure. In other instances, the residential structure was attached to a bunker on one of its ends, or was sandwiched between two bunkers.

In the Maginot Line itself, the main line ouvrages occupied key terrain. CORF selected and/or designed all the positions and components of the ouvrages, casemates, abris and special blockhouses. Interval positions were placed to cover lines of advance and relay information to the forts. The interval casemates and most of the casemates of the ouvrages were oriented for flanking fires so that they could support each other. They were also designed to engage the enemy in close combat and thus were not equipped with heavy artillery.

The artillery ouvrage had a number of standard features, even though no two forts were identical. Each ouvrage consisted of two parts; the combat section and the support section. The combat section included several concrete blocks, normally of two levels, that came in several types and usually had one main function. The block types included casemate positions, turret positions, and a combination of both. In addition, each block functioned primarily as an infantry or an artillery position. In most cases the entire block was covered with earth and rock with the exception of the casemate weapons positions. Most blocks also sported a small non-movable turret, known as a cloche, that became the trademark of the Maginot Line. [6]

The casemate blocks could be classified under two basic types, according to their function. The first was the infantry casemate position, which usually mounted a single 47-mm anti-tank gun. However, those positions built before these weapons came into production, held a smaller 37-mm anti-tank gun. The anti-tank gun shared a firing embrasure with a water-cooled twin machine gun, known as jumelage de mitrailleuse or JM. The infantry casemate sometimes had and additional position for JM or a single automatic rifle, known as *Fusil Mitrailleur* or FM.

Along the fagade, in front of the weapons crenels, a small

---

[6] AM Cloche

moat known as *fosse diamant,* served as a receptacle for shell casings and the gases of expended ordnance and concrete debris off the fagade caused by artillery and bomb hits. Its function was to keep the firing embrasures from being blocked. A grenade launcher, or *lance-grenade,* ejected small grenades into the fosse to prevent the enemy from crossing it and attaching explosives to the embrasures. The *fosse diamant* was a standard feature on all casemates.

On the roof of the infantry casemate could be found one or more cloches that provided small-arms and mortar fire in all directions. The firing rooms were located in the upper level of this type of block, above a rest area. The roof of the infantry casemate normally consisted of 3.5 meters of concrete with an earth covering that could resist 420-mm artillery. In addition, the rear-facing wall was usually about 1.75 meters in thickness so that it could be breached by friendly heavy artillery if the position had to be recaptured.

The second type of casemate block was the artillery casemate, which usually mounted three 75-mm guns. As'in most casemates, its exposed facade faced to the rear and its firing chambers were angled so that the guns covered an angle of approximately 45 degrees to the flank. Some artillery casemate blocks featured a single 135-mm howitzer-like weapon, a special type of weapon with the characteristics of a mortar and a howitzer, known as a *lance-bombe*. Other types of artillery blocks normally mounted a pair of 81-mm mortars, but these were usually at the lower level and fired out of the fosse. Each artillery block usually had an M-3 magazine-not found in infantry blocks-equipped with a set of overhead rails that hauled ammunition cases in and out to the firing chambers.

In most infantry and artillery casemates, armored air vents attached to the wall drew air into the block's filter-room. In some of these blocks, an emergency exit allowed access to the surface and was used for patrolling the fort's super-structure. More commonly, however, the emergency exit opened into the fosse from the lower level. This exit was sealed by an armored door and was covered by an interior firing position for small arms. The length of the fosse was usually covered by an FM crenel. The turret blocks also came in two categories, according to their function: infan-try turret blocks and artillery turret blocks. They included no more than one turret but could have several cloches. Most also had a small armored air vent that drew air into the filter room. Used air was normally expelled through the cloches. A *monte-charge,* or small lift, carried ammu-nition up to the turret. The turret-similar to the earlier models-had more armor, rotated 360 degrees, and eclipsed. Both eclipse and rotation operations could be car-ried out manually as well as electrically in all turrets. Dif-ferent types of turrets were used for machine guns, 81-mm mortars, 135-mm howitzers and 75-mm guns. At a later date, turrets that combined different types of weapons were added to the inventory.

The infantry turret block, included one of three types of turrets: a machine gun turret and two types of mixed-arms turrets. The machine gun turret mounted a JM. Plans were made to add a 25-mm gun at a later date, however, this gun was not ready for mounting until the onset of the 1940 campaign. The mixed-arms turrets were developed for the New Fronts.

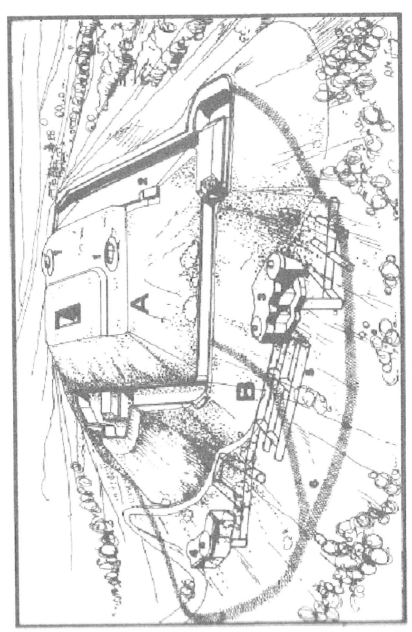

One type mounted two JMs, each with a 25-mm gun. The other had two machine guns with a 25-mm gun. It also had a 50-mm mortar that fired through the roof even when the turret was retracted. The mixed-arms turret also included a periscope for observation. The turret was usually located in a commanding position above the block to give maximal fields of fire. [7]

The largest turrets were located in artillery turret blocks for 75-mm guns. Like the machine gun turrets, they stood on a slight concrete rise that facilitated direct fire. The 135-mm howitzer and 81-mm mortar turrets sat in a small concrete depression to reduce their silhouette since these weapons used a high trajectory. The shells from the 75-mm gun and 135-mm howitzers were returned to the lower level in turrets and casemates through a funnel or hopper known as an *entonnoir,* into a toboggan, ending in a storage area inside the fort. All the artillery turrets mounted two weapons, but only the 75-mm turret had an observation position. In addition to the turrets, the ouvrage had cloches that came in several types and sizes. The GFM *(Guet* and *Fusil Mitrailleur* or observation and automatic rifle) was the most common type. It came in various sizes but normally had three or four crenels and special mounts for an episcope, an FM, and a special 50-mm breech-loaded mortar. Most cloche types also had a roof mounting for a small observation periscope. Access was by a ladder, but in most cloches the floor could also be raised and lowered. The cloches served as an exit for the fort's filtered air. The rush of air leaving the block made such a din that it

---

[7] Fort Suchet and Gros Ouvrage of Barbonnet in Alps. Fl Suchet

1. Turret with 2 x 155-mm guns
2. Observation position = 3O of Barbonnet
3. Block 2 artillery casemate with 2 x 75-mm gur
2 x 81-mm mortars, and 1 GFM cloche and 1 Lance Grenade cloche
4. Entrance - Block 1 with 1 cloche
5. Caserne
6. Anti-Infantry Obstacles

was difficult to hear in cloches, besides being drafty and uncomfortable. The greatest weakness of these cloches was that they usually towered above the block, and, unless they were heavily camouflaged, they were quite vulnerable to direct enemy fire.

The JM cloches mounted a pair of machine guns that covered a limited sector across the fort's surface. These cloches had a small observation position on each side of the JM crenel. They were usually placed flush with the roof of the block and presented a smaller target than other types of cloches.

A special type of mortar cloche was designed for many of the blocks. It was flush with the surface and consisted of a special breech-loaded automatically fed 60-mm mortar. The purpose of this cloche was to shower the block's surface and surrounding area with bombs. These cloches, called *cloches lance-grenade,* were never ready for use because their weapon was not perfected. In addition to the GFM cloches for observation, CORF designed special observation cloches that mounted no weapons. One type had narrow observation slits and a small roof periscope. The other type was flush with the surface and mounted a huge periscope that rose above the ground. When not in use, the periscope was lowered and the cloche opening was sealed with an armored covering. Some ouvrages had special observation blocks exclusively endowed with these special cloches. In this case, the command post was usually situated below the observation block. In each combat block the crew, whose number varied from twenty to forty men, slept in a special rest area situated at the lower level. These men were rotated back to the service area in shifts, but during the war many simply preferred to stay in their block rather than haul their gear back and forth. Each block had a filter room, rest area, storage for small arms ammunition, latrine facilities, and a stairway connecting it to the subterranean level of the fort. Some of the smaller blocks-those for observation only that had just a single cloche or weapons position-did not always have these features. However there were few of this type in the Maginot Line Proper. Most artillery blocks had a chamber for an M-3 magazine and elevators for .'.auling ammunition from the subterranean gallery to the combat level.

The underground gallery "system was situated below most of the blocks, especially the artillery blocks, at a depth of twenty to thirty meters, depending on the terrain. The gallery system consisted of secondary access tunnels that connected the combat area to the main gallery, which was normally at a depth of about thirty meters.

Additional facilities for the artillery blocks were located in the tunnels below, and included a machine room for operating the elevators, an M-2 magazine for maintaining a larger supply of ammunition for the guns above, and a room for expended shells. The access tunnels were usually sealed off from the main gallery by a set of armored air-pressure doors. In the majority of the ouvrages the main command post was located near the main gallery together with offices for the artillery, infantry, and engineer commands and a communications room. Telephone lines linked the command post to all parts of the ouvrage and order transmitters were found in the firing chambers of the gun rooms. In only a couple of ouvrages was the command post situated at a level between the subterranean works and the combat blocks.

A power sub-station, located near a point where the combat area of the fort began, received electrical power from the service area. Its transformers and converters stepped *down* the power for redistribution to the combat blocks and other facilities. The power lines and the communications wires ran back to the service area along the main gallery. With few exceptions, the ouvrages had a rail system that connected the service area to the access tunnels through the main gallery. This was necessary since the length of the main gallery between the combat and service areas was up to 500 meters long, and the distance between the entrance block and the most distant combat blocks could easily exceed 1,000 meters. The train engine normally operated only in the main gallery, where it received its power from overhead cables and carried almost exclusively supplies and ammunition. The troops had to walk, or in the case of larger forts like Hackenberg, they were supplied with folding bicycles. At one or more points the main gallery was sealed off by armored doors designed to halt any enemy soldiers that might penetrate that far. In addition, **at** several points along the gallery there were special explosive-filled niches that would block the gallery when detonated. There were even internal blockhouses in a few of the forts.

All galleries had a slight incline so water could flow out of the fort through a drain located beneath the floor, which emptied at the side of a hill. Most drains were large enough for a man to crawl through and could serve as an emergency exit. A weapons position covered the length of the drain. The main gallery was usually wide enough or two sets of tracks near the EM, but the secondary tunnels only accommodated one set of tracks. Most ouvrages were also provided with a secret emergency exit that was invisible from the surface because its upper chamber was filled with sand. When this sand was released into an empty room below, it allowed the men to enter the upper chamber and climb a ladder to the surface.

The main gallery began in the service area, near the entrance block. The gros ouvrages normally had two entrance blocks: one for the munitions called *entree des munitions* or EM, and one for the men, called *entree des hommes,* or EH. The EM was a large block that faced the rear and contained one or two firing chambers for antitank guns, JM and FM like the infantry blocks. The roof of this block usually had two GEM and a lance-grenade cloche.

A diamond fosse protected the exposed [8]face of the block in front of the weapons crenels and the entrance. A perma-

---

[8] Combat block 1 at the fortress Limeiln (ouvrage Four-à-Chaux, Alsace), showing signs of German testing of explosives inside some fortresses between 1942 and 1944

nent concrete bridge spanned the narrow fosse and a heavy iron grating barred access to the entrance tunnel. The grating was covered by a firing position for an FM at the end of the tunnel, adjacent to a heavy armored door. In front of the armored door and weapons position was a sliding bridge over a deep pit, known as a tank trap. This arrangement was standard for EMs designed for train cars of a narrow-gauge military railroad and for trucks. Those entrances that were not designed for railroad use had a slightly different design. Trucks and rail cars could be off loaded behind the armored doors, where the small train cars of the ouvrage awaited. This unloading area was defended by one or two interior blockhouses located in front of a second armored door leading to the main gallery. Depending on the elevation, access to the main gallery was either direct, by an incline using a special engine to move the cars at an angle, or by elevator. The incline was considered to be the most desirable for the EM, while the elevator was preferred for the EH.

The EH was smaller than the EM and had an "L" shaped entrance, a narrower entrance corridor, and no tank trap. A removable metal bridge spanned the fosse and the armored door sealed the end of the "L" shaped entrance, out of the direct fire of the enemy. In a few ouvrages a single entrance was used both for supplies and men and was called *entree mixte* or mixed entrance. It resembled the EM rather than the EH, which was too small for the protected unloading and movement of supplies.

The service area housed the *caserne,* or barracks area, and associated facilities. The caserne was designed to accommodate about.one third of the garrison. It included showers, latrines, a large filter room, a well, water storage, kitchen, storage rooms for food stocks and wine off the kitchen, an infirmary and, more often than not, a small detention area. The larger ouvrages also had an operating room and a dentist's office. Since there was no mess hall, the troops had to eat in the corridors, on shelves attached to the walls. The officers, however, were allowed the luxury of rheir own mess area. Electric heaters kept the temperatures in the caserne at comfortable levels.

In addition, the service area normally contained the *usine,* or engine room. In the gros ouvrages it held four diesel engines, two of which were used to maintain operations and the remaining two were kept in reserve. These engines supplied the fort's electrical needs. The fumes from the usine were expelled into the fosse of an entrance block, through special escape vents. In rare cases, when the usine was too far from the entrances, a special chimney block had to be built. Associated with the usine were the fuel and water storage areas, the converters, the transformers, and a work room. In peacetime or prior to combat, power arrived from the National Grid by underground cables after leaving a special fortified military sub-station by aerial cables.

Another important feature of the service area were the magazines. The M-l, or main magazine, was usually located near the EM. It had smaller annexes for fuses and other types of explosives. Most ouvrages had an M-l, except Schoenenbourg, one of the most prominent exceptions, which had a special M-l/M-2 magazine near its combat blocks. To protect the rest of the ouvrage from the effects of accidental explosions, special protective measures were taken. They included a sprinkler system and curved access galleries to deflect the force of the explosion. In addition, the main gallery could be quickly sealed by a special seven ton armored door that was designed to slam shut automatically in the event of an explosion.Finally, the service area housed workshops and garages for the maintenance, repair, and storage of the underground train located in the main gallery.

The surface of the ouvrage was protected by wire and anti-tank obstacles. Normally, the service and combat areas were surrounded by separate sets of obstacles. However, in some cases the individual blocks were similarly protected. The antitank obstacles consisted of several rows of rails embedded at various heights which connected most of the ouvrages. In the few ouvrages with two separate sets of combat areas, each set was covered by these obstacles. In some cases an anti-tank ditch and/or wall ran between the two areas and covered their individual blocks as well.

Originally, plans for the ouvrages called for encircling moats, but these turned out to be too expensive, especially during a period of economic depression. As a result only a few small sections were actually built, as mentioned. There were no mine fields because the French had not developed anti-personnel mines, but some anti-tank mines and booby-traps (anti-personnel) were implanted. The petits ouvrages were similar to the gros ouvrages but they had fewer combat blocks, and the few that had artillery mounted no more than 81-mm mortars. A number of petits ouvrages had originally been planned as gros ouvrages but were not completed as such. In most cases, their mission was either altered or became more circumscribed.

The few petits ouvrages that had a separate entrance block either had a very small entrance for men, like Lembach, or a mixed entrance, like Immerhof. This entrance was smaller than the EM of a gros ouvrage, and looked more like the EH. In most petits ouvrages, there was no special entrance block, but two or more of their infantry casemates included a regular entrance. Most petits ouvrages consisted of one to six blocks. The monolithic ouvrages were rather large because they had no subterranean galleries. Consequently, all their service facilities and mortars, which fired through the fosse, were at the lower level. In some petits ouvrages, the underground facilities could not be placed thirty meters below the surface because of the terrain. The usines of the petits ouvrages held fewer engines, and all their facilities but the combat blocks were built on a smaller scale.

Another type of structure in the Maginot line was the interval casemate found in the main line between ouvrages and designed by CORF. These casemates followed standard blueprints and were similar to some of the infantry casemates of ouvrages mounting anti-tank guns, JM and FM. The main difference was that the CORF casemate had its own small usine since it was an independent position. Some were double casemates, meaning they had firing positions on both flanks. Only the cloches were devised for observation and defensive firing to the front. Like the casemates of most petits ouvrages, the CORF casemates had an armored door entrance that faced to the rear and often a diamond fosse. Each casemate sheltered a garrison of about two dozen men and one officer. Communication was by telephone, via underground cable linked to adjacent positions and ouvrages.

The CORF observatories were smaller than the casemates and were manned by a few men with communications equipment. They were located at key points with a good view of the surrounding terrain. Their job was to keep the artillery ouvrages informed of the enemy's movements.

Abris, or troop shelters, were found to the rear of the other positions of the main line. They were like small casernes with facilities for a command post and came in two types: the cavern abri and the monolithic surface abris. The cavern abris generally had two small entrances, each defended by a small arms position that led to the subterranean facilities below. [9] The monolithic abri generally consisted of two levels and had two GFM cloches above. This type of abri was similar to the casemates of an ouvrage in that it was covered by a layer of earth, (except on its rear-facing facade), and was usually built into a reverse slope or a hill.

When the war began, new types of non-CORF positions ap-

---

[9] At least one had three entrances.

peared and still newer types were added when work began on the New Fronts. These included a mixed variety of non-CORF casemates and blockhouses. Many old FT-17 tank turrets and chassis set in concrete became observatories and small bunker-like positions. During the "war, the army built many non-standard blockhouses throughout the line.

The Sarre Gap was defended not only by dams for flooding, but also by a number of small blockhouses. The *Service Techniques du Genie* (STG), or Technical Service of the Engineers, designed fortifications to cover areas not protected by CORF works and, after 1938, built some STG type casemates mainly in the Sarre Gap. These STG positions were smaller and usually held fewer weapons. A few were designed to mount a cloche that was not installed in time for the campaign.

The support positions, which included permanent casernes,

were generally located behind the main line of resistance. However, there were small temporary casernes near each ouvrage. Only the RF of Metz had fortified sub-stations for relaying power from the National [10] Grid to the ouvrages. Supply, ordnance, engineer depots, and even some positions for heavy artillery were also located in the rear area. At Thionville the French rearmed the gun turrets of the three old German Feste of Illange, Koenigsmacker and Guentrange with 105-mm guns to support the main line. [11]

---

[10] Machine gun turret of block 8 of the gros ouvrage of Rochonvillers in its lowered position.

[11] In 1933, the short-barrel German 105-mm guns (100-mm according to German nomenclature) of Ft.Guentrange were replaced with long-barrel weapons. It appears that the German-built complex at Mutzig also maintained a few batteries in a supporting role.

Although they were not a part of the Maginot Line Proper, the Rhine Defenses were built at the same time. They included no forts along the Rhine, except for old ones, and consisted mostly of casemates located along the river and behind the river line. These casemates consisted of a single level because the water table did not allow for underground construction. Each was a typical CORF casemate with its own facilities to operate independently with a platoon-sized force. Most had a GFM cloche. Over a hundred casemates occupied the river

and village lines, but even those on the river provided only flanking fires. These river position covered the key crossing points and had to be heavily camouflaged, yet they were not difficult to detect. The village line had the largest casemates. A large number of smaller blockhouses mostly occupied a position between the casemates of both lines.

The blockhouses in the Rhine sectors were similar to the many non-standard types built by me army and only held a few men. Between the river and village lines a number of abris and blockhouses guarded key points, and roughly, formed a second line in the heavily wooded terrain. In a few sectors defensive positions near the 111 River created a fourth line.

The SF of Haute Alsace, with only seven casemates and over forty blockhouses running from Sierentz to Folgens-bourg and then parallel with the Swiss border, was the on-ly sector not dependent on the Rhine as a natural barrier. Here the French established a defensive line southeast of Blotzheim and south along the Swiss border.

The Maginot Extension and Maubeuge

The Maginot Extension was part of the New Fronts built to extend the western terminus of the Maginot Line. The new ouvrages lacked some of the features of the Old Fronts and were slightly different. Some of the changes included a new type of entrance block that no longer used a rolling bridge, but a heavy metal portcullis that came up from the floor near the entrance. In addition, whereas the forts of the Maginot Line were designed to support each other and create interlocking fires, :hose of the extension were spaced so far apart that they could not adequately do so, not being able to assist more than one neighboring ouvr-age at a time. The sub-sector of Marville (part of the SF of Montmedy and attached to the SF of La Crusnes when the war began) was a heavily wooded and hilly region with a number of STG casemates and other smaller positions to defend it. The 75-mm gun turret of the ouvrage of Ve-slones in the extension covered the entire sector. The 75-mm gun turret of the ouvrage of Fermont, the last artillery fort on the Maginot Line Proper, also covered much of this sector.

The sub-sector of Montmedy held four of the new ouvrages: two petits ouvrages, and two gros ouvrages. One of the two petits ouvrages was protected by both gros ouvrages, while the last ouvrage on the line, La Ferte, was covered only by one of the two gros ouvrages. Furthermore, the gros ouvrage were not within range of each other and could not provide mutual support. The two gros ouvrages had a single 75-mm gun turret block each. One was outfitted with an older turret of World War I vintage, and a mixed arms turret block that was basically an infantry position. Both ouvrages had several mixed arms cloches, but these forts were not as powerful as those of the main line. The petit ouvrage of Thonnelle, located between the two larger forts, had a mixed arms turret block, two other infantry blocks and an entrance block. The smallest ouvrage, at the end of the extension, was La Ferte with only two combat blocks, one of which mounted a mixed arms turret. The main differences between the ouvrages of the main line and those of the Maginot Extension, were the extensive use of mixed arms turrets and cloches and the new and more economical type of entrance block. In addition, the artillery ouvrages were smaller in size, had fewer artillery blocks, and were not designed to support each other effectively. Finally, the petits ouvrages of the Maginot Extension were generally better armed than many of those in the Maginot Line Proper.

The New Fronts also included, among other areas, the SF of Montmedy, the SF of Maubeuge, and the lightly defended SD of the Ardennes. The SF of Maubeuge received new fortified works in 1936, after work had already begun on the New Fronts elsewhere. Four petits ouvrages were added to four old forts that partially surrounded the town of Maubeuge. Of these, three consisted of two blocks, and one of three blocks and all four included one mixed arms turret. A similar ouvrage was built in the SF of Escaut. Even though these forts are identified as Maginot ouvrages, they were of inferior quality and were even less suited to function within the Maginot scheme of defense than those of the Maginot Extension.

The Little Maginot Line (Alpine Defenses)

The Alpine or Southeastern Front included some of the most impressive Maginot ::rtifications. Three SFs ran from the Swiss border to the Mediterranean Sea. Mountainous terrain formed almost impenetrable gaps between the fortifications. The f Fs included the following from north to south:

SF of Savoie 5 gros and 5 petits ouvrages, 1 casemate, 4 abri and 7 avant-postes
SF of Dauphine 4 gros and 12 petits ouvrages, 1 observatory, 5 abri and 4 avant-postes
SF of Alpes Maritimes 14 gros and 17 petits ouvrages, 27 casemates, 2 observatories 1 abri, and 14 avant-postes*

*The sub-sectors of Tinee-Vesubie and Mounier are included here, but when the war began they were part of the 65th Division and detached from the SF of the Alpes Maritimes. A Demi-Brigade of Alpine fortress troops occupied most sub-sectors of the Alpine Front.

The ouvrages of the SF of Savoie sealed the Arc Valley and the approaches to Modane. Other works defended the Valley of the Isere leading to Chambery. The ruvrages of the SF of Dauphine blocked the approaches to Briancon. The largest sector, the SF Alpes Maritimes, closed the southern approaches through the Maritime Alps and shielded Nice. The entrance block of its last ouvrage rested near the reach adjacent to Menton, while the rest of the ouvrage perched at a higher elevation directly above. Several more ouvrages of the SF of Alpes Maritimes actually rverlooked the sea.
The Alpine ouvrages did not conform to the CORF designs

of the Maginot Line Proper. In fact, they were usually smaller and held smaller garrisons. In addition, their service areas lay virtually within the combat areas. The firepower of the gros ouvrages usually equaled that of the forts of the Northeastern Front, but some petits ouvrages were more like shelters than actual combat positions.

Some ouvrages were located in hilltop positions in valleys, while others were either built into mountain sides or on mountains tops. Some had two subterranean gallery levels instead of a single level, but none had train engines since the wagons needed to be pushed only short distances. Their usines normally held three diesel engines, but did not rely on the outside electrical power grid. Because all the facilities were so close together, their entrance blocks were always of the mixed type, and were normally located close to the combat blocks. However, they were quite secure because the mountain terrain permitted much greater overhead cover than in the Maginot Line Proper. The combat blocks usually consisted of two floors and housed artillery combinations unlike similar blocks in the Northeast Front. Indeed, in the Alps it was not unusual to find an artillery block with 81-mm mortars and 75-mm guns or mortars. Many blocks had firing chambers on both levels often covering two different directions. Monte Grosso, the largest ouvrage of the Little Maginot Line, housed the only 135-mm casemate and turret in the Alps. In the SF Alpes Maritimes, Monte Grosso, L'Agaisen, and Mont Agel mounted the only 75-mm gun turrets in the Alps. The latter ouvrage had two of these turrets.

Many of the Alpine gun casemates faced forward, requiring additional concrete protection and added armor. The artillery was concentrated in two or three blocks in most cases. Turret blocks were seldom used in the Alps because the surrounding terrain did not allow a 360 degree unobstructed field of fire. Like the Maginot Line Proper, the Little Maginot Line relied on interlocking fields of fire for its defense. In most cases the terrain was so rugged that anti-tank obstacles were unnecessary, although wire obstacles remained in use.The garrisons of the gros ouvrages averaged 160 men in the SF of Savoie, 200 men in the SF of Dauphine, and 290 men in the SF of Alpes Maritimes.

The petits ouvrages of the Southeastern Front were small and unlike similar positions in the Northeast Fronts. Normally, they mounted nothing larger than JMs and held no diesel engines. They were also classified as active abris since they seldom had more than a few cloches or embrasures and usually mounted only light weapons.

Most of the Alpine ouvrages were not finished because priority was given to the Northeast Front. In addition, the construction of such positions in the Alpine sectors involved a great deal of money because of their location and the ruggedness of the terrain. Some of the ouvrages were almost inaccessible in the winter because of the snow and in the spring because of landslides that often blocked their access roads. A few, located high in the mountains, were reached by a type of ski lift with small cable cars known as a *telepherique*.

The Alpine defenses also included a line of avant-postes that were, however, very different from those of the Northeast. They were designed by the STG and usually built by military labor (Main d'oeuvre or MOM). Seventeen of the twenty-five avant-postes built after 1935 were sited near the frontier of the SF Alpes Maritimes. Many were multi-block and connected by trenches or tunnels, but none could be considered as strong as an ouvrage. Their main defensive advantage was in their location, since many lacked roofs over their thin walls.

In some places the advance line included upgraded older fortifications. For instance, in the early 1930s the late nineteenth-century fort of La Turra, located on a ridge dominating the pass of Mont Cenis in the SF of Savoie, received a new caserne and two gun casemates for 75-mm field pieces that opened onto the rock cliff overlooking the plateau below.

Some older fortifications to the rear of the main line were also modernized to support the newer positions. Thus the two-block gros ouvrage of Barbonnet was built into the old fort of Suchet whose old 155-mm Mougin turrets served as long range support.

The Coast Defenses

The French coastal defenses did not receive the same priority as the Maginot Line because it was unlikely the Germans would present a serious threat from the sea. From 1932 the 3,000 kilometers of coast line were divided into four naval districts, each commanded by an admiral. During the First World War many of the large guns were removed to be used at the front and they remained with the army after the war. Nonetheless, the French continued to maintain coastal fortifications, which were mostly concentrated in their major ports. However, with few exceptions, these installations had become obsolete before 1939.

The 1st Naval District extended from Dunkirk on the Belgian border to St. Malo, covering most of the 1,100 kilometers of the North Sea and Channel coast line. Dunkirk, Calais, and Boulogne were relatively small ports. The navy set up light defenses at Dunkirk where sand dunes and embankments dominated a large part of the coast. To the east of Dunkirk, a coastal battery and searchlight unit occupied a position north of the old Fort des Dunes (west of Zuydcoote), and further east was the Battery of Bray-Dunes. West of Dunkirk lay gun batteries at Ouvrage Quest and at Fort Mardyck, also equipped with a searchlight. All these defenses were oriented seaward.

Further along the coast, the port of Calais included the Battery de la Digue, located opposite its West Mole and guarding the approach to the port. The ship basin on the northeast end of the town was covered by a battery and searchlight position at Bastion II. A battery at Bastion XII, defended the channel entrance toward the city in the proximity of old Fort Risban.

A battery position with turret guns lay west of Calais at old Fort Lapin. In 1928 there were eight old 240-mm and 190-mm guns and four railway pieces at Calais. By the beginning of the war, the defenses included no gun heavier than 120-mm. However, many weapons were in open emplacements with a 360 degree field of fire like the battery of 138-mm guns at Cap Gris Nez. The French made little effort to protect either Calais or Dunkirk from land assault. However, they did plan some water barriers for the protection of Calais.

The port of Boulogne was more extensively protected than Dunkirk or Calais. At the east end of its ship basin, north of the town, stood the gun battery of La Creche with its searchlight. Batterie de la Digue was located on the mole and Batterie du Bassin lay inside the port. Batterie du Mont de Couple, with a searchlight, and Batterie d'Alprech were on the southwest side of the town, on either side of Le Portel. Batterie d'Equilen stood about three kilometers to the south, landward defenses were absent and the town had to rely on its old medieval walls for protection.

Further down the coast lay the two most important seaports of the 1st Naval District: Le Havre and Cherbourg. Le Havre in particular was not only an important commercial sea port, but also the key to the Seine and, therefore, to the important inland port of Rouen. The harbor of Le Havre was defended by three batteries, and the mouth of the Seine by two. Two old forts from the Vauban era overlooked --T.e northern part of the city. In 1928 its weapons included four old 240-mm guns, two 140-mm naval guns, and two 95-mm coast guns. However, these guns may have been retired and not part of the batteries mentioned, before the war began. On the south side of the mouth of the

Seine, the small harbors of Trouville and Deauville were given a battery of guns. All of these defenses overlooked the net and mine barriers installed at the mouth of the river. All these important measures were taken recause the Le Havre area was considered to be one of the most important access points on the northern coast.

However, Cherbourg, which served as a naval base and headquarters for the admiral commanding the district, was the most heavily defended port in the district. Here, the moles created an inner and outer anchorage area. The outer moles linked several islands defended by forts. On the coast, up to ten kilometers east and west of the city, stood the artillery batteries. To the east lay Batterie Brulay, with its 135-mm guns and large, but still unfinished concrete observation post. There were two more batteries between Batterie Brulay and the city. Additional batteries were still under construction when the war began, including Batterie Tourville with its 340-mm Mle 1912 guns originally intended for the *Normandie* class battleships. Work on this position stopped in June 1940. Three others were situated west of the city. Old Fort du Roule, on the south side of the city, overlooking Cherbourg and its harbor, was one of the old Vauban positions protecting the city.

The 2nd Naval District began at St. Malo and ended south of Brest on the southwest corner of Brittany. It encompassed the easily defended major naval base of Brest, headquarters of the commander of the 2nd Naval District. Its old Vauban forts formed part of the outdated defenses of the landward and seaward fronts. However, sixteen newer battery positions protected the approaches to the anchorage outside of Brest. Not all the positions were completed in time of the war. For instance, the battery of Minou had only four of its guns. To the west of Minou lay Batterie Toulbroch with its 240-mm guns in open and unshielded concrete positions. South of the anchorage of Brest, on the southern end of the Crozon Peninsula, was the Batterie of Cap de la Chevre with its modern concrete command post completed in 1939. The guns of this battery, like the others, were mounted in armored shields, on pedestal positions. A mobile anti-aircraft and searchlight battery was also used. To the west of the Brittany Peninsula, the island of Ouessant served as an advance post with a gun battery on its eastern and western ends. The old fort of St. Michel, located on an island near Brest, had received two 75-mm gun turrets in 1910, one of which was still operational when the Germans incorporated the fort into their Atlantic Wall.

The 5th Naval District covered about 1,300 kilometers of Atlantic coast. It began where the 2nd Naval District ended, and continued to the Spanish frontier. The naval port of Lorient, almost defenseless in 1928, was fortified with batteries at the mouth of the river leading to the harbor. Additional defenses were being erected along this stretch of the coast when the war began.

The mouth of the Loire, leading to St. Nazaire, was covered by a battery of 194-mm guns. Further down the coast La Rochelle and La Pallice were also protected by battery positions that included the batteries on the Island of Re. Batteries for 164-mm and 240-mm guns were projected for Royan, at the mouth of the Gironde. Their mission would be to cover the approaches to Bordeaux. Most of these positions, including those of the 1st and 2nd Naval Districts, were improved, completed and incorporated into the German Atlantic Wall between 1942-1944.

The 3rd Naval District, which included the major seaport of Marseilles and the main naval base of Toulon, encompassed the entire Mediterranean coastline and Corsica. Marseilles, like Toulon, was heavily defended by fortifications going back to the Vauban era. In addition, it was protected by a number of coastal batteries mostly concentrated on the fortified islands of Ratonneau and Pomeque that guarded the harbor entrance. The most notable of these defenses were a 305-mm gun battery, consisting of weapons from a *Danton* Class battleship, located outside the port and a few 240-mm coastal guns.

Toulon was protected by a number of gun batteries, including eight 240-mm coastal defense guns. Its defenses were increased during the latter part of the 1920s. Two new twin gun turrets with 340-mm guns were taken from the *Normandie* Class battleships and installed in the Cepet Battery at Toulon. The other minor ports along the coast up to Menton were given smaller batteries that included no gun larger than 120-mm. As in the other districts, all the batteries of the 3rd Naval District were also designed for landward defense. Unfortunately most of these batteries were also obsolescent. In 1943 they were modified and put to use by the Germans.

The Maginot Line in World War II

In September 1939, as the army mobilized, the troops of the Maginot Line quickly occupied their defenses. However, as no German attack materialized in 1939, the defenders of the Maginot Line soon became bored with garrison duty. The only major action at that time consisted of a barrage of German propaganda. While waiting for something to happen, the Maginot troops were put to work creating a number of intermediate positions of non-standard type and improving the existing defenses.When the German offensive finally took place in May 1940, the French fortress troops were ready, only to find that they would not be in the main theater of operations: the Maginot Line had forced the Germans to avoid a direct assault on the French frontier and seek a different invasion route.

In the meantime, the garrisons of the ouvrages of Schoenenbourg and Hochwald, bored with routine operations, sought and received permission to install old 120-mm guns in open positions on their forts and fire upon German positions. Some forts of the RF of Lauter, which were within reach of the German border, also fired occasional volleys from their 75-mm turrets. [12] As the German offensive broke through the Ardennes, a German infantry division went after the last ouvrage on the Maginot Extension, the petit ouvrage of La Ferte, with heavy artillery and air support. On May 17, 1940, two huge 210-mm mortars joined in the bombardment, inflicting little damage to the ouvrage, except to the surrounding obstacles.

---

[12] The term main d'oeuvre or MOM creates some confusion. It refers to military labor, and some work; have been identified as MOM bunkers, abris, etc. This only means that military labor built therr. and the design could have come from the STG or there regions' engineer command. In many cases groups of MOM bunkers would be named for a commander such as Billotte Bunkers.

On May 18 the two nearby casemates with 75-mm guns were abandoned by their garrisons. German assault engineers worked their way up to Block 2 of La Ferte. [13]
The neighboring ouvrage of Le Chesnois strove to drive them off with its 75-mm gun turret but it was too far away to be effective. The mixed arms turret of La Ferte was partially blown out of its well and its weapons destroyed with hollow charges. By May 19, after a whole day of fighting, the Germans penetrated Block 1 and found the crew dead, apparently asphyxiated in the subterranean gallery. Between June 12-14 the garrisons of the other three ouvrages received orders to sabotage them, and the extension was abandoned completely. Thus came about the Germans' first victory against the Maginot Line, a victory that had more value in the war of propaganda than in actual fact.
On May 14 the Germans bombarded the ouvrage of Schoenenbourg with 280-mm guns, and later with a 420-mm, in an effort to divert attention from their offensive through the Ardennes. [14] It wasn't until a few days later that it became clear that the Germans were crossing the Meuse between Sedan and Dinant and had no intention of assaulting the Maginot Line.
Between May 20 and May 23 the four petits ouvrages at Maubeuge fought valiantly until they were eliminated one by one. In some cases the Germans deployed Stuka bombers, assault engineers, flame throwers and/or heavy artillery against them. Further north, the isolated petit ouvrage of Eth lasted until May 26, fighting off the German attacks for four days. Ironically, while the men of the Maginot Line resisted undaunted, the Germans continued their race to the sea and the bulk of the Allied forces floundered

[13] GO Fermont Block 4, Artillery Casemate. Interior back at all three gun positions
[14] The German First Army had two 420-mm pieces. One was a Czech Skoda weapon and the other of German origin (possibly a Big Bertha?).

and retreated.

The interval troops had been on the defensive since the campaign began, and were in the process of being removed from the Maginot Line Proper and the Rhine Defenses when the German Army Group C finally struck in June. At the time, German Army Groups A and B had already started a new campaign, breaking through the final defensive positions between the Maginot Line and the sea. The German infantry divisions that had begun to move around the Maginot Line in the vicinity of Longuyon were engaged by the gros ouvrage of Fermont.

In a retaliatory move, Fermont was placed under heavy bombardment. High-velocity German 88-mm flak guns, which proved successful in penetrating the cloches of La Ferte, were trained on the rear face of Fermont's artillery casemate. They almost succeeded in penetrating the concrete wall after firing repeatedly at the same spot, but they withdrew one round too soon. The crew of the damaged block effected repairs under cover of darkness. A few days later, on June 21, Fermont withstood another heavy bombardment and beat back a German ground assault.

The Germans showed little interest in engaging the great forts in the RF of Metz. On June 14, Operation Tiger was launched in the Sarre Gap. Several German divisions forced back the remaining French covering forces and fanned out behind the Maginot Line. On June 21, the Germans laid siege to several petits ouvrages on the end of the RF of Metz, which were well beyond the artillery range of the gros ouvrages. A couple of these small forts were saved by the 81-mm casemate mortars of the petit ouvrage of Laudrefang. Nonetheless, the Germans, attacking from the rear, were able to reduce and capture a few of these petits ouvrages with the help of their high-velocity 88-mm guns. Two of the petits ouvrages on the Sarre end of the RF of the Lauter also fell between June 21-24.

In the RF of the Lauter, German troops were able to penetrate through the lightly defended gap in the Vosges, between Bitche and Lembach. Heavy artillery, including the 420-mm howitzer, was trained on the ouvrages of Hochwald and Schoenenbourg. The latter, heavily bombarded between June 20 and 23, sustained only one damaging hit when a shell penetrated near an artillery block leaving a fracture in the combination M-l/M-2 magazine below. The aerial Stuka bombardment only succeeded in damaging the fosse of an infantry block.

June 15 marked the beginning of Operation Bear, an assault across the Rhine. The undermanned garrisons of the Rhine Defenses strove to repel the invaders, but were no match against the 88-mm guns that quickly knocked out the vulnerable casemates on the river. The Germans succeeded in taking the first line and penetrat the next line of casemates because most of the supporting troops had been ordered to withdraw with the French Second Army Group.

When France surrendered, many ouvrages still held on, not giving up until directed to do so by a representative of the French government. The Germans soon rccupied the forts and began to exploit them for propaganda purposes. They removed many of the weapons and some of the equipment for use elsewhere. The Germans also found other uses for a few of the forts. For instance, Hackenberg became an underground factory and Four-a-Chaux was used as a target for weapons tests.

In 1944, the Germans failed to use the Maginot Line systematically even though the ouvrages could have been useful against the advancing Americans since many of their weapons fired toward the flanks and rear. One of the few ouvrages to be turned against the Allies was Hackenberg, whose artillery casemate (Block 8) with its three 75-mm guns stopped the American advance in November. The day was saved by a French officer who directed the Americans to a blind spot from which 155-mm self propelled artillery blasted away the weak rear wall of the block.

The Germans made a belated attempt to defend their old forts of the Metz ring, previously renovated by the French for use as headquarters and support bases. They also defended the forts of Thionville, which had been rearmed by the French to support the Maginot Line. The Americans had a difficult time eliminating these forts, but they succeeded in capturing both Koenigsmacker and Guentrange. In the RF of Lauter, the ouvrage of Simserhof and Schiesseck changed hands in combat in 1944. The American 100th Division found these ouvrages impervious to their artillery despite the fact that they were not fully armed. Finally, a major battle raged over Simserhof. The American troops had to fight on its surface, destroying die positions occupied by the Germans one by one with explosives.

The Little Maginot Line

Since the Southeast Front had been stripped of most of its divisions even before the Germans embarked on the last phase of their campaign in the West, the Italians, who entered the war in early June, believed they could easily penetrate the French defenses. However, they soon found out how wrong they were. On June 20, when the Italians launched their assault, many parts of the Alpine front were still covered with snow, severely hampering their maneuvers. Their effort to penetrate the Arc Valley and take Modane failed dismally. They never even penetrated the line of avant-postes at Mont Cenis. The old masonry fort of La Turra, firing its two 75-mm guns through galleries in the cliff brought them to a standstill. One gun was pulled out and positioned to fire down on an advancing column of Italian light L-3 tanks. Further down the front, on June 24, Italian troops tried to overrun the two ouvrages of Pas du Roc and Arrondaz near the border south of Modane. However, the two forts, mutually supporting each other, successfully repelled the attack.

At Briangon the French ouvrages engaged in a duel with the huge Italian fort of Chaberton, despite the fact that they had not been designed for this purpose. With the help of the ouvrages' observation positions, a battery of French 280-mm mortars destroyed most of the 149-mm gun positions on top of Mount Chaberton between June 21-24.

In the Southeast the Italians concentrated their effort against the SF of Alpes Maritimes. Here again, the main attack, which began on June 22, failed to even break the line of avant-postes. Near Menton the tiny avant-poste of Pont St. Louis held out until the end of the campaign, denying the Italians the use of the coastal road. However, despite Pont St. Louis's valiant stand, the Italians took the railroad tunnel beneath it and attempted to advance behind it to take Menton. Alas, victory would elude them once more. As they emerged from the tunnel, they ran into a barrage of fire from several of the ouvrages in the area. To counter the cannonade, the Italians brought forth a naval artillery train, which was promptly damaged. Italian forces actually managed to storm the last ouvrage of the line, Cap Martin, but had to withdraw after a desperate fight. It must be recognized, however, that during the attack the Italians achieved something the Germans never did: to reach the superstructure of a gros ouvrage.

Thus the Alpine forts remained undefeated. Unfortunately, their victorious campaign was negated by the surrender of the French armies and government to the Germans.

The Coast Defenses

Some of the coastal defenses took part in the defense of Dunkirk, Calais, and Boulogne. At and near Dunkirk the Battery of Bray Dunes fired its three 164-mm guns at German troops from May 28 until its ammunition was expended on June 4, 1940. The Battery of Zuydcoote, with three 149-mm and two 75-mm cannons, did likewise.

The 155-mm guns of the 3rd Naval [15] Mobile Battery also took part in the action until June 3, when they were destroyed. If the events of the Pas de Calais area took on epic

[15] The entrance to Ouvrage Schoenenbourg along the Maginot Line in Alsace

overtones, those off the coast of Menton owed more to the comic opera. In late June 1940 the Italians assembled an armada of fishing boats, motor boats, and other private vessels as well a squadron of MAS [16] (motor torpedo) boats, and two submarines. The armada departed on June 22, but it soon became clear that the mismatched fleet would not be able to travel in unison. The smaller vessels were soon left behind, some, not equipped for such a long voyage, were actually stranded in high seas. By the time Menton was sighted, what remained of the small armada was too widely scattered to be effective. In addition, it became apparent that the engines on many of the vessels were too loud to approach the French coast undetected. Finally, the troops on board were too exhausted by the long trip and seasickness to consider swimming ashore.

Thus the operation was aborted with no bloodshed.After the fall of France, the Germans worked on the unfinished defenses and restored the completed ones for use in their Atlantic Wall by 1942.

The myth of the Maginot Line

The existence of the Maginot Line was never intended to be a secret. To the contrary, since one of its major purposes was to deter attack, it was important that potential enemies know of its existence. In any case, it would not have been possible to keep it secret. France was a democratic society, and the debates surrounding its construction and funding were public knowledge and widely discussed in the press. Beyond that, the scope of the construction was massive and could not have been hidden, especially since all of the fortifications in north-eastern France were constructed in areas of France that Germany had occupied from 1870 to 1918 and that still contained a portion of the population that was sympathetic to Germany. Con-

---

[16] Fort position Maginot Line, France

certed efforts were made to keep the details secret however. The plans of individual works and their exact locations were classified information. Photographing construction sites was prohibited. The actual sites occupied by the
completed works were off limits. All this meant that the
public had little real information about the fortifications.
There are indications that the French government made efforts to exaggerate their strength and extent in an attempt
to increase their effectiveness as a deterrent. While a few
fairly accurate reports describing various aspects of the
Maginot Line did appear in the press in the 1930s, most
published reports were full of fanciful exaggeration. Frequent mention was made of an impregnable line of fortifications running from the English Channel to the Swiss
border. Reports spoke of all the forts being connected together by an underground rail network. Others claimed
that the forts were invisible from the air. In 1936 the *Daily
Express* of London published what was purported to be a
cutaway drawing of one of the '£30,000,000 Forts of the
"Maginot Line".' It showed a seven-level, hundred-metre-
deep structure that looked more like an underground hotel
than an actual *ouvrage*. There was even a streamlined express train shown running through one level. But it was
not just press accounts that kept the Maginot Line in the
public eye. There were novels that centred around the
Maginot
A plan showing the overlapping potential fields of fire of
the close-in defences of the combat block area of the gros
ouvrage of Michelsberg. The twin machine guns and antitank gun of the infantry casemate block at the right and
the c/odie-mounted twin machine gun at the bottom fire
along the line of obstacles (not shown) connecting the
works together.The plan does not reflect dead ground, but
in general care was taken during construction to avoid
dead ground to the maximum extent possible. (Eric Hal-
ter)

Line and in 1938 even a feature film, *Double crime sur la Ligne Maginot.*

As late as 1939 the French government was still engaged in deception. While it did release photos and newsreel footage taken inside Maginot Line *ouvrages,* the purported exterior views actually showed pre-World War I forts built by the Germans while they had occupied Alsace-Lorraine. All this fed the myth of an invulnerable Maginot Line and it is clear that much of the public, and perhaps even some within the French military, bought into the myth, holding exaggerated expectations as to the Maginot Line's ability to save France from invasion - expectations that were doomed to disappointment.

The German view

Based on their public statements, it seems clear that at least some individuals -.vithin the German military were also taken in by the myth. However, the German intelligence services were not. An extensive German military report ; Dmpiled in 1935 and 1936 quite accurately described the Maginot Line fortifications, not only correctly identifying their general locations and relative -Tiengths, including those in the Alps, but also providing details of their irmament. A subsequent report prepared in 1937 contained accurate, detailed olans of several *ouvrages,* plans that were too detailed to have been drawn simply rom memory by a German military attache who had been given a quick tour on them. Both reports contained inaccuracies, but they do show that at least some sections of the German military had a much clearer understanding of the strengths and weaknesses of the Maginot Line than did the general public. It is not known how the Germans obtained the information on which these reports were based. Certainly, spying played a significant role, but some information may also have been obtained from those directly involved in building the fortifications. Construction had required more labour than was available from the French work force. As a result, large numbers of foreign labourers had been employed including many from Germany.

Pre-war life in the Maginot Line

Specialised units of fortress infantry, artillery and engineers were raised to man the fortifications. The fortress infantry units both manned the interval casemates and the infantry weapons of the *ouvrages* and provided the infantry component of the interval troops whose mission it was operate outside the fortifications, supporting them and containing any possible hostile penetration of the line. Like the infantry, the fortress artillery units had a dual role. They manned both the artillery integral to the *ouvrages* and the field artillery that supported the interval troops and provided offensive firepower forward of the line. In north-eastern France and along the Rhine River alone the field artillery totalled more than 1.200 pieces. The vast majority of these were 75mm and 155mm guns and howitzers but there were a small number of heavy guns ranging in calibre from 220mm to 370mm. The mission of the fortress engineer units was to operate and maintain all of the specialised equipment within the fortifications other than the weapons. They also operated most of the communications equipment.

The Maginot Line fortifications were organised geographically, primarily into fortified sectors, the majority of which were further divided into subsectors. Beyond that most of the fortified sectors in north-eastern France formed part of either the Metz or Lauter Fortified Regions. Fortress unit organisation roughly corresponded to the geographic organisation. In addition, the artillery was organised into groups for co-ordination purposes. Each fortress unit was made up of both active duty and reserve soldiers. The active duty component consisted in large part of the highly trained specialists who were required to keep the works ready for war and who could man them at a moment's notice in the event of a surprise attack. The reserves were drawn from the local area so that they could be rapidly mobilised to reinforce the active duty troops and bring them up to wartime strength.

The soldiers of the fortress units wore special insignia that made them easily recognisable, the most prominent being a distinctive beret badge bearing the motto of the Maginot Line *'On ne passe pas'*, usually translated as 'None shall pass'. Not surprisingly given their mission as France's first line of defence and the immense amounts of money that had been spent on the Maginot Line, the fortress troops considered themselves to be among the elite of French Army and they were renowned for their high morale.

The Maginot Line works, especially the *ouvrages,* were cold, damp, dreary, and generally uncomfortable places in which to live. Consequently, permanent barrack complexes were provided for the regular army portion of the fortress troops. These were constructed at intervals along the line close enough to the fortifications so that the troops could conveniently train in them and maintain them while living in relative comfort. Immediately adjacent to each *gros ouwage* a small complex of buildings was constructed to provide temporary accommodation for those troops whose duties required them to spend longer periods at the *ouvrages.* These buildings were constructed of wood so that they could easily be knocked down in the event of wan

Training and preparing for war

The fortress units trained in the works they garrisoned, but because the fortifications were located in civilian areas it was not possible to actually fire their weapons. To circumvent this limitation, mock-ups of infantry weapon emplacements were built at local firing ranges where automatic rifles, machine guns, and in most cases anti-tank guns could be fired. To practise live fire with artillery weapons, the artillery officers and non-commissioned officers periodically travelled to the vicinity of the town of Bitche in the northern Vosges mountains, where a *gros ouvrage* was situated in a military training area and artillery live fire was possible.

The garrisons carefully surveyed the area around each *ouvrage* so that fire could quickly and accurately be brought to bear on any target that came within range. To make it easier for observers to pinpoint targets, annotated panoramic photographs of the surrounding area were prepared for each *cloche* and similar photos were prepared for the *ouwage* command posts.

In March 1936, in response to Germany's re-militarisation of the Rhineland, the fortress troops were mobilised and moved into the fortifications for the first time. Problems were encountered with the works themselves, especially dampness and poor lighting. Difficulties were also experienced integrating the various components of the garrisons. As soon as the crisis was over, steps were taken to address the problems. Lighting was improved where possible and the problems associated with damp were alleviated somewhat although they were never completely solved.

In an effort to improve the functioning of the *ouvrage* garrisons, officers were sent to study the way the crews of naval ships operated. The result was the adoption of a naval-style organisation for the *ouvrages* with the garrisons being divided into watches similar to those used on ships.

Germany

After the Franco-Prussian War, the leaders of the Second Reich (1871-1918) exacted France to seek retribution for its losses. In addition, fearing that a potential Franco-Russian alliance could lead to a disastrous two-front war, they decided to each a number of forts and associated defenses on both the eastern and western wders of Germany. In the west, the Germans established fortress rings around Strasbourg and Metz, often building on old French forts, as in the case of Metz.

By the turn of the century, the Germans, responding like the French to advances in warfare, developed new and stronger forts. They extended the defenses of Strasbourg to Mutzig and those of Metz to Thionville. They also developed a new type fortification known as *Feste*. The preliminary work at Mutzig consisted of angular type forts and detached batteries employing turret positions. The Feste was further refined at Thionville and Metz. Located at prominent points and usuty covering much of a hill top, it consisted of one or more large batteries of four guns each in an armored turret. All its other facilities were built into the ground, including the large earth-covered casernes. Only the rear facades, a number of coffres, fantry positions, and observation points were exposed. Most of the *Feste* was surrounded by a ditch or moat, and infantry obstacles. A tunnel system linked most of concrete positions, and an engine room, or usine, provided the needed power. hen World War I began, these forts were still unfinished. None of them had a chance to participate in combat until World War II. At the end of the Great War, virtually all of the German *Feste* in the west ended up in France. The only one reaining in German territory, Istein, was destroyed, since Article 42 of the Treaty of Versailles specified that:

"Germany is forbidden to maintain or construct any fortifications either on the left bank of the Rhine or on the right bank to the west of a line drawn 50 kilometers to the East of the Rhine."

Thus the Treaty of Versailles left the Rhineland virtually defenseless. In the west only the obsolete fortresses of Ulrn and Ingolstadt were allowed to stand, in East Prussia, the obsolete defenses at Konigsberg and Ldtzen, and in the east, the outdated fortifications of Küstrin, Breslau, and Glogau.In addition, the treaty directed that "The fortifications, military establishments, on the Islands of Helgoland and Dune shall be destroyed," thus unmasking the approaches to the mouth of the Elbe and Wesser Rivers and associated ports as well as the Kiel Canal. However, Article 195 allowed Germany to maintain certain coastal defenses in their "existing condition." Those defenses included positions at Cuxhaven and Wilhelmshaven on the North Sea, and Pillau and Swinemiinde on the Baltic Sea. Thus, during the 1920s Germany had been virtually stripped of its defenses. With a navy of six obsolete battleships and an army of ten divisions, the armed forces could do little to defend its naval bases or frontiers.

Nonetheless, the Germans did not give up easily. After World War I, the outlawed General Staff surreptitiously continued to operate, but defense was not its primary concern. Despite this attitude the German fortress engineers not only continued to maintain the few remaining fortifications, but also illegally improved their condition. However, the Inter Allied Commission, set up after the war, foiled several German attempts to build defenses on the eastern frontier. Until 1935, the German army was unable to build anything more than some bunkers along the Oder River and create water defenses on the Nischlitz-Obra Line, which later became part of the future Oder-Warthe-Bend Line. On the western frontier they completed only a small number of positions along the eastern side of the Rhineland, as allowed by the restrictions of {he Versailles Treaty. After 1933 the situation changed, but fortifications remained of secondary importance as the General Staff concentrated on resurrecting the German army and transforming it into an offensive machine to be reckoned with.

Feste Kaiser Wilhelm II—Muteig 1893-1914

The German army reinforced its frontier positions in Alsace and Lorraine inasmuch as time allowed. The position at Mutzig-Molsheim was designed to block the Bruche River valley between Strasbourg and the Vosges River and stop the advance of French troops coming down the plain between the Vosges and Rhine from the vicinity of Belfort, from Toul or Epinal, or through the Vosges along the valley of the Bruche.

Work on the Mutzig-Molsheim position began with the construction of Ostfort in 1893 and continued into the next century. Both Ostfort and Westfort were completed by 1897. Concrete infantry shelters, casernes, and new battery positions were then subsequently added. All of these positions were dispersed over the plateau and finally encircled by wire obstacles, forming a single combat unit identified as Feste Kaiser Wilhelm II.

Ostfort and Westfort served as battery positions mounting four 150-mm howitzers in single-gun turrets. Battery 2 was located at Westfort and Battery 5 on Ostfort. Even though they were not retractable, these turrets oscillated for loading and firing. These steel 150-mm howitzer turrets substituted for the older iron 210-mm howitzer turrets that had originally been in the plans. These new turrets proved more efficient, less vulnerable to enemy fire, and less complex. The two forts also included several small retractable 60-mm gun turrets and armored observation positions. These small eclipsing turrets for 57-mm guns (listed as 60-mm) were small and effective for close defense but proved to be too expensive to justify their use in future festen.

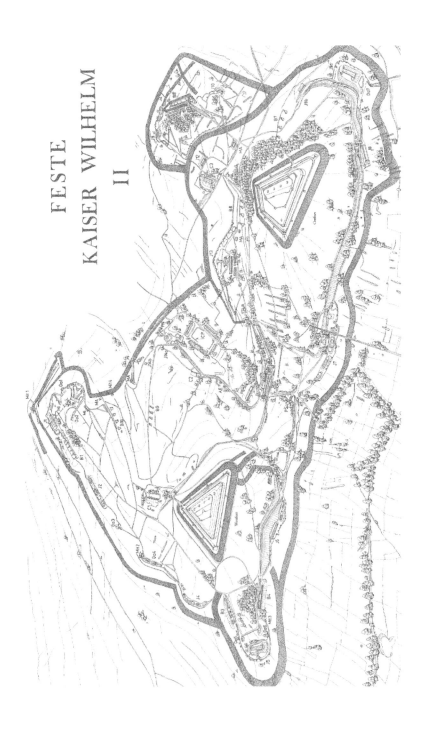

FESTE KAISER WILHELM II

Both Ostfort and Westfort included an *usine* (a power plant with diesel power generators and transformers), a well, a kitchen, and a bakery that served the support positions for the garrison. These two triangular-shaped forts included an encircling moat with coffres mounting 53-mm rapid-fire cannons in the counterscarp that characterized older forts of the 1870s and 1880s generation.

Individual concrete batteries dispersed over the plateau included numbers 1, 3, and 4 , each mounting 105-mm guns in shields. Battery 1 had four turrets and the other batteries had three turrets. These were naval-type guns and shields which, with only 80-mm of armor, lacked sufficient protection against the high-explosive shells. Each of these battery blocks contained its own kitchen and munitions storage area. Battery ; 6 was the largest position and was an armored battery with four turrets with each mounting a 100-mm (actually 105-mm) cannon. This was one of the first armored battery blocks built and included a usine, kitchen, and well. Battery 1, 3, and 4 were of a style not favored in later works built after 1899. Battery 1 was only a month older than Batteries 3 and 4 which had a new design for ammunition entrance that was not repeated in future batteries. These types were basically designed as a matter of economy. It was a long concrete construction with places for mounting the four guns with shields (a naval design), and between each gun position was a storage area or shelter built into the structure. Normally at each end was a position for an armored observation cloche.

Battery 6, the armored battery position, whose construction began in 1904 and was completed by 1908, became the favored type of artillery position for the newer and stronger festen. It included positions for four turret guns located along the center line of the elongated rectangular structure that was about one hundred meters in length. The turret positions were surrounded by curved frontal armor set in the concrete that could stop any artillery round that penetrated the concrete before it reached the position beneath the turret. The armor greatly increased the cost of building this kind of position. The heavy armored turrets also included mechanisms to rotate them and to deliver the ammunition from below. Battery 6 included space for a power plant and kitchen, and mounted a single observation cloche. Some of these features became standard in most later-day armored battery blocks.

The second building phase at Mutzig, which began in 1900, saw the construction of Battery 6, more concrete trenches, shelters for the infantry and munitions, three large bombproof casernes, and a number of armored observation positions. Caserne II was completed in 1901 as work began on Casernes I and III. These large rectangular concrete structures consisting of several levels were completely covered with earth, except for their rear face. Only dozens of small ventilation vents on the roof revealed their location from the surface. Each included latrines, a heating system, a kitchen, a bakery, and all the -facilities needed to serve the garrison. The largest, Caserne I, accommodated 720 men and the smallest, Caserne II, only 360 men. The entire garrison of the feste was 6,500 men and the three casernes could take over 1,600. None of these casernes had a power plant.

New types of infantry shelters, some of which were experimental, also appeared at Mutzig during the second phase of construction. They varied in size, but included latrines and a water supply. Two of them had an observation cloche. Shelter J-16, a very large infantry shelter, included not only the standard features, but also a kitchen, a bakery, a power plant, and even a hospital. The power plant was not added until 1914 and was the third to be installed at the feste. Westfort was the first position to receive a power plant in 1895, and Battery 6, was the second in 1904. All eighteen shelters of varying size were completed by 1914.

Two guard posts or blockhouses watched the entrances into the feste and four casemates for machine guns protected
the perimeter. One of these, Machine Gun Casemate 1, was
a double coffre linked to infantry shelters 1 and 16 (J-l and
J-16) by a tunnel completed just before the war. During
the war, Russian prisoners prepared countermines in the
tunnel between J-l and Machine Gun Casemate 1.
Observation positions with armored cloches
set in a concrete structure independent of other positions
appeared early in the first decade of • the new century. Of
seven of these observation posts, two, dating from the
1890s, mounted a *Panzerbeobachtungsturm* 94 *(P.B.T.
94)*, which was an observation turret that could rotate and
retract. There are only two other turrets of this type in existence at Graudenz in the east. A smaller non-movable
cloche, *Panzerbeobachtung-stand* 96 *Leicht (P.B.St. 96,*
light), was used on Battery Blocks 1,3, and 4. *Panzerbeo-
bachtungstand 05 (P.B.St. 05)* was used on Battery Block
6 and three artillery observation blocks. P.B.St. 05 was
larger and heavier than the light-version P.B.St 05 (Light),
which were found on two artillery observation blocks. A
newer version was found on infantry shelters J-ll and J-12.
The independent armored observation position used at
Mutzig was also an innovation in fortifications.
Communication was improved with the creation of telephone links between Caserne I and all batteries and
trenches in 1903. A radio station was added to Ostfort in
1902 and in 1903 telegraphic communications linked all
the casernes to Ostfort and Westfort.
By the end of the first decade of the twentieth century
most of the feste was surrounded by barbed-wire obstacles
of a depth of up to twenty-five meters, but work on this
barrier continued through the First World War. Feste Kaiser Wilhelm II was essentially the experimental feste. It included many innovations such as an advanced ventilation
system, its own usines or power plants to ensure a power

supply, and mobile observation positions. This was where most of the features and new equipment were tested and evaluated in the 1890s before they were incorporated in the other festen.

(Source: *Le Fort de Mutzig: Feste Kaiser Wilhelm II 1893-1918by* Bernard Bour and Gunther Fischer, France, 1992.)

From the ruins of the Second Reich

World War I resulted not only in Germany's defeat, but also in its partial dismemberment. The victorious Allies ignored American President Woodrow Wilson's caution to seek a "Peace without victory" and attempted to cripple Germany with one of the harshest treaties of the century. When the new German government, the Weimar Republic, sent its representatives to the Paris Peace Conference of 1919, it was faced with the alternative of signing the treaty or face an Allied occupation of Germany. The German government had little choice but accept the terms since Germany was racked by revolution led by the political Left and Right. As the formations of the German army disbanded upon returning home, many of their veterans joined the *Freikorps* formations led by their former officers. The Freikorps put down a revolt led by Spartacists (German Communist Party supporters) in Berlin in January 1919, but were defeated in Bavaria by a Communist force of twenty thousand men. At the same time, they challenged territorial claims to German territory by their new eastern neighbors. In March 1919, the government created the *Vorlaufige Reichswehr* or Provisional German Defense Force, which numbered almost fifty brigade-size formations largely taken from the Freikorps, giving it a strength of about 400,000 men. The new Socialist government of Bavaria was smashed by the provisional army troops sent by the Weimar government in May 1919. In June, with Allied encouragement, a Republic of the Rhineland declared its independence from Germany, but in a week the Weimar government again used the army to quell the revolt.

Although this provisional army was large and effective against civil disorder, it did not have the ability to face an invasion of the Western powers. Thus, amid this civil strife the German representatives had no alternative but to sign the Treaty of Versailles at the end of June 1919. The armistice required the Germans to:

1.   Immediately evacuate all invaded countries including Belgium, France, and Luxembourg along with Alsace-Lorraine within fifteen days of the armistice.

2.   Surrender in good condition: 5,000 guns, 25,000 machine guns, 3,000 trench mortars, 1,700 aircraft.

3.   Evacuate all German armies from all territories on the left bank of the Rhine, which were placed under Allied or American control.

4.   Allow a ten-km-wide neutral zone to be established along the east bank of the Rhine, with Allied held bridgeheads at Mainz, Koblenz, and Koln, and extending from the Dutch to the Swiss frontier.

5.   Withdraw its troops from the former Austria-Hungary, Romania, Russia, Turkey, and East Africa.

6.   Surrender all operational submarines in specified Allied ports within fourteen days or destroy them if not seaworthy. Send sixteen battleships and battle cruisers, eight light cruisers, and fifty destroyers to designated locations to be placed under Allied guard. The remainder of the fleet was to be concentrated in specified German ports to be disarmed by the Allies.

Thus, after the signing of the treaty in June, the German armed forces were reduced to almost no navy—in November 1918 the bulk of the fleet arrived in Scotland to surrender—no air force, and a large but poorly armed army. Koln, Koblenz, and Mainz were occupied by British, American, and French troops, making it politically impossible for the Germans to negotiate further. [Note: British troops left Koln in late 1929 and the French were replaced in Koblenz by the Americans, who remained there until 1923, and withdrew from Mainz in the summer of 1930.]

In addition to requiring Germany to pay huge sums in reparations, the Treaty of Versailles stripped it of territories that included Alsace-Lorraine and a large part of West Prussia with plebiscites to be held in Silesia and the Saar. These German prizes from earlier centuries were important to Germany's industrial base. The Rhineland, which included the Ruhr, Germany's industrial heart, was demilitarized, and three bridgeheads were occupied by Allied troops. This provision left Germany virtually defenseless in the west since the vast majority of its fortified sites were located in the demilitarized zone and the lands returned to France. In the East the situation was only slightly better since the nineteenth-century fortresses of Konigsberg and Lotzen remained in German hands, but they were in East Prussia, which was cut off from the remainder of Germany by the establishment of a coastline for Poland. The major German port of Danzig became a free city under the administration of the League of Nations. Some older fortifications at Kiistrin, Breslau, and Glogau remained in German hands, but any fortifications of significance were destroyed or neutralized. Feste Istein on the Rhine was the only armored feste to remain in German territory and, like Helgoland, was closely scrutinized by the Allies. Its turrets and cloches were dismantled and its blocks destroyed by mid-1920, thus losing its military value. According to the terms of the treaty, only the old fortifications of Konigsberg, Kiistrin, Glogau, Breslau, Ulm, and Ingolstadt were allowed to be maintained, but not renovated. None of them included antiaircraft weapons and their facilities and weapons were obsolete. However, the treaty actually placed no restrictions on the development of antiaircraft weapons, only specifying that "All fortified works, fortresses, and field works situated in German territory to the west of a line drawn fifty kilometers to the east of the Rhine shall be disarmed and dismantled," (Article 180) and it forbade any reconstruction of these positions. Essentially, the Germans kept the right to maintain only a few fortifications on their eastern and southern borders.

Except for Danzig, Germany retained most of its key harbors, but the fortifications which protected them were specifically neutralized as required by Article 115: "The fortifications, military establishments, and harbors of the Islands of Helgoland and Dune shall be destroyed." The same terms applied to the approaches to Bremerhaven, the Jade, and the naval base at Wilhelmshaven. The treaty further specified that the Germans were forbidden from reconstructing any similar installations. Those coastal fortifications that the Germans were allowed to retain could only be maintained in their existing condition. They included the defenses at Cuxhaven and Wilhelmshaven in the North Sea and Swienmunde and Pillau in the Baltic Sea.

The German navy was allowed to maintain six old battleships, six light cruisers, twelve destroyers, and twelve torpedo boats, but under special restrictions regarding their replacement. The German navy was forbidden to have submarines. In addition, Germany was denied the right to maintain an air force even though General von Seeckt and others attempted to have the treaty modified to allow some aircraft. Finally, to make certain that the new Germany would remain virtually at the mercy of its neighbors, the German army was restricted to a strength of 100,000 men, which meant at best ten weak divisions including seven infantry divisions of about 11,200 men each and three cavalry divisions of about 5,500 men each. Armored vehicles were forbidden although the police were allowed to have a certain number of armored cars. On September 30, 1919, the Transitional Army or *Ubergangsheer,* replaced the Provisional Army and was reduced almost by half to about twenty brigades. It was not until January 1,1921, that the army further shrank to the 100,000-man limit and the *Reichswehr* (German armed forces from 1921-1933) was established to administer the *Reichsheer* (army) and the *Reichsmarine* (navy).

The Versailles treaty also imposed restrictions on military service, requiring enlisted men to serve twelve years and officers twenty-five years in order to prevent the creation of a large reserve. This meant that a massive mobilization would bring forth largely untrained recruits with an insufficient number of officers on active duty to train and lead the new formations. As a final touch, the Allies included a clause in the treaty that required Germany to acknowledge responsibility for causing the war and accept all war guilt. Clearly this was retaliation for Germany's treatment of France after the Franco-Prussian War. [17]

As in the case of the Treaty of Frankfurt of 1871, the terms of the Treaty of Versailles laid the seeds of the next war as the Germans soon referred to this document at the *Ver-*

[17] Hitler (right) in the Sigfried Line

sailles Diktat. It did not take long for the reactionary forces of the Right to react. During the autumn of 1919, Adolf Hitler took control of the newly formed National Socialist Party ("Nazis") in a German beer hall. In March 1920, half a year after signing the treaty, the Freikorps was on the march again. The Ehrhardt Brigade moved on Berlin and attempted a coup against the government, declaring Wolfgang Kapp the new chancellor. At this time the Freikorps had little popular support and the Transitional Army refused to join it, thus allowing the revolt to fail. Germany's Weimar government returned to power and order was restored. While the situation stabilized, the new Nationalist Socialist Party formed a paramilitary group known as the *Sturmabteilung* (Storm Detachments or *SA),* which consisted of many former members of the Freikorps. By 1923, the Nazis numbered seventy thousand members in Bavaria. In 1924, they launched an unsuccessful coup which landed Hitler in prison where he wrote his infamous *Mein Kampf.*

As a result of Germany's inability to pay the huge reparations required by the treaty, the French and the Belgians had occupied the Rhineland the year before which created a great deal of ill-will in the country, but did not significantly improve the Nazis's position. The remainder of the 1920s was little affected by the reactionary forces led by the Nazis as Germany's reparations payments were adjusted to a more manageable rate and the country finally began to prosper.

The German military did not sit idly by as the new prosperity improved the situation of the country. Instead they worked on rebuilding Germany's armed forces and defenses in secret. For instance, while the Allied Disarmament Commission supervised the destruction of German fortifications, the Germans managed to prevent complete destruction of the installations at Helgoland, and damage was limited at certain facilities and underground works which would facilitate the reconstruction of the fortress at a later date. The Inter-Allied Military Commission remained in Germany from 1920 until 1925, but it paid more attention to violations of the 100,000-man army limit and the illegal existence of the General Staff operating under another title than the fortifications. Thus improvements on the fortified positions on the eastern border went largely unnoticed. The three engineer battalions of the new Reichswehr quietly modernized the five old forts near Kixstrin to protect the route leading to Berlin and worked on a defensive water system between the Warthe and Oder Rivers. Further up the river at Glogau, they built emergency positions to protect the vulnerable frontier from a possible Polish invasion.

The German frontier was irregular and quite as vulnerable as its industrial regions. The Western Front was virtually indefensible. Germany's industrial heart, the Ruhr and the Rhineland, were occupied or demilitarized and the Saar was practically lost. Germany's second most important industrial region in Upper Silesia was in an area that formed a vulnerable arm only about one hundred kilometers wide projecting between Poland and the new Czech state, making it difficult to defend. The remaining industry was scattered throughout central Germany, but it would not be able to sustain Germany in any but a short war. In addition, East Prussia was isolated from the remainder of Germany by the Polish Corridor which was from seventy-five to one hundred kilometers wide. The valuable agricultural lands of East Prussia could be quickly lost since the small Reichsheer did not have enough troops to defend it effectively and protect the other eastern borders at the same time. Fortunately for Germany, its new borders "were secured by the Locarno Conference.

The Germans decided to create a line of small bunkers in the east, which was dubbed the "skeleton line" in American military summaries of the period. The idea was to expand and reinforce this sketchy line when the time was right. Construction was begun along the Oder River to protect Upper Silesia and outside of Glogau on a bridgehead that would support future offensive operations. More work was done in front of Kiistrin, Konigsberg, and in the lake area around Lotzen.

After 1925, the Inter-Allied Military Commission remained in Berlin and, surprisingly, relied only on Germans to do the field investigations. It was not until 1926 that their reports exposed much of the illegal work. When the Inter-Allied Military Commission was disbanded at the beginning of 1927, the Conference of Ambassadors decided on the fate of these new positions in February 1927. Boguslaw Perzyk and Janusz Miniewicz summarize in *Miedzyrzecki Rejon Umocniony (The Fortified Front of the Oder-Warta Rivers)* the new rules that were imposed by the Conference of Ambassadors. Fortifications were banned from most of East Prussia, a zone between the Oder River and the Polish border, and an area about fifty kilometers behind the Polish border in Pomerania. This forbidden zone covered most of the German frontier. Of the new positions that had been built, the conference allowed the Germans to retain thirty-four installations near Konigsberg, fifteen near Lotzen in East Prussia, and eight on the west bank of the Oder near Glogau. They ordered the destruction of another twenty-two positions near Konigsberg, eight on the right bank of the Oder at Glogau, and five near Kiistrin. These numbers appear rather insignificant since they do not represent an impressive amount of work, except at Konigsberg. The positions built at Kiistrin were little more than concrete shelters for the equivalent of one or two squads. The only firing embrasures were in the interior, covering the entrance of these simple positions.

The Germans refrained from further work on defenses after this. Instead, as they had done between 1923 to 1925, they carried out reconnaissance work for future defenses during the next few years. The German situation in the East was considered more critical than in the West because after the Russo-Polish War of 1918-1920, it appeared that a strong Poland had emerged in territories taken from Germany, Austria (former Austria-Hungary), and Russia. The new Poland was emerging as a major force in the East after defeating a Soviet invasion and laying claim to its old territories, which included a variety of fortified positions such as the Austrian fortress of Przemysl, which had been considered the strongest in Europe after Metz, Verdun, and Krakow before 1914. Poland also inherited several Russian fortress positions including Warsaw and Brest-Litvosk. From the Germans, the Poles obtained the fortifications of Graudenz, Kulm, Thorn, and Posen. The Poles themselves did not lack fortification experts since their new army included generals like Emil Gologorski, the inspector general of engineering for the Austro-Hungarian army in 1912 and the designer of some of the works at Krakow. The Polish victory over the Soviets left the Germans with a nation on their eastern border that, at least on the surface, appeared well protected with fortifications and had an army strong enough to challenge the Reichswehr.

To defend the isolated territory of East Prussia the Germans had the fortress of Konigsberg. The border region with Poland was protected by natural defenses offered by the terrain, such as lakes and forests, which supplemented the very old forts of Boyen and Lotzen and a large number of new infantry works, bombproof shelters, and batteries built to extend the defenses of the forts. The positions in the southeast bordering Poland included only the few new and small positions at Glogau and Breslau, allowed to stand by the Conference of Ambassadors. Between there and the Baltic Sea only the partially completed defenses of Kustrin barred a Polish approach towards Berlin, which was only about 175 kilometers from the border. In 1921 Czechoslovakia had formed the "Little Entente" with Yugoslavia and Romania, which further endangered the German position in Upper Silesia. This entire eastern frontier was a cause for great concern for the German political and military leaders throughout the 1920s.

Rise of Nazism

The political, economic, and social factors of the early 1930s led to rapid change, and the military passed from a period of retrenchment in the 1920s to one of massive expansion and defiance of the so-called *Diktat of* 1919. The Great Depression hit Germany as hard as the other industrialized countries. This was the turning point when the people found themselves being pulled by the forces of Fascism to the Right and Communism to the Left. Fascism offered more immediate relief from their problems. The SA Brown Shirts increased to a membership of over sixty thousand by 1930. The Nazis offered the industrialists and middle class an alternative to the spreading fear of Communism which would eliminate them. Unlike other Western governments, the Weimar government did not seem to instill confidence in its population to maintain control and the result was that many Nazis were elected into the German *Reichstag*. The methods used to take over the reins of government are well known from this point. Hitler, attempting to make the final bid for power, actually failed in his attempt to win the presidency from Paul von Hindenburg in 1932, but his political party was still able to dominate the government and helped put him into power as chancellor in 1933. The army feared that the growing SA would become a rival military force unless this paramilitary group were subdued. This was done in 1934 in an agreement made between Hitler and the army and later they would have to swear their loyalty to him. Hermann Goring organized the secret air force, although the work had been done before and without him. Only the navy was able to maintain a non-political stance.

In 1933 General Werner von Blomberg became the defense minister and General Freiherr von Fritsch became the *Chef der Heeresleitung* or commander-in-chief of the army, with General Ludwig Beck as chief of the Truppenamt. The first two were receptive to more modern ideas and technology, but Beck believed in the older methods. Finally, Beck allowed the formation of the first panzer division in the 1935. Still, in the early 1930s, despite the modernization of the army and its expansion in 1934, it virtually had no real ability to wage offensive war and was too widely distributed to successfully defend the borders of Germany which were only lightly protected. Despite the preparation for the expansion into twenty-one infantry divisions, the army lacked the trained reserves from which to draw. They were available to draw from some militia units of mixed value but the only relatively reliable formation was the East Frontiers Guards or the *Grenzshutz,* which amounted to forty thousand men or more. The Reichswehr had helped subsidize this force for years to protect the eastern borders. There were also some security police formations made from veterans of the post-war Freikorps and other units that could be drawn from, but their numbers were probably similar to those of the Frontier Guards. This situation began to change in 1934 as the government turned into a dictatorship under Hitler and all opposition was removed. A ten-year, non-aggression pact with Poland in January 1934 temporarily secured the eastern border as Germany prepared to break the restraints of the treaty that had limited its military forces.

Rearming and fortifying the Reich: the Wehrmacht prepares

By 1936 the *Heer* (army) increased to thirty-nine divisions, the number of regiments continued to grow, and German industry began to be mobilized for complete rearmament. Meanwhile, the projects of the military engineers were implemented as fast as possible in the east to secure the border with Poland.

The German Army High Command directed work to be done along three positions on the Polish frontier: the Oder Line covering Schlesien, the Pomeranian Line on the Pomeranian frontier, and, between them, an advanced position east of Kustrin and Frankurt on the Oder, which b'ecame the first German fortified front by 1936.

As planning and construction were beginning, a major change took place in the organization of the military service for fortifications. [18] Until 1933, Group Command 1 and Group Command 2 were staffed by officers of the *Pioniere* (engineers). Each of these command groups was in charge of several *Wehrkreiskommando* (military district headquarters) staffed by military engineers responsible for recommending and directing construction operations in the military region under their command. The *Wehrkreiskommando* were further subdivided into one or more fortress or fortifications command offices. In October 1934, a major reorganization took place when the *Inspection der Ostbefestigungen* (Inspectorate of the Eastern Fortifications) and the *Inspektion der Westbefestigungen* (Inspectorate of the Western Fortifications) were founded in Berlin and placed under the *Oberkommando des Heeres* (Army High Command). Each of these inspectorates were further subdivided into *Festungsinspektionen (Fest.Insp.)*—Fortress Inspectorates. As the army expanded, so did the number of engineer officers.

---

[18] Siegfried Line

By August 1936, the Inspectorate of Western Fortifications moved from Berlin to Wiesbaden and set up its own fortress inspectorates. In addition in 1936, *Festungs-Pionier-Stabe (Fest.Pi.St.)*, or Fortress Engineer Staffs, were formed to provide closer supervision of the work on the defenses. The actual construction work was mainly in the hands of civilian contractors and workers, who, in many cases, were drawn from youth groups.

Early in the 1930s, some work had already been done on these positions. Janusz Miniewicz and Boguslaw Perzyk claim in *The Pomeranian Wall* that by 1932 twenty troop shelters had been built at Neustettin (today Polish Walcz) and reinforced positions for heavy machine guns at Deutsch Krone (today Polish Szczecinek). Barbed-wire obstacles and steel stakes were placed the following year to hamper enemy advance. Between the Oder and the Pomeranian Lines obstacles were erected on the planned fortified front that eventually became the Oder-Warthe Bend (OWE). After Hitler took full control during 1933, the work on these fronts continued at a faster pace.

Terrain reconnaissance on the Pomeranian frontier, the Oder position to the south, and in East Prussia had been carried out in 1928 and 1929. General Otto-Wilhelm Forster, who as a lieutenant colonel had participated in the reconnaissance work, pointed out in *Das Befestigungswesen* that East Prussia was considered the most vulnerable piece of German territory because it could be quickly isolated. Thus construction of fortifications began in 1931 in the Heilsberg Triangle and additional work was done in the Samland Fortress in 1932. The Samland Fortress was given two fronts: an eastern one on the Deime River from Kurisches Lagoon to Labiau following the river to its junction with the Pregel River at Tapiau, and a southern front that extended from Tapiau to the marshland of Frisching, along the Frisching River to Tharau, and on to the Frisches Lagoon at Bradenburg. These two fronts formed the main line of protection for Konigsberg. Even though the positions along these fronts were weak, Type-C strength, combined with the water barriers they would be sufficient to form a line of resistance against an enemy advance. The *Heilsberg Stellung,* or Heilsberg Triangle, a small fortified area about forty kilometers south of the south front of Samland was the only area in East Prussia that was allowed to be fortified by treaty specifications. The *Heilsberg Stellung* was actually not a triangle but a large semicircle that extended from the front at Konigsberg, passed through Heilsberg, and ran to the Baltic coast. According to some sources, it also included the Samland Front. To the east of Heilsberg, near the frontier, was the Lotzen Position, which relied on the lakes and woods to form a bastion against a surprise Polish advance upon Samland. It is here that the first antitank obstacles in the form of wooden posts were created. By the end of the decade, wooden posts and, later on, concrete obstacles became standard antitank barriers on most fronts.

Oder-Warthe Bend (OWB) - The East Wall

In 1934, most of the defenses in the east consisted of little more than field fortifications; however, serious construction was under way. According to Otto-Wilhelm Forster, work had actually begun on the OWB (Oder-Warthe Bend) Fortified Front in mid-1933 with the first positions of Type-B strength. Although strong Type-A works had been projected at first, the engineers came to the conclusion, according to Forster, that the Polish artillery did not warrant fortifications stronger than Type-B. By the time construction began on the OWB Line, the numerous streams, lakes, ponds, and swamps in the area had already been harnessed to form barriers. Dams had been built to control flooding and bridges had been prepared for demolition. Between 1934 and 1938 the OWB Line became a giant

training and experimental area for developing fortifications, whereas only components and even individual types
of fortifications were built and tested at Hillersleben in
central Germany west of Magdeburg. Clearly, building an
entire fortified line at a place like Hillersleben solely for experimental purposes would have been uneconomical. Testing fortifications on the OWB Line offered the possibility
of experimenting while securing the frontier at the same
time. A closer examination of the OWB reflects the development of various types of German fortifications in the
1930s, ranging from the massive type of combat block reminiscent of the French blocks in the Maginot Line, to the
smaller class of positions used for defense in-depth.

The OWB fortified position began as the Nischlitz-Obra
Line. Its southern end was anchored on the Oder River
(Polish Odra) where it was linked to Lake Nischlitz; its
northern end was anchored on the Warthe River from
where it continued westward to join with the Oder. The
Oder itself flowed westward and then northward, passing
through Frankfurt and Kustrin where it merged with the
Warthe, creating an effective water barrier oh the north,
south, and west. Most of the terrain to the east between
the two ancho'rs of the Nischlitz-Obra Line, devoid of natural barriers, needed to be fortified so the eastern edge of
the quadrilateral formed by the fortified line and the rivers
could be sealed. This area would eventually become known
as the Oder Quadrilateral. [19]

----

[19] Type 10 Lines programme bunker seen from the back.

In 1934 some of the natural water obstacles of the Nis-chlitz-Obra Line, such as lakes, ponds, marshes, and streams, were improved upon. Small concrete positions were built to protect the area, dams and sluices were built at five sites south of Lake Nischlitz, and rolling and sliding bridges were built over the streams. The rolling bridges consisted of two sections, one of which was mechanically slid back into the other on the friendly side of the crossing. The bridge machinery was housed in a room below the bridge and on the safe side. The rotating bridge consisted of a main span that pivoted ninety degrees. Interestingly enough, not all of these bridges were of metal, some were made of wood, which made them easier to destroy. The pre-existing concrete bridges had to be defended or de-stroyed in case of attack.

Some of the machinery and sluices were later improved with Type-A concrete construction with walls 3.5 meters thick, and also included a weapons position with an em-brasure for a light weapon to protect the door. For in-stance, Position 602 protected a sluice adjacent to a defended road bridge with a sliding span. Besides Position 602, four other sluices in the southern sector, to the south of Lake Nischlitz, were protected by similar fortified positions in 1935. However, not all water barrier positions were similarly protected. In some cases, wooden dragon's teeth were installed on the friendly side of the canal or water obstacle where the banks were soft.and the enemy could ford the river. When the water level rose these obstacles disappeared from sight. Great care was also taken to camouflage these defensive positions. For instance, Position 602 was camouflaged to look like a barn. Often plants native to the area were planted around these positions because they could conceal structures far more effectively than man-made camouflage. Water obstacles received first priority because they were key to an effective defensive system in the area.

Much of the OWE Line remained on paper, without actually being built. Nonetheless, the work that turned it into a major line of fortification began in 1935, with the construction of twenty-five concrete positions with a strength of B, Bl, and C, a number of which had armored components. Most machine-gun bunkers had a strength of C, but some were Bl. Some of the earliest fortifications built on the OWB Line were C-type bunkers, known as *Hindenburg Stands,* made of brick on the lower level and reinforced concrete on the higher level and rectangular in shape with dimensions of about eight meters by six meters. The entrance section broke the symmetry of the rectangle. The lower level, usually found below the surface, included a small kitchen, a rest area for the garrison, and quarters for the commander. The upper level housed a combat room, whose front wall consisted mainly of an armored shield with a firing position for a heavy machine gun, a troop room adjacent to the stairway leading down, a protected entrance with an outer door covered by a small-arms weapons embrasure in the wash closet, and a garage for a 37-mm antitank gun or, possibly, a 75-mm infantry gun. The antitank gun was pulled out by its crew and moved to an open firing position usually located above and in front of the bunker. As in most German fortifications, simple instructions were painted onto the walls at certain key points in the Hindenburg Stands. These instructions, not much different than those in WWI-era forts, included warnings to close the crenel shutter while the lights were on, color codes to identify the various wires and cables, instructions on how to operate the heaters, and so on. These fortifications were mainly designed for field troops without specialized training in fortress duty. A total of twelve Hindenburg Stands were built on the OWE Line between 1934 and 1935.

In 1935 more impressive positions of the B- and Bl-type were built on the OWB Line, based on plans prepared during the previous year. The Bl-type constructions generally consisted of a single level and had concrete walls one meter thick. B-type fortifications *(B-Werke}* consisted of two levels with walls half a meter thicker than the Bl. Over a dozen of these massive positions were erected on the Nischlitz-Obra Line in 1935. Except at a key point on the road to Berlin where four were built as a group, these bunkers stood alone along the line.

Large bunkers of this type were designed for all-around defense. Although their features varied, most included at least one combat room with a wall formed by an armored plate with an embrasure for a heavy machine gun. A three-embrasured, cupola-like position that might be termed a half cloche, was embedded in the concrete wall and provided a field of fire of about 180 degrees from its crenels. Either a flanking combat room for a machine gun or more simple small-arms embrasures covered the entrances. Some bunkers had one or two entrances secured by armored doors and most designs also included a chamber covered by an interior embrasure. In the entrance hall there was usually a decontamination area with some type of shower arrangement. Some B-Werke included the new six-embrasure cloche in the roof which afforded all around coverage and/or had a position for a small observation cloche. A few even included a garage for a 37-mm antitank gun. The interior facilities were complete with quarters for the garrison, latrines, a kitchen, a communications room, a power source, and an emergency exit.

The most important yet weakest sector of the Oder-Warthe Bend Fortified Front was the central sector known as *Hochwalde*. Unlike the northern and southern sectors, which had the advantage of water obstacles, the Hoch-walde or Central Sector had to rely on concrete and steel to create a barrier. It was here that most of the *Werkgruppen,* groups of fortified B-Werke positions constituting a new type of fort, were established. The individual B-Werke of a werkgruppe were similarly equipped with the stand-ard weapons, but differed in size, shape, and type and number of combat and observation positions. Most werk-gruppen or fortified groups were connected by under-ground tunnels and many were also linked to the huge tun-nel system of the Central Sector. Eventually, the B-Werke were often referred to as *Panzerwerke* (armored works), but this term was generally applied to all positions of any type built during the war. On the East Wall, the term *B-Werke* continued in use.

The entire area encompassed by the new fortified front was placed under the strictest security; overflights were carefully restricted and rigid ground security was main-tained. The *Fest.Insp.III* at Kiistrin, which was in charge of the operations, delegated the supervision of the actual con-struction to *Fest.Pi.St.6* and *Fest.Pi.St.7,* which were setup in 1936 at Kiistrin and moved in 1937 to Sternberg and Zie-lenzig respectively. However, work on the first B-Werke had started long before the formation of either of these two fortress engineer staffs.

Before construction could begin, the network of roads in the area had to be improved. Most of these military roads consisted of a gravel surface, but where necessary, cobbles were used as well. In areas too soft for heavy vehicles, concrete slabs were laid to form tracks for the vehicles to follow. The year 1934 saw the birth of the first two positions of *Werkgruppe Ludendorff,* situated on a rise known as Fox Hill (today Lisia Gora), on a bend of the Obra River, which was crossed by a north-south road connecting Althofchen Miihle to the main east-west road from Schwiern to Kustrin. The first of the B-Werke to be built was number 522, an unusually shaped position that later became the entrance block for Ludendorff. Its upper level consisted of a firing chamber facing to the rear with two flanking firing embrasures, each of which covered one of the two armored door entrances. Each of these doors opened into an L-shaped entrance hall covered with a small drawbridge which opened up to cover the interior armored door at the end of the "L." One of these entrance halls had direct access to a large decontamination room, a rather unusual arrangement, because in other B-Werke the decontamination facility was located in a niche, at the angle of the "L." A six-embrasure cloche for all around defense was embedded at the front of the upper level and overlooked the concrete bridge over the Obra. The lower level, located below the ground behind the upper level, included the engine and filter rooms, barracks or rest areas, and two emergency exits. The roof of the lower level was not covered by earth and served as a loading position that was accessed from the main road by a path of concrete slabs. Inside the lower level, a shaft led down to an underground tunnel that led to the next two positions built, initially also designated as position 522. Later, a large subterranean caserne was added to the underground facilities and was linked to additional blocks built in 1937 and later. The other two positions identified as 522 were later redesignated as 866 and 867 and the entrance became 865. Position 866 was an experimental casemate with an armored plate pierced by an embrasure for a 37-mm antitank gun and another similar armor plate for the roof of the firing chamber for the antitank gun. This position was small and had a single level plus a three-embrasure half cloche and it covered the concrete bridge over the Obra. The other position, 867, completed by 1936, was an even smaller two-level block which included a three-embrasure half cloche also facing toward the concrete bridge. A tunnel was made of prefabricated sections. Three additional blocks were planned and built after 1936 and completed by 1938. During the war additional smaller supporting positions were added and the group was designated, as *Werkgruppe Ludendorff.*

Positions 863, 864, and 868 were added before 1939. Position 863 was a small, three-level block with a three-embrasure half cloche *(dreischartenturm)* that covered a bend in the Obra River with its machine gun. Position 868 was even smaller and consisted of a six-embrasure cloche *(sechsschartenturm)* placed almost at the center of the werkgruppe. Position 864, located between 863 and 868, which served as another entrance block and included a six-embrasure cloche, was a more typical B-Werke because it included two entrances with armored doors that opened into an L-shaped tunnel, each of which was covered by an embrasure for light weapons. A small drawbridge in the inner arm of the "L" covered a four-meter-deep trap. A niche with a decontamination shower and basin was located at the corner of one of the L-shaped corridors. A flanking machine-gun casemate covered the entrances. Position 864 also included a cloche for an M-19 50-mm automatic mortar, one of the standard features on most of the B-Werke. It may have also had a standard fortress flamethrower in the roof, but this is difficult to confirm because the blocks were heavily damaged by the Germans in 1945. Unlike most similar positions, 864 consisted of a single level but it had an elevator shaft and a stairway that led to a gallery that linked it to the other two positions and a large under-ground caserne. Werkgruppe Ludendorff was surrounded and subdivided into three sections on the surface by barbed-wire obstacles. Compared to most other werkgrup-pen of the East Wall, Ludendorff was unique because of its number of blocks and their unusual types, which is not surprising since it was the first werkgruppe and was used as a testing ground.

While Werkgruppe Ludendorff was still under construc-tion, work began on other werkgruppen. By 1939, two ad-ditional groups were built in the northern sector, but un-like Ludendorff, they only consisted of a single position each. These two one-block werkgruppen were linked by a tunnel to two detached cupolas. Because Ludendorff was experimental it had six blocks while most werkgruppen had three to four blocks. On the southern section of the Oder-Warthe Bend Fortified Front, only one werkgruppe of four blocks was built. On the critical central sector, which lacked natural obstacles, nine werkgruppen were built. Seven of them were connected to the huge tunnel system.

Work on the tunnel system was done in the greatest se-crecy. Old mine shafts in the area were linked to the new galleries, creating about 32.5 kilometers of underground works ranging from twenty to forty meters below ground level before excavations were halted in 1938. The entran-ces to this vast tunnel complex lay about two kilometers to the rear of the main line. The main gallery, which had a railway system planned for it, branched off into many sec-ondary galleries that led to the magazines, casernes, en-gine rooms, and links to several werkgruppen.

The werkgruppen of the Oder-Warthe Bend Fortified Front shared certain characteristics that had resulted from experiments at Werkgruppe Ludendorff and at the testing grounds in Germany. Before construction, various types of concrete, reinforcement, and armor for cloches were meticulously tested. The first cloches were tested at Meppen in 1934, but installation on the werkgruppen did not occur until 1938 because they were expensive and required time to produce. These cloches were made of chrome molybdenum steel (about .5 percent to .7 percent molybdenum content). The essential element, molybdenum, had to be imported from the United States. The weapons of the cloches were purely defensive and included a roof-mounted flamethrower, a 50-mm automatic mortar (the M-19), machine guns, and antitank weapons.

Werkgruppe Scharnhorst is the best preserved position today because, unlike Werkgruppe Ludendorff, it was not destroyed even though the Germans took special measures to prepare all these fortifications for destruction if necessary. Begun in 1937, Scharnhorst was largely completed in 1938 when work was stopped. It included three blocks: 716, 717, and 716a, which was added as an entrance position since, with the exception of Ludendorff, most of these werkgruppen had no special entrance block. The planned strength for Scharnhorst was B-alt. Its entrance included the standard protection in the form of a flanking machine-gun position, a decontamination niche, the drawbridge obstacle, and gas-tight armored doors. Its all-around defense was assured by a six-embrasure cloche *(Sechsschartenturm)* located above a shaft that led down to a subterranean gallery connected to the other two blocks. Position 717 had a single entrance door and, in addition, features similar to 716a, a 50-mm automatic mortar cloche, a flamethrower in the roof, two six-embrasure cloches, and an observation cloche. A shaft led down to the subterranean gallery and caserne, which included an engine room and air filters. Position 716 was similar to 716a, but had no ground-level entrance. The main tunnel system was accessed from Scharnhorst's underground works. A fourth position had been planned but wasn't built. The individual positions were usually served by a crew of thirty to fifty men. The remaining werkgruppen were essentially similar in design.

In addition to the combat blocks, obstacles such as barbed wire, the famous concrete dragon's teeth known as *Hockerhindernisse,* and even an antitank ditch were laid out on the OWE line. The dragon's teeth were concrete pyramidal structures that were arranged in rows by various heights and were designed to impede the advance of tanks. In addition, plans were already drawn up for the construction of several panzer batteries, which were to include individual block positions for guns in turrets. These batteries would have belonged to the A-Werke category, consisted of three blocks, and mounted one heavy armored turret with a 105-mm gun for long-range fire. In actuality, only the foundation was laid out for Panzer Turret 3 block of Panzer Battery 5, which was linked to the southern end of the tunnel system. Some work was done on three other battery positions, but the project ran out of funds and material. Four additional panzer batteries for 150-mm howitzers never went beyond the planning stage. The turrets for these artillery batteries could be produced at a rate of two per year. With war looming, none were completed even though Hitler did not order all work to cease on these batteries in 1938. Nonetheless, in 1938 these East Wall fortifications were given a lower priority than the West Wall and most of the other Wehrmacht projects. At the time that Hitler visited the Oder-Warthe Bend Fortified Front in November 1935, construction was just beginning on many of the larger positions and he agreed for the work to go ahead. It is likely that Hitler was not very enthusiastic about the project, but went along with the recommendations of the military simply to defy the restrictions of the Treaty of Versailles. When he returned in 1938, Hitler was infuriated by what he beheld. Apparently he had not given these fortifications much thought for about three years and was astounded by the huge appropriations and efforts expended on an extravagant tunnel complex and the large B-Werkes that mounted so few weapons.

Expansion of the German Armed Forces

The year 1938 brought some drastic changes to Germany's fortifications program. Although Hitler had allowed a massive fortifications program to develop in the East between 1934 and 1938, he turned his eyes increasingly toward the West in 1936. In addition, he encouraged industry to gear up and arm and equip the newly created *Wehrmacht,* which replaced the Reichswehr in 1934. Thanks to the system instituted by von Seeckt in the 1920s, the German army began to expand rapidly into its twenty-one infantry division program in 1934 and 1935. In March 1935, the West watched paralyzed as Hitler formally announced Germany's intentions to break with the Versailles *Diktat* and ordered conscription for the creation of thirty-six infantry divisions in order to expand the Wehrmacht into a force of over 500,000 men. Most of these thirty-six divisions acquired all three of their infantry regiments, their artillery regiment, their engineer battalion, and their antitank battalion by mid-1936, but equipment shortages began to develop. A Four Year Plan for economic development and rearmament was developed in the fall of 1936 to prepare for full militarization. Before 1935, the government had spent just under 9 percent of its budget on the armed forces. That amount would rise to almost 16 percent in 1935 and steadily increase at about 7 percent or more a year until it reached 42.7 percent in 1938. By then, the army was able to form as many as fifty-one divisions of all types.

Germany's admirals, not to be left behind, proposed an ambitious naval building campaign to acquire capital ships and U-boats, and the Luftwaffe requested large numbers of aircraft. In addition, as early as 1933 Hitler considered the tank a key weapon in future campaigns. He got the idea in the summer of 1933 when he visited Heinz Guderian, one of the founders of the German panzer arm, at the Kummersdorf testing ground and was given a thirty-minute demonstration which included a platoon of the experimental *Panzer I*. After watching the tank platoon and other motorized platoons, Hitler declared "Thats what I need ... That's what I want to have!"

The fortifications in the East were considered important only until the Wehrmacht was able to expand into a force large enough for major offensive operations. German industry was not able to produce the first cloches for the fortifications until 1938, but even before that time the fortress engineers had to compete for steel products with other big consumers: the panzer force and the Kriegs-marine. Aircraft and weapons also drew upon other valuable resources, such as bauxite and copper, that were needed for the construction of fortifications.

Between 1935 and 1936 Germany's political and military situation changed drastically. At the time Hitler had endorsed the work in the East, and he could r.ardly fortify the western border since the Rhineland was still demilitarized. To -.he south, his bid to dominate Austria in 1934 failed when Italy threatened with intervention, but the mountainous terrain provided sufficient protection for his reace of mind. The Czech frontier was vulnerable, so Hitler ordered the construction of a few small and weak bunkers along the main routes into Germany in 1935. However, the threat from Czechoslovakia was relatively minor so work on this frontier received low priority and limited funds. To the east, Poland, which possessed a large army, was considered the most serious threat to Germany, so the defenses in East Prussia and the East Wall along the frontier from Pomerania to Silesia were given first priority.

Strategic and Economic Planning

In the 1930s, the General Staff planned to build the fortifications in the East in three phases, which involved the
building of a skeleton position, the reinforcement of the
position, and the completion of the line. The first phase
saw the construction of a skeleton line called *Sicherheit-
sausbau* (security position). This initial work was meant to
prevent the enemy from penetrating the front and to delay
his advance long enough to allow troops to assemble for a
counterattack. To more offensive-minded generals, this
work would also support and serve as a base for an advanced guard. During the first phase only the most important permanent combat positions and observation posts
were built. Plans were made to expand existing anti-infantry and antitank obstacles and a rudimentary communications system was established. During the second phase,
called the *Verstarkungsaubau* (reinforcing the position),
all remaining bunkers needed to ensure enfilading fires
along the entire line were built. The number of positions
was also increased to give depth to the line and additional
obstacles were added. The third and final construction
phase, called *Armierangsaubau* (building of field fortifications), involved the completion of the line by covering gaps
and providing additional support for the permanent positions. However, at the eve of World War II, this work was
only partially completed. During this last stage, work was
done near or on the frontier so as not to disrupt agricultural activities until necessary. Special shelters for construction and maintenance equipment for completing the
work on the defenses called *Armierungsschuppen* were
built and readied for use.

The East Wall was a necessary commitment for Germany
while the Wehrmacht expanded and the Luftwaffe built up
its inventory and trained pilots. The Reichsmarine was a
special problem because its involvement in a war with Po-

land or Czechoslovakia would be minimal, but it would play an important role in a war with the western powers and therefore it needed capital ships and submarines.

By 1935 the German army consisted of three army groups and had grown to r.venty-nine divisions organized into ten army corps. This force included two cavalry divisions, and in October 1935 it acquired the first three panzer divisions f quipped with light Panzer I tanks that mounted only machine guns. April 1935 marked the debut of the Luftwaffe under Hermann Goring. Until then the air force units had been hidden in other organizations, but they were quickly incorporated into the new Luftwaffe and assigned to one of six *Luftkreis-Kommandos* or Air Force Service Area Headquarters. There were thirteen *Flieger-Gruppen* (wings) and nineteen *Flak* (antiaircraft) battalions, which were taken over from the army. In 1935 the Luftwaffe numbered twenty thousand men and just under two thousand aircraft, but it was far from a formidable force. The first fighter group was *Jagdgeschwader* f/G) 132, which included Arado and Heinkel biplanes: Ar-65, Ar-85, and He-51. The first monoplane fighters, Messerchmitt BF-109 and Heinkel He-112, were still in the design stage and were not tested until the Spanish Civil War more than a year later. A bomber force was built around a number of Junkers Ju-52 airliners designed for Lufthansa, which were converted at the factory into bombers in March 1934. The first bomber group, *Kampfgeschwader KG* 154, was formed with two dozen of these aircraft and three Do-lls, formerly used as cargo carriers. The Junkers Ju-86 was still being developed as a medium bomber. Thus most of Germany's two thousand aircraft were models not designed for combat.

The development of the Reichsmarine was somewhat slower. In the first half of 1935, it had laid down only two new battleships and its surface fleet still consisted of obsolete battleships and two pocket battleships that were no match for any fleet outside the Baltic. Thus in 1935, Germany was not yet ready to take on any of the western powers and certainly not Poland. Construction on the East Wall had to go forward until Hitler could select the time and place to implement the ideas espoused in *Mein Kampf* and by the Nazi Party. The year 1936 constituted a turning point because the attention of the French and British had been focused on Mussolini's invasion of Ethiopia since the latter half of 1935. As that war was coming to a close Hitler prepared to make his first bold move in regard to territorial questions in March 1936. The previous year a plebiscite held in the Saar region returned that territory to the Reich and with it came the valuable economic resources that gave a boost to the German economy and helped arm the Wehrmacht. However, Germany was prevented from protecting the Saar which lay in the demilitarized zone created by the Versailles treaty. Surprisingly, Hitler, who had already openly violated the treaty by creating the Luftwaffe and the new panzer force and exceeding the 100,000-man limits for the armed forces, did not set off any alarms in the west.

In 1936 Germany, whose expanding military was still vulnerable and whose East Wall was still under construction, had little chance of stopping the French despite the fact that France's air force was obsolescent and its army had little appetite for offensive action. Clearly the situation called for caution, bluff, and clever political maneuvering. On March 7, Hitler sent only three battalions into the Rhineland and ordered the small number of aircraft available to the Luftwaffe tc fly back and forth across the demilitarized zone. The German army was instructed to withdraw if the French appeared. However, the French army contented itself with moving into the newly completed Maginot Line, occupying support positions, and waiting. Poland, ready to break its non-aggression pact with Germany-proposed to strike at it simultaneously with France but was turned down. Thus Hitler's limited fortifications in the East missed an opportunity to show their worth. After the occupation of the Rhineland, plans were immediately drawn up to fortify Germany's Western Front and thus secure its most vital economic region

In July 1936, the Spanish Civil War broke out, providing an opportune diversion for the Germans. It not only drew the attention of the great powers away frorr. Germany, but it also gave the Germans the opportunity to test their new equipment and tactics by sending a military force into Spain. As German troops of the Condor Legion and the Fascist Italian forces sided with Francisco Franco 5 Nationalists, the French, the British, and even the Soviets were sucked into the vortex. The association with the Spanish Nationalists was even more fruitful for Germany than the previous arrangement with the Soviets that had allowed the Germans to train men and evaluate equipment at bases within Russia. Now German troops, including air units, could actually test their tactics and equipment under actual battleground conditions. Only the Soviets entered into a similar relationship with the Republican government. Great Britain and France only sent aid depriving themselves of the opportunity to battle-train their troops.

Meanwhile, as the strength of the Wehrmacht slowly grew, Germany's isolation crumbled when Hitler was able to forge an alliance with Mussolini, who stil smarted from the West's rebuke of his Ethiopian adventure. Later in the year, the Berlin to Rome Axis was created.

To continue to expand the armed forces of the Reich it was also necessary for Germany to become economically self-sufficient. In September 1936, Hitler announced the Four Year Plan for economic development and rearmament and put Goring in charge. The main emphasis was on the expansion of iron ore resources for the steel industry, the development of synthetic rubber production, ;r.d the expansion of oil resources. During the latter part of the 1930s, Germany became only second to the United States in the production of iron and steel, but success was achieved through private industry led by the Krupp Werks. Goring also established the Hermann Goring Werks near Hannover largely as a state-financed industry to develop the iron-ore deposits near Hannover. Although -.his venture did not achieve great success, it did increase production. Germany's r reduction centers were concentrated in the Rhineland south of Koln, and in northern Germany around Hannover. However, much of the German iron ore was of low quality (low metallic content), which led to a heavy dependence on swedish iron ore, which was shipped to Narvik, Norway, and from there along the Norwegian coast to Germany. As a result, the security and neutrality of these two nations played a decisive role in German strategy. On the other hand, Belgium and France had significant iron-ore fields close to their borders with Germany, which whetted their neighbor's appetite.

In addition to iron ore from Scandinavia, Germany had to import other key elements for the production of steel for weapons, ships, and fortifications, such as molybendium from the United States and chromium from Turkey. To minimize dependence on foreign sources, strategic stockpiles had to be created in the event of war. Germany also needed oil for its modern war machinery such as tanks, aircraft, and vehicles. Synthetic oil production from both lignite and coal was expanded until the eve of the war. By 1940 Germany achieved 80 percent of its intended oil production under the Four Year Plan. The synthetic oil industry was concentrated in central Germany, around Halle and Magdeburg. In 1936 the industry expanded to the area north of Koln. Despite all these efforts, German oil production and refining continued to rely heavily on imports. Of the oil imported in the 1930s, up to 50 percent came from Romania and nearby Austria.

Since rubber could not be produced in Europe, the synthetic rubber industry took on particular importance. In the mid-1930s, Germany possessed the largest rubber manufacturing industry in Europe, but it was largely dependent on raw material from Southeast Asia. Any conflict involving one of the western powers could seriously jeopardize its supply. To remedy the situation, the German petrochemical industry came up with Buna, a synthetic rubber derived from petroleum by-products. The industry was dominated by the IG Farben cartel, which was allowed to take the lead in the production of Buna. By the time the war began production was in full swing. There were only nine Buna plants, concentrated around Halle, Mannheim, and near Koln, but they produced most of Germany's needs.

Despite its best efforts, Germany could not make itself totally independent from the rest of the world, because it did not possess all the natural resources so necessary to its industry. Such was the case for the air industry, which needed to import bauxite from countries like Yugoslavia for the aluminum so vital to the production of aircraft. Other products such as copper, needed for electrical wiring in ships, aircraft, and fortifications, and the production of shell casings, also had to come from sources beyond the borders of the Reich.

Control of the economy was critical to rearmament and to construction of fortifications, but in Germany it reached the point of being absurd. One of the main forces in guiding Germany's economic recovery was Dr. Hjalmar Schacht, a skillful economist who had been president of the *Reichsbank* during most of the 1920s and was reappointed when he also became minister of economics. However, when Goring was appointed economic leader and given the responsibility for the Four Year Plan, he came into conflict with Schacht, causing the minister's resignation in 1937. Under the Four Year Plan of 1936 the ministers of labor, agriculture, and transport came under Goring's domination as well. Walther Funk, who replaced Schacht as the minister of economics, retained the position until the end of the war, but remained subservient to Goring. In 1938 the economic situation became even more confused when Hitler created the *Oberkommando der Wehrmacht (OKW* or Armed Forces High Command) with General Wilhelm Keitel as the chief of staff and himself directly in charge. While the minister of economics attempted to guide the economy, the key decisions for armaments production came out of the OKW through the office of *Wehrwirt-schafts- und Rustungsamt (WiRuAmt)* (the War Economy and Armaments Branch), created in 1939 by the transfer of the *Heereswaffenamt (HWA* or Army Armaments Branch) to the OKW. The person at the top of this chain was Hitler, and his directives essentially decided what each branch of the service would get as they competed for resources. From allotments of resources to fortifications, to battle-ships, to aircraft, the final decisions would be made by the Fiihrer regardless of the military establishment's actual needs. To make matters worse, according to Alan Milward in *The German Economy at War,* a full war economy did not become a reality until well into the war because Hitler was more interested in short, quick wars known as *blitz-kriegs.* This byzantine arrangement led inevitably to waste of resources and inadequate allocations. Late in the 1930s, when Hitler demanded more aircraft production, Goring turned away from a heavy strategic bomber program to in-crease the number of aircraft produced. During the war Hitler stopped work on the surface fleet, although it is questionable that he saved much by interrupting the work on naval vessels already under construction.

The work on the East Wall and the new West Wall put ad-ditional demands on the economic system, which involved not only material resources but labor as well. One solution to the labor problem was the creation of the *Reichsarbeit-dienst (RAD* or the Reich Labor Service) in mid-1935, which oversaw a six-month compulsory service for all young men between ages nineteen and twenty-five. This service provided a sizable force for government and military projects. Thus, when a youth turned nineteen he left the Hitler Youth, which was made compulsory late in June 1935, and served in the RAD. This organization grew out of an idea of Konstantin Hierl, a member of the Nazi Party, who suggested such an organization in the late 1920s when it began as a voluntary organization of the Weimar Republic. At the same time, a similar Nazi Party organization had formed. In July of 1934 the two organization merged to form RAD, which remained under Hierl's leadership.

As the Four Year Plan moved towards making Germany more economical independent for natural resources, another element was developed to increase the effectiveness of the Wehrmacht. This was the German transportation system, which included railroads and roads. Germany's railroad network was one of the largest in Europe, but it strained under the pressure of serving both industry and passengers while having to be ready for military use. To solve some of the transportation problems, Germany began to develop a new autobahn system, which would consist of a network of four-lane, paved roads, forming the world's first super highway system for rapid transit. Work began in 1934, providing jobs for over 15 percent of the nation's unemployed who went to work on its construction and in associated support industries. Between 1935 and 1939 about three thousand kilometers of new roads were completed and fifteen hundred more kilometers of roads were under construction, which represented more than half of the amount authorized by the government. Stettin was linked to Berlin and more road work pushed the system eastward. The section between Berlin and Breslau was still incomplete, but the highways from Berlin to Munich and from Munich to Kassel via Stuttgart and Frankfurt on the Rhine were finished. The autobahn from Bremen to

Hamburg and Lübeck was completed, but work to link Hamburg to Berlin was still in progress. Thus the auto-bahn system still needed much work when the war began in 1939. The man responsible for the autobahn system was Fritz Todt, the inspector general of German roads. To build the transit system he designed, Todt formed an organization (eventually called *Organization Todt* [OT]), that consisted of work crews for construction roads and bridges. Many of its workers were older men until after the war began when it was heavily supplemented by young conscripted non-Germans who would form up to 80 percent of the labor force after the first major conquests.

As the Reich geared up for war in 1936, it did not neglect its navy, which received a portion of the steel and resource allotment. The *Scharnhorst* and the *Gneisenau,* the first major warships to replace the "pocket battleships," were laid down in 1935. These two compromise battle cruisers carried 11-inch guns, like the smaller "pocket battleships," but included an additional 11-inch gun turret and more armor. These ships were built at the end of a Five Year Program designed to produce new destroyers and smaller vessels that had begun in 1932 under Admiral Erich Raeder, who had taken over as commander-in-chief of the navy from Admiral Hans Zenker in 1928. Zenker and his staff had designed the *Deutschland* class in an attempt to have functional warships and yet conform as much as possible to treaty requirements. Raeder, on the other hand, disregarded the treaty requirements as much as he dared, by ordering larger, improved battleships of the *Deutschland* class that could no longer be classified as "pocket battleships." The new warships were built as a result of another diplomatic victory won in June 1935 when the British signed the Anglo-German Naval Treaty, allowing the Germans to create a fleet equaling 35 percent of the strength of the British fleet that included five battleships, two aircraft carriers, and forty-five U-boats. No sooner was the treaty signed than the Germans went to work on the two new battleships. That same month the first submarine, U-l, which had been secretly under construction with several others at Kiel since 1934, went into service. By 1936 twenty-five of these small 500-ton coastal submarines were available, but their number was not sufficient to alarm the British and French.

In 1936 a greater commitment was made to rebuilding the *Kriegsmarine*—the new name for the navy. Work began on the *Bismarck* and the *Tirpitz,* two new 45,000-ton battleships that mounted 15-inch guns. These projects were long-term commitments, needing about three years to complete. Hitler had wanted even larger battleships with twice the displacement and guns of up to 20-inch, but the navy officials managed to convince him of the impracticality of such a warship. The Reich could not expect to have a sizable surface fleet before 1941, yet it was imperative to have a navy ready to protect the iron-ore sea routes from Sweden and Norway.

Late in 1938 the Kriegsmarine, under Admiral Raeder's direction, proposed its Z Plan, which was approved by Hitler in January 1939. This plan proposed building or completing Hitler's six H-Class, diesel-powered, super battleships that displaced over 56,000 tons and mounted 16-inch guns. Two battleships similar to the *Bismarck,* two similar to the *Scharnhorst* (the 11-inch guns on this type were to be replaced with 15-inch guns by 1942), three battle cruisers with 15-inch guns displacing 32,000 tons, two aircraft carriers, five heavy cruiser, four light cruisers, forty-seven destroyers, fifty-four torpedo boats, and two hundred and twenty-nine submarines of all types were to be completed by 1944. Additional units, including nine more battle cruisers, additional cruisers, numerous destroyers, and torpedo boats were slated for completion by 1948. This ambitious plan promised to be a major drain on Germany's industrial assets since it would require more resources than those alloted to the army and Luftwaffe. According to Jak P. Mall-mann Showell, author of *The German Navy in World War Two,* Admiral Donitz opposed the Z Plan, preferring instead to have three hundred U-boats that would cost as much as four battleships and would have required fewer resources. However, Hitler approved the Z Plan, opting for a large surface fleet.

As the European powers became enmeshed in the Spanish Civil War during 1937, Germany stepped up its efforts to defend its borders. Since the East Wall was well under way, much effort was diverted to the new western defenses. Hitler threw up a new smokescreen early in 1937 by publicly demanding a return of Germany's former colonies. Meanwhile, relations with the U.S.S.R. had cooled and the Germans became increasingly suspicious of an alliance between the Soviets and the Czechs. Later in the year they tried to neutralize Poland by signing a non-aggression agreement. In the West, Hitler promised to protect Belgian neutrality in an effort to keep that part of Germany's western frontier protected. Soon, the world's attention became distracted not only by the Spanish Civil War, but also by the Japanese invasion of China after the Marco Polo Bridge Incident in July 1937. The Germans, in need of such raw materials as tungsten, first tried to support the Chinese but then decided to ally itself with the Japanese.

When Hitler demanded a greater number of aircraft for the Luftwaffe, Goring canceled all plans for four-engine strategic bombers in favor of smaller planes to meet the demand. The army had expanded from three to four army group headquarters and since 1936 assembled thirty-nine divisions, which included three panzer divisions equipped mainly with light tanks. On November 5, 1937, Hitler informed the leaders of the Wehrmacht that the time had come to prepare for war and for Germany to create the *Lebensraum* that he had promoted in his early preaching.

Major Fortifications

The East Wall

In East Prussia, Pomerania, and parts of Poland, glaciation from the last Ice Age left a region of moraines dotted with lakes with no unusually rough features. None-theless, on the edges of the North European Plain, there was no lack of natural defenses, despite the fact that most of the moraine did not exceed more than a couple of hundred meters in elevation. In fact, the terrain turns to mud after heavy rains, seriously impeding progress off the roads. To overcome this problem the German government built an autobahn running from Berlin past Breslau and Stettin to Königsberg and Elbing. The segment between Königsberg and Elbing remains in its original state to this very day, only one double lane completed for most of its length. Another autobahn ran from Berlin to Frankfurt-on-the-Oder, making possible rapid reinforcement of all the defensive positions in the east.

The East Wall occupied large sections of the frontier, including the isolated defensive positions of East Prussia primarily protecting Konigsberg. Although it con-unued to be developed throughout the war, it was never actually completed. The East Wall consisted of three distinct lines: the Fortified Front of the Oder-Warthe-Bend, the Pomeranian Line, and the Oder Line. In addition, the Ortelsburger, Lotzen and Christburg Positions formed the border defenses of East Prussia. Finally, the position known as Fortress Samland constituted the final interior line running from the Frisches Lagoon (Vistula Lagoon) to the Kurisches Lagoon (Courland Lagoon) well in front of Konigsberg. The small positions of the Heilsberg Triangle south of the fortress area, which were of little value by the end of the 1930s, are usually overlooked. At Konigsberg, the old fortress ring acted as the last line of defense.

The main defensive line of the East Wall was the Oder-

Warthe-Bend (OWE) Line, which was intended to cover the direct route to Frankfurt-on-the-Oder and Berlin. Intended to be the main defensive front, this position received the most attention. It was planned as a quadrangle extending from Kustrin on the Oder, along the Netze River to the Warthe. Directly to the south the main lines of fortifications covered the gap between the Warthe and the Oder rivers. The intended path of the defenses followed the Oder downstream past Frankfurt to Kustrin. Most of the area consisted of hilly and swampy terrain dotted with a number of lakes.

Before 1939 the OWB Line was the only German fortified front, representing the main defenses on the Eastern Front. It extended for approximately 80 km. The sides of the quadrangle remained uncompleted. The heavily defended sections began near Schwerin (Skwierzyna), at the confluence of the Warthe and Obra Rivers and ran south along the west bank of the Obra to the vicinity of Meseritz (Miedzyrzecz). The line then continued southward to the Oder passing west of Schwiebus (Swiebodzin), a road junction on the main highway toward Frankfurt on the Oder, and then reached the Oder east of Krossen (Krosno Odrz).

The OWE Line included three sectors: Northern, Central, and Southern. The Central Sector, about 15 km long, was the shortest, occupied the terrain with the most relief, and had the heaviest concentration of modern fortifications. Dominated by hills more than any other, this sector was covered by fields, and had hardly any woods at all before the war. The other sectors, also running in the midst of fields, relied heavily on the many lakes and watercourses for defense.

The Oder Line hugged the river between the cities of Glogau and Breslau and was located over 20 km behind the border in most places. South of Breslau the terrain became hilly and more easily defended, especially in the industrial region of Upper Silesia. Between Breslau and Frankfurt there were some low and marshy patches along the river, particularly on the east side of the Oder, down river from Glogau.

The Pomeranian Line began where the Netze River merges with the Warthe River and followed the line of lakes to a point north of Scholochau where the terrain became hilly and began to resemble the morainic regions of East Prussia. [20] For the most part, the main positions were not near the river but ran close to the border. The small wooded moraines that dominated the region were amenable to defense. The plan to extend the line to the sea was never carried out.

The main border defenses of East Prussia began east of

---

[20] Construction of dragons teeth on the West Wall in 1938.

Elbing, near the coast at Braunsberg (Braniewo), followed the Passarge River to Wormditt, turned eastward along the Alle River to Bartenstein (Bartoszyce), then hooked around and covered the town of Allenstein. They were known as the Christburg Position.

The Lotzen Position ran north to south using the heavily wooded Masurian Lake Region for defense. An intricate network of marshes and lakes and a tangle of moraines turned much of the area into a wilderness. This formidable terrain, which extended from Lyck to Osterode and included the Ortelsburger Forest Position, covered the border southeast of Allenstein, joining the Lotzen Position. Access through this region was via easily defended narrow defiles. Both of these positions ran from 20 to 40 km behind the border. The main line, Fortress Samland, began near the sea at Brandenburg, hugged the Frisching River to its source, turned north to Tapiau, and followed the Deime River to the sea.

The West Wall

According to German propaganda, the West Wall ran from the Swiss border to the point where the Rhine enters the Netherlands and consisted of the Army Position, which closely followed the border, and the Air Position which was further back and formed an air defense zone. In reality, the strength of the first position was grossly exaggerated and the second position was never developed beyond an elementary stage. Nonetheless, in World War II the West Wall was the fortified line with the greatest depth in relation to its length.

The West Wall ran along the Rhine and the elevated terrain of the Black Forest in the Upper Rhine Valley and through the wooded and low rolling terrain of the faar region. Further north it passed through the wooded and rough terrain of Hunsruck and Eifel, along the remainder of the Belgian border to the Dutch border, and on to the sea. The West Wall almost ceased to exist along most of the relatively flat terrain near the Dutch border, before it reached the point where the Rhine enters the Netherlands. The West Wall, which spanned over 400 km, consisted of four major sections: Aachen, Trier, Pfalz (the Palatinate), and Oberrhein (Upper Rhine). The main de-rensive positions were the Aachen Advanced Position, the Orscholz Position in the Trier sector, the Hilgenbach Position, the Sprichern Position in the Pfalz, the Fischbach Position, the Ettlinger Position, and the Korken Wald (Forest) Position on the Upper Trine. Most of these positions formed switch lines or oblique lines running off the main line of the West Wall.

The West Wall was located in excellent defensive terrain consisting of hills, — any woods, and forests with the Rhine barrier forming a front line on the Upper Rhine or a final defensive position in other sectors. Only in some sectors, such as the Pfalz, did the Germans sacrifice the advantage of good defensive terrain to move their fortifications closer to the border at the insistence of Hitler.

Coast Defenses

In the North Sea, the German island base of Helgoland was restored to its role as the main position for the protection of the approaches to the ports of Wilhelmshaven, Cuxhaven, and Hamburg. It was located about 50 km from both the mainland to the south, southeast and east. The East Frisian Islands, beginning with Borkum Island in the west and Wangerooge in the east, covered the North Sea coast up to the approaches to Wilhelmshaven. Borkum, Norderney, and Wangerooge mounted the main defenses. The North Frisian Islands, with Sylt Island serving as the main defensive position, shielded much of the coastal region along Schleswig-Holstein. This coastal defense region was known as the *Coast Defense-Naval Command North Sea*. The fortress commander for the East Frisian Area was headquartered at Wilhelmshaven and the commander of the North Frisian Area, in Cuxhaven. In September 1939 the fortress commands became coastal commands and in February 1941 the two regions were unified as the *Coast Defense, German Bight*.

On the Baltic Sea, the pre-war *Coast Defense-Naval Command Baltic* included three autonomous zones: the *West Baltic Coastal Command,* which covered the coast :<f Schleswig-Holstein, Mecklenburg, and the main defenses near Kiel, the *Pomeranian Coastal Command,* concentrated at Swinenmünde (Swinoujscie), and the *East*

The West Wall - Shield for Aggression

After the occupation of the Rhineland, Hitler gave great importance to the construction of fortifications on Germany's western border. Some work had already been done in 1935 on the inner border of the fifty-kilometer demilitarized zone on the east side of the Rhineland. It included defenses along the Main River up to the Tauber River, about thirty kilometers east of Frankfurt on the Main. A second line about fifty kilometers east of Mannheim followed the Neckar River and part of the Enz River and ended west of Stuttgart. The largest works built in both of these lines consisted mainly of Type-C and Type-D bunkers and a few Type-Bis with half cloches and some troop shelters, which were added later. Additional light bunkers built between Siegen and Wesel constituted the Hindenburg Line, according to Polish researchers Rogelski and Zaborowski. This line offered little to no protection for the industrial regions of the Rhineland. In 1936, Hitler presented the General Staff with the mission of defending the Rhineland with what he termed the "Limes." Like the French in the 1920s, the German military leaders weighed the advantages of a continuous line of heavy fortifications over a line with great depth consisting of smaller fortifications. General Erich von Manstein, who served on the General Staff, had proposed in 1935 a fortified line, similar to the Magtnot Line, along the border with France, Luxembourg, and Belgium. However, because of the political situation at the time, he had suggested setting up blockaded zones within the demilitarized Rhineland that relied upon the terrain. After the reoccu-pation of the Rhineland, he again proposed heavy fortifications along the border and lighter fortifications in areas where the terrain provided a sufficient obstacle. Apparently his proposal was endorsed by the fortress engineers as well as General Forster. However, the idea of a deep line of lighter fortifications was also considered attractive. The resulting plan was a compromise. Eventually, however, the idea of defense in depth prevailed and plans for building a number of heavy fortifications were mostly abandoned.

A document called *The Army Service Regulations for fortress Engineers* based on experiences with the Eastern fortifications set out a three-stage process for the creation of a Western fortified front. The first phase called for tactical and technical surveys and the development of both tactical and technical plans. The second phase involved the preparation of construction plans and designs. The third phase involved the actual building. The first phase had already begun in secret before the occupation of the Rhineland. Considering the time allotted to all three phases, the building would have begun in 1938 or 1939 and been completed in about 1942.

The original line was supposed to run from the vicinity of Aachen to the Rhine, south of Karlsruhe and from there it would follow the Rhine. While work went or an intense propaganda campaign was launched in order to allay Allied fears : German aggression to the West and to convince everyone that Germany's interests lay in the East. By making the West Wall appear to be a response to the Maginot: Line, Hitler and his military establishment hoped to convince the West that thev contemplated no westward offensive. Even though the military engineers move: ahead as fast as possible with construction, disregarding their own *Regelbaute.* (standard design), by 1937 only 640 bunkers had been built, many of them of the weak Type-C and D and some Bl. Some of the work included machine-gur. bunkers covering bridges on the Upper Rhine, the Ettlinger Barrier, consisting an antitank ditch and about fifty bunkers of mostly Type-C, and the extension of the Neckar-Enz Line. Streams and vineyards in the Rhineland were to serve **as** antitank obstacles. Ditches were dug and equipped with staggered rows of wooden posts, like in the

East, when these natural obstacles were not available.

The Fortress Engineer Program of 1937 called for building positions of Type B1, C, and D with emphasis soon shifting to Type-B when Hitler interfered. A shortage of resources and insufficient financing pushed the completion date to 1948. In March 1937 that date was moved further back to 1952 because concrete and steel fortifications were considered secondary to warships and tanks. In addition, the new autobahn system received priority for materials over fortifications.

In 1938 serious changes took place as Hitler became directly involved in military affairs. Hitler's first objective was to draw Austria within the sphere of the Reich. Next, he prepared to launch an assault on Czechoslovakia. To secure his western borders he directed a complete change in policy with regard to construction of the new West Wall since a propaganda blitz was not enough to deter a possible French offensive when he struck against the Czechs.

Late in February 1938, Hitler demanded self-determination for the German minority of Czechoslovakians living in the Sudetenland. At the same time, he moved forward with his invasion plans and encouraged local Sudeten Nazis to engage in a campaign of agitation against the Czech government. Meanwhile things had progressed in Austria to the point that Nazi support had risen and the time was ripe for a takeover. After Nazi-inspired rioting in Austria, Hitler ordered the army to cross the frontier on March 12, 1938, and by the next day the entire country was annexed to the Reich. The Austrian armed forces included seven infantry divisions of three regiments, one light artillery regiment, and one engineer battalion each. In addition, the Austrian army included an infantry brigade a mobile division with four motorized rifle battalions, two dragoon regiments, a tank battalion, a motorized pionier battalion, and an aviation and flak unit. All of these formations were quickly incorporated into the Wehrmacht and plans were revised for the invasion of Czechoslovakia, which was now threatened from a new front on its southern borders. The annexation of Austria with its mountainous terrain secured Germany's southern front and added its resources for the Reich.

Case Green, the new plan for the conquest of Czechoslovakia, was ready in April. In May the Czechoslovakians began to mobilize and the French and British, bound by treaty, were expected to come to their aid. The Soviets also insisted they would not abandon their ally. Poland, on the other hand, took a neutral stance because of pre-existing animosity toward Czechoslovakia. Although Hitler seemed confident that Poland would not maintain the ten-year non-aggression pact it had signed with Germany in 1934, he did not expect it to break the agreement over a dispute with Czechoslovakia and was more concerned about his Western front. A war with Czechoslovakia would most likely mean war with the West, which might well cut off the vital imports of raw materials. Before he forced the issue with Czechoslovakia, therefore, Hitler had to secure the front against Poland, and, more importantly, the industrial region of the Rhineland against France. Upon inspection, he found that work on the West Wall was not satisfactory and that work on the East Wall had taken a direction that did not coincide with his own views.

A surprise visit to the East Wall on Thursday, June 30,1938, provoked Hitler's wrath. He was particularly infuriated after his inspection of the Hochwalde sector of the OWE Fortified Front when he came to the conclusion that the massive tunnel complex could only serve as a trap to thousands of men if the vulnerable entrances were smashed by heavy mortars of 305-mm and larger caliber guns. In addition, the large B-Werke served by the tunnels consisted of huge blocks that merely housed small infantry weapons, which, in his opinion, did not justify the large garrisons. The Fuhrer opined that millions of reichmarks

and vast economic resources had been wasted on these positions. He resolved to put his personal touch on the building of fortifications and issued a directive to that effect.

Surprisingly, Hitler's dissatisfaction did not bring an end
to the work on the East Wall. Instead, positions already
under construction were to be completed. Furthermore,
plans went ahead for the erection of massive A-Werke,
which were largely destined for mounting armored batteries. In the Hochwalde, or Central Sector, three batteries
mounting three single 105-mm gun turrets each and four
batteries with three 105-mm howitzer turrets were
planned. In addition, plans were made for thirteen Type Al
positions that would each mount a 100-mm gun in a turret
or casemate. They were referred to as "silent works" because they were not to be committed to battle until enemy
armor had already engaged in the assault. Positions
mounting a 50-mm gun in a turret or a 105-mm gun in a
casemate reached the planning stage, but work had barely
begun on a couple blocks of the armored batteries when
construction was interrupted.

Dieter Bettinger and Martin Buren in *Der Westwall* have
describe the distinct building stages in the development of
the West Wall. The first stage of the Fortress Engineer Program started in 1936 when light positions and barriers
went up. The second, was one of grandiose planning of
eleven A-Werke and twenty B-Werke. The A-Werke were
to be almost as impressive as the ouvrages of the Maginot
Line, but they were never built and the B-Werke were to be
similar to those of the East Wall. Then in the spring of
1938, after Hitler decided to become more personally involved, the "Limes" Phase began. The West Wall was
dubbed the "Limes Position," a name derived from ancient
Roman border fortifications. The West Wall was to be
heavily reinforced before October 1, 1938. In June 1938,
Hitler scaled back the construction on the East Wall, noting in a memorandum of July 1 that it had already served

its purpose. He wanted the work on the West Wall to pick up its pace and in May he put the entire project in the hands of his road builder, Fritz Todt. Beginning in May, with plans for operations against Czechoslovakia underway, Hitler wanted the western fortifications significantly strengthened. The Fortress Engineer Staffs in the West had not been able to accomplish the objective during 1937, partially because resources did not flow freely to meet the demands of construction. Only about 40 percent of the steel required for the building of the "Limes" was actually delivered. In addition, they did not have the power to mobilize the civilian sector like Todt did. The plans prepared by the army required phases of reconnaissance through construction that took too long. In addition, the staffs were only in charge of coordinating the work, which had to be contracted out, or assigned to labor units. The completion date for the West Wall, based on resources allotted and time schedules, was then estimated at about 1954.

The situation changed quickly when Todt took over and was able to redirect significant resources from the economy and speed up the construction schedule by emphasizing mass-production of positions, using many civilian contractors, and ignoring the phases laid out by the army engineers. He promised Hitler four hundred to five hundred bunkers a week in order to meet the completion date of October 1938. Albert Molt, an engineer officer serving with the *Inspektion der Westbefestungen* at the time, observed in *Der Deutsche Festungsbau von der Memel zum Atlantik* that Todt's policy led to a clash between the civilian sector and the fortress engineers. Todt sought a quick and simple solution for the construction of these new bunkers, disregarding at times elements in design deemed important by the military professionals. Some compromises had to be made and about sixty to seventy *Regelbauten* (regulation designs) had to be agreed upon, but generally speaking, Todt's workers used the simplest plans because they were not skilled in this type of work and were not able to produce more sophisticated designs.

Ignoring the carefully laid phases of the fortress engineers, Todt assembled a huge labor force using about one thousand private construction firms organized into twenty-two brigade-size construction units and put them to work as quickly as possible. On June 22, Hitler gave this force the name of Organization Todt or OT. Todt set up his central headquarters at a hotel in Wiesbaden. In addition to the OT, he was able to call upon the fortress engineers and army units, including the engineer battalions and infantry units of General Wilhelm Adam's Army Group 2. This put at his disposal not only a force of up to 90,000 soldiers, but also 340,000 OT men and 100,000 men from three hundred detachments (company-size units) of the expanded RAD. Todt also had much of the railway system at his disposal, which enabled him to use over eight thousand railcars. Many barges and thousands of trucks were also drafted into transporting materials to the Western Front. However, the amount of heavy equipment was limited and the bulk of the construction was done by manual labor. The heavy equipment was limited mostly to cement mixers needed for preparing the concrete and, when necessary, cranes for large beams. Todt's goal was to produce over eight thousand positions by November 1938, but this was a gargantuan task and whether he actually succeeded is a point in question, even though Martin Gross claims in *Der Westwall* that he actually completed twelve thousand bunkers by that time. However, the quality of Todt's work is questionable. General Forster, inspector of engineers and fortifications, commented in the Limes Program of 1938 that the line was little more than an "improvised line of border defense" that consisted of a mere twenty positions per kilometer. A close examination of some of the more heavily defended sectors of the "Limes," such as the one at Aachen, seems to indicate that Forster was probably correct for the most heavily defended sectors. The density of positions per kilometer was probably even less in the more lightly fortified sector.

On June 30, 1938, during his fateful second visit to the East Wall, Hitler had been taken to the nearly completed Werkgruppen Scharnhorst and Lietzmann and the huge tunnel system. The next day, after returning to Berchtesgaden, he dictated a forty-page memorandum dated July 1,1938, in which he presented his views and directives in regard to the construction of fortifications. Claiming that his experiences as a frontline soldier in World War I made him a better judge of what needed to be done than his engineer officers, he insisted that defense in depth was important and that field fortifications had already proved themselves more effective than permanent fortifications. He insisted that armored batteries were not adequate to serve the needs of defenders and that massive permanent fortifications that required crews of 70 to 150 men only served to keep soldiers out of the battlefield and did nothing to prevent the enemy from advancing.

In the memorandum, Hitler set forth his own theory of fortifications and their role in the battlefield. He insisted on smaller, decentralized strongpoints that provided firing positions for every man of the garrison. According to him, the role of the concrete bunker was solely to protect the infantry during non-infantry actions and preserve its strength until the time came to attack. The bunker was to be of sufficient strength to protect the troops from most heavy artillery, but not super-heavy artillery, and to include necessities of life such as wells and latrines, storage space to keep the troops from making unnecessary trips for supplies, and protection against gas-saturation attacks. For the artillery, Hitler insisted on concrete shelters to protect the crews and ammunition, and that most artillery positions should be beyond the range of enemy artillery. Antitank guns had to be placed in forward areas to engage the enemy. Hitler was particularly impressed with the flamethrowers of the last war and wanted them included as a defensive feature of the larger bunkers.

In his memorandum he also covered numerous other issues, from signal communications to the proper use of barbed-wire obstacles, mines, and camouflage. He also made it a point to analyze the work on the East Wall, which he did not find entirely satisfactory, and directed all cloches to be sent immediately to the west since in 1938 the threat from the east was minimal. In addition, Hitler stipulated that the various types of cloche should be installed not only in large structures, but also in smaller ones to make them less vulnerable. Finally, he concluded by expressing his concern for enemy aircraft and explained the proper use of batteries of infantry divisions inside the defensive zone.

Months later during the fall of 1938, Hitler, dismissing the views of engineer officers like Forster, decided that the West Wall should be advanced toward the border in order to fully protect several major German cities and virtually every inch of the territory of the Reich. He proclaimed that "... not a foot of German soil should be occupied by the enemy." Between 1936 and 1938, the more carefully planned positions had been built on good defensive terrain, now they were to be moved up to the frontier. Todt once again did his best to oblige him, despite objections from the commander of Army Group 2, General Adam, who did not approve of the type of fortifications Hitler wanted. After the Czech crisis, Adam was removed and Todt continued working.

As work on the Limes Position forged ahead during the summer of 1938, the Sudeten Germans agitated against the Czechoslovakian government with more vigor and France and Great Britain began making preparations for war. Strangely, at the end of June, the British unilaterally agreed to allow the Germans to build 16-inch gun battleships larger than 35,000 tons in order to appease them. Throughout the month of July, France and Great Britain continued to support Czechoslovakia, while British Prime Minister Chamberlain tried to mediate the crisis. In mid-August the German army called up 750,000 men for military service and began maneuvers near the Czechoslovakian border. Hitler was ready for war even though the Wehrmacht was not. The army, which began expanding from thirty-nine to fifty-one divisions, included three panzer divisions and one parachute battalion (from the Luftwaffe). With the exception of about one hundred Panzer III and IVs and about 625 Panzer Us, most of its fifteen hundred tanks were Panzer Is with machine guns. The Luftwaffe had three *Luftflotten* (air fleets) consisting of a total of six air divisions and twenty-two air groups with a total of about 2,900 aircraft. Over eleven hundred of these aircraft were bombers and nearly five hundred were reconnaissance planes. There were less than seven hundred fighters planes. Air defense was assured by seventy-four flak battalions equipped with a variety of weapons. Nor was the Kriegsmarine ready to challenge the British above or below the waterline.

Czechoslovakia, &i the other hand, was able to mobilize twenty-five to thirty divisions that were relatively well-equipped. Like the Germans, the Czecho-slovakians had built a series of fortifications to protect their frontier from their enemies, mainly Germany. Their heaviest fortifications, built with the help of French advisers, were patterned after the Maginot Line but were largely unfinished. These heavy fortifications were concentrated along a section of the northern border with Germany. The remainder of the border area was covered by lighter fortifications, which were mostly complete or near completion. There were few vulnerable, largely unprotected sectors. The Czechoslovakian air force consisted of a number of relatively modern aircraft. In addition, Czechoslovakia had some powerful allies such as the Soviet Union, which had offered to back it up from bases in Slovakia. If France, with or without the help of Great Britain, had taken action against Germany, the Wehrmacht would have been hard-pressed since the majority of its divisions and its most offensive units would be engaged against Czechoslovakia. If Poland had decided to intervene at that point, which was highly unlikely, Germany would not have had sufficient units to defend the East and West Wall simultaneously. In addition, the German army had not yet developed the anti-personnel mine for mass production, one of the most formidable obstacles of modern warfare. Thus the chief of the General Staff, General Ludwig Beck, who felt that a German assault on Czechoslovakia would most likely end in disaster even if the French failed to intervene right away, resigned on August 18, and several other officers hatched a plot in the event their Fuhrer went ahead with his war plans.

Hitler in the meantime paid a personal visit to the West Wall on August 28 and, with the help of skillful propaganda, convinced the leaders in the West that this line of fortifications was much more formidable than it actually was. Early in September, negotiations continued while Hitler set the date for the invasion for September 27. The French called up their reserves while British Prime Minister Chamberlain did all he could to stave off a conflict. On September 15, Chamberlain flew to Berchtesgaden to see Hitler. The Soviet Union prepared for war and Poland laid claims against territories in Czechoslovakia. Soon, Great Britain and France asked Czechoslovakia to give in to the German demands and the Czechs complied on September 21. The next day, when Hitler made further territorial demands, Czechoslovakia mobilized. French and British forces likewise began to mobilize, but at the end of the month Chamberlain called for a conference.

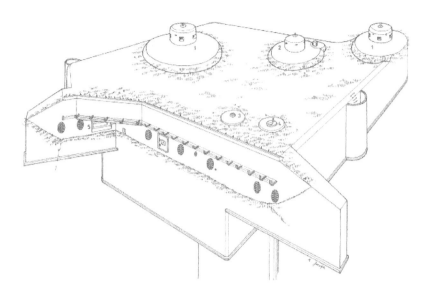

Terms and Features of B-Werke on the East Wall

Beobachtungsglocken—Observation cloche non-movable turret) which was small in size with narrow openings.
Dreischartenturm—Half cloche with three embrasures for weapons. These armored positions were built into the concrete side of a bunker. Feshmgsflammenwerfers—Fortress flamethrower mounted in its own armored position in the roof, which allowed its nozzle to cover 360 degrees. The fuel tanks usually were located in a well-protected room in the bunker. *Luftungskuppeln* Very small ventilation dome located in the roof of a bunker. Maschinengranatwerf —M-19 automatic mortar or grenade launcher mounted in a room with its tube in its own armored cloche. Notausgange—Emergency exit usually located in a wall, earth covered on the outside. Its lower section was filled with sand, which had to be released from the inside so the crew could ascend a "D" shaped well to the surface. Panzerabwehr—Antitank defense. Panzerkasematte—Armored casemate. Sechsschartenturm—Six-embrasure cloche with six posi-

tions for two machine guns and side openings for periscopes. [21]

Werkgruppe—After the end of World War I, the term was applied to many large fortifications, but it was also inappropriately given to groups of bunkers that had no relationship to each other and no links. By a directive of June 9, 1939, all German fortifications were to receive the designation of *Panzerwerk* (Pz.W.) "In order to emphasize the strength of our fortifications. . . ." This was essentially a propaganda ploy that had nothing to do with the actual nature and strength of a position.

	Thickness of:		
Strength	Concrete /	Armor Turret /	Armor Plate
A	3.5 m	600 mm	250 mm
A-1	2.5 m	420 mm	250 mm
B-neu	2.0 m	250 mm	200 mm
B-alt	1.5 m	250 mm	200 mm
B-1	1.0 m	120 mm	100 mm
C	.6 m	60 mm	60 mm
D	.3 m	60 mm	30 mm*

The term *B-Werke* referred to the strength of the bunker in relation to thickness of armor and concrete. Some fortified positions could be of mixed type. During the 1930s and 1940s, three types of B-Werke emerged based on their

---

[21] Not all sources agree on these figures. These figures come from Bettinger and Buren's *Der Westwall*, which was based on extensive research. Manfred Gross in *Der Westwall zwischen Niederrhein und Schnee-Eifel* quotes different sources that put Type D armor at 50-mm and B-1 with a range from 100-mm to 160-mm. He also puts B-l concrete at a range of 1.0 meters to 1.5 meters which may be due to the fact that some B-*Werke* had walls of both thicknesses.

strength. The oldest type was classified as B, and was later reclassified as *B-alt,* and was followed by types *B-l* and *B-neu.* The following strengths were used and first established in the mid-1930s and modified early in the war:

Although most *B-Werke* were fairly uniform in design, some of the early ones included a number of non-standard features that were eliminated from later plans. The entrances to the *B-Werke* were mostly standardized and included small drawbridge-like floors that lifted up in front of the armored door to create a trap just within the entrance. In general, the *B-Werke* were armed for close combat and did not house any heavy artillery for long-range action. Late in the 1930s plans were made to expand some of the *B-Werke* and equip them with revolving turrets for 50-mm guns. Some plans also included 105-mm mine throwers and others showed casemates or turrets for 37-mm anti-tank guns, 50-mm antitank guns, or 105-mm cannons. None of these plans came to fruition.

On October 1, 1938, German troops occupied the Sudetenland, which included most of the Czech fortifications. The German engineers were not only able to study these positions, but, more importantly, they were able to strip many of them of their equipment and obstacles and install those in their own fortifications. Of particular value were the Czech 47-mm fortress antitank guns.

Within six months, on March 15,1939, the German army occupied the rump of the Czech state, which provided the Reich with new economic resources. Czech military equipment was used to bolster the strength of the Wehrmacht, especially a large number of tanks that were superior to the German Panzer I and II. Many of these Czech tanks later served to fill out medium tank companies of a number of new panzer divisions. In addition, the Czech munitions industries like the Skoda Works, which was only second to Krupp, were added to the patrimony of the Reich. To add insult to injury, the green uniforms of the Czechoslovakian army were issued to the workers of Organization Todt as they continued to labor on the West Wall.

The Road to War

In 1939, Hitler's Wehrmacht finally reached the point where he needed no longer to rely on bluff and subterfuge to bully the rest of Europe. The German military machine was now capable of engaging in a war with the West even though its forces were still at a disadvantage. The army stood at fifty-one divisions and was capable of expanding to just over one hundred divisions on mobilization. This made it possible to launch a campaign on one front, while still having a reasonable number of divisions to garrison the other front (either the Eastern or Western) in a relatively short war. The occupation of Czechoslovakia in March 1939 allowed the panzer force to expand from three to six divisions. An additional three light divisions joined the one created in 1938. Still over 2,100 tanks were Panzer I and II models and only 361 medium Panzer III and Panzer IV were available. However, three hundred Czech medium tanks helped strengthen these divisions. In contrast, Poland and France had no armored divisions, although the French had already formed several armored cavalry divisions and would soon create their first armored divisions.

In addition, a parachute division was formed in the summer of 1938, later known as the 7th Air Division, which consisted at first of only a couple of *Fallschirmjager* (light parachute infantry battalions) and the 16th Regiment (from the 22nd Division) for air landing operations. By the summer of 1939, the 7th Air (Parachute) Division, part of the Luftwaffe, consisted of two parachute regiments. The 22nd Infantry Division became a *Luftlande* or Air Landing Division, although only its 16th Regiment was trained for such operations. The Ju-52 three-engine transport, the workhorse of the Luftwaffe derived from a passenger airliner and bomber became the primary troop transport and general transport aircraft.

The Luftwaffe was organized into four air fleets or *Luftflot-*

ten. The number of aircraft rose from just under 3,000 in 1938 to 3,750 in 1939. The bomber force consisted of about 1,200 medium bombers, but had no heavy bombers for long-range strategic operations. The number of dive-bombers for close ground support had increased from about 200 in 1938 to 335 in 1939. The number of single-engine fighter aircraft stood at 1,240, but these were modern Me 109 and FW 190 models. By 1939, the combined air and ground forces actually formed a formidable force that was more than a match for its Polish, French, Belgian, and Dutch neighbors.

The Kriegsmarine, however, was not yet ready to engage in war and Plan Z was far from complete. On the eve of the war, the High Seas Fleet, or *Flottenstreitkrafte,* still had to rely on its two old World War I veteran battleships, its two new battle cruisers, the *Gneisenau* and the *Scharnhorst,* and its three pocket battleships, which included the newly completed *Admiral Hipper.* The only heavy cruisers were the *Deutschland* and the *Blilcher,* the latter not finished until a month after the war began. The escort force consisted of six light cruisers, twenty Z-Class destroyers, and a number of torpedo boats and minesweepers. This fleet might have been able to maintain mastery of the Baltic, but it had little chance of matching the British or French navies. The U-boat arm, which could take offensive action, numbered just over fifty U-boats, only half of which were designed for operations in the Atlantic.

Even though Germany now enjoyed the added industrial resources of Austria and Czechoslovakia, its economy was not ready to support a prolonged war without many quick victories. However, the situation on the defensive fronts was much better. In the fall of 1938, Hitler's order to move the West Wall forward toward the border as part of his new Aachen-Saar-Program, began the last phase of West Wall construction before the war. Showing little concern for tactical considerations, he made the sealing of the German border his first priority. When the defensive line was moved toward the border, Aachen, Trier, and Saarbrucken finally found themselves behind the West Wall. The 1939 line included new types of bunkers, many of which were no longer as simple as those built by the OT. In front of Aachen about one hundred new bunkers covered a sector of about eight kilometers between Bocholtz and Vaals. In front of the bunker line ran an almost continuous line of dragon's teeth whose density was not great because the city of Aachen was not too far away. In August 1939, the West Wall was extended from the area near Briiggen northward toward Kleve, along the Dutch border, because Hitler was afraid of being outflanked on the Lower Rhine. This new extension was named the Geldern Position. This was part of the work that Manfred Gross refers to as the Border Watch Program that seems to have begun in 1938. Additional construction on the West Wall took place during the first year of the war with more simplified positions being added.

The massive labor effort on the West Wall was well publicized and the fortifications were made to seem much more imposing than they actually were. In the West, many analysts became convinced that Germany's investment in such a project meant that it did not have any aggressive intentions, and that it was merely concerned with securing its borders, much as France was doing with its Maginot Line.

Meanwhile, construction on the West Wall went on. New types of bunkers, more economical, better designed, and easier to build were introduced. In 1938 antitank obstacles called *Hockerhindernisse,* or dragon's teeth, supplemented and/or replaced the old wooden-post obstacles known as *Pfahlhinderneiss* that had been designed in 1936. These small, reinforced concrete pyramids of various heights were laid out in four rows on a concrete base, which consisted of two parallel beams connected by a lateral beam. The height of each of these "teeth" increased from front to rear. They were designed to stop *a* 20-ton tank. In 1939 the dragon's teeth were upgraded to stop a 36-ton tank. The new design consisted of larger teeth, five rows, and an additional pyramid placed in the intervals between those of the new row. The five-row dragon's teeth were about twelve meters wide, that is about twice as wide as the four-row type of 1938. The 1939 type included a third parallel concrete base and the lateral bases that linked with it were set at a slight angle from the middle concrete base. The first row of teeth was about .7 meters high and the last, 1.5 meters high. In some cases an anti-tank ditch was placed in front of the first row. Barbed-wire obstacles, usually placed behind the dragon's teeth, were often put among them. Roads leading through the dragon's teeth were flanked by large, concrete structures with slots for steel beams.

Another type of obstacle employed in the West Wall was the steel curved frame or *Hemmkurvenhindernisse* that could stop tanks of up to 36-tons. These were placed together to form a continuous row with their forward face presenting a curved wall that a tank could not negotiate. Martin Gross reports in *Der Westwall Zwischen Niederrhein und Schnee Eiffel* that by 1940, 42.7 kilometers of the wooden stake obstacles had been completed, although the original plans in 1937 had called for 84 kilometers. Seventy-six kilometers of dragon's teeth were also finished. Additional obstacles included the famous Czech hedgehogs or *igelhindernisse,* which were found in large quantities around the Czech fortifications, but had the capacity of stopping only 12-ton tanks.

Although images of long rows of dragon's teeth extending for kilometers became associated with the West Wall, these obstacles were of limited value because they gave away the location of the forward edge of the main defensive front. In actuality, the most significant defensive feature of the West Wall was the land mine. Several countries had developed new types of antitank mines since World War I, but Germany took the lead by mass producing the Tellermine or T-mine in 1929. This pressure mine was replaced in 1935 by the Tellermine 35, which was different in design and slightly heavier. Also in 1935, the Germans designed the first mass-produced standardized antipersonnel mine. The antipersonnel mines of World War I had simply consisted of artillery shells with specially attached fuses. The *Schrapnellmine* of 1935, known as the Schu or S-mine, was the first antipersonnel mine manufactured as such. When stepped on, it was projected about one or two meters above the ground by a small charge and then detonated like a shotgun, spewing over 350 steel balls for a distance of up to 150 meters. Both antitank and antipersonnel mines were produced and stockpiled in large quantities before the war. Generally speaking, the Germans deployed mines around most of their fortifications except the East Wall. Minefields were found between the dragon's teeth and the line of barbed-wire obstacles behind them or behind the barbed-wire obstacles deployed in depth to protect the numerous bunker positions. Mike Caroll states in *The History of Landmines,* that the German minefields included a mixture of antipersonnel and antitank mines at a ratio of 1:2. Minefields were not laid until the outbreak of war or when mobilization was imminent, for two reasons. First, the mines could deteriorate and detonate by accident in peacetime. Second, it was standard policy not to hinder agricultural activities in the border areas, so that the final field fortifications and obstacles were not added until absolutely necessary. By 1939, Hitler's armed forces were in much better shape than in 1938 and were capable of offensive action with a relatively formidable barrier to protect their Western Front.

German Land Mines

Throughout World War I shells were used as mines in booby traps in Europe. Rudimentary mines made from pipes
were deployed by the Germans in Southwest Africa. However, it was not until the tank made its appearance on the
battlefield that the need arose to standardize antitank
mines. After World War I, the Germans took the lead in
the development of mines. In 1928 the first model of *Tellermine* went into mass production. In 1935, the Germans
became the first to perfect a standardized mass-produced
antipersonnel mine called the *Schu* mine or *"S"* mine,
which went by various names during the war. The French,
who ran into it first, called it the "Silent Soldier." The Eng-
lish-speaking Allies gave it the nickname of "Bouncing
Betty" because, when activated, a small charge blew it
about a meter or more above the ground before it exploded. Antilifting devices were added to some of the
mines to prevent the enemy from removing them. Later,
wooden and glass mines went into production in order to
foil mine detectors.

Germany's policy was not to plant mines to complete 'the
permanent lines of fortifications until the threat of battle
was imminent, so as not to disrupt the agricultural activities in the border regions. Before World War II, the Germans mass produced and stockpiled large numbers of antipersonnel and antitank mines in preparation for deploy-
ment. Based on some estimates, the Germans probably deployed more than 150,000 land mines during 1939. After
1941 these numbers rose to more than one million and, as
Germany prepared for defensive operations, exceeded ten
million in 1944. However, when Rommel was given the
task to improve the Atlantic Wall in 1944, he found that
there were not enough mines to meet his needs.

Mines were generally laid in rows spaced either one, two
or four meters apart. Antitank minefields with *Tellermine*

35 usually consisted of eight, twelve, or sixteen rows while antipersonnel minefields of *S-35* mines consisted of either two, four, or six rows when the rows were two meters apart, or four, eight, or ten rows when the rows were four meters apart. Mines planted in a line were usually spaced two or four meters apart, but in some cases S-mines were spaced only a half meter apart if the space between rows was only one meter or if the Sc/zu-mine *42* was used. The Sc/iu-mine *42* was planted in one, two, or three rows.

According to American intelligence, the Germans changed their standard method for setting up minefields late in the war. No longer were dense minefields laid in front of the main line of resistance, as was the case during most of the war, instead mines were more dispersed throughout the minefields. Also, the more traditional minefields were placed within the main line of resistance. German engineers were instructed to carefully establish reference points for laying out the minefield and establish four corner points from which to plot the location of the mines. Minefields were laid out in distinct patterns, except in areas where no future offensive action was contemplated where the mines were laid in an irregular pattern. Antitank minefields also included antipersonnel mines.

The minefields were clearly marked with several types of signs including a special sign for dummy minefields. The side facing the enemy was generally not marked, but this was not always the case when dummy minefields were created. Signs were also used to indicate paths through the minefield and everything was carefully recorded by the engineers and sent on to the higher command.

Blitzkrieg to victory 1939 to 1942

In the late 1930s, the Third Reich was prepared to fulfill the agenda Hitler laid out in his *Mein Kampf*. The main instrument for transforming his dream into reality was the Wehrmacht, which had greatly expanded in the years since he ascended to power especially with the creation of the Luftwaffe and the panzer force. His strongest weapon, however, was propaganda, which could not win him victories without the threat of a strong Wehrmacht. The Spanish Civil War of 1936-1939 had helped the German military leaders hone their skills. The "Fifth Column," which helped take Madrid from within, became a tremendous propaganda ploy. German military intelligence, the *Abwehr,* formed its own special group for behind-the-line operations, organized into small combat units for unconventional warfare. During the first year of World War II, this special group expanded into company-size formations that formed a battalion, which, in turn, became the Brandenburg Regiment in late 1940. Other special units designed for offensive operations were the *Fallschrimjäger,* parachute infantry battalions formed into a division-size unit between 1938 and 1939. These special units for offensive operations, which generally required extensive specialized training, represented a small percentage of the total forces of the Wehrmacht. The bulk of the army consisted of less specialized troops serving mainly in the infantry, artillery, and supporting services. Many of these more traditional formations were not only necessary in offensive operations, but also in maintaining the defensive positions of the Reich.

The quality of the troops in the infantry formations ranged from first-class troops to entire divisions of older troops formed only for security and defensive purposes. The fortifications of the West and East Wall were designed for all types of troops. The German *pioniere* (sappers or engineers), were further subdivided into units such as combat engineers, assault engineers, construction engineers, and so on. These were the troops responsible for clearing the line of advance and lines of communications for offensive operations and also for preparing the defenses.

In the 1920s, there were only seven battalions of these troops, which served as part of the seven infantry divisions. Their small but highly skilled staffs had been in charge of planning and organizing work on fortifications. During the 1930s, the number of engineers expanded to match the number of divisions, but there was also a greater need for engineers at higher echelons.

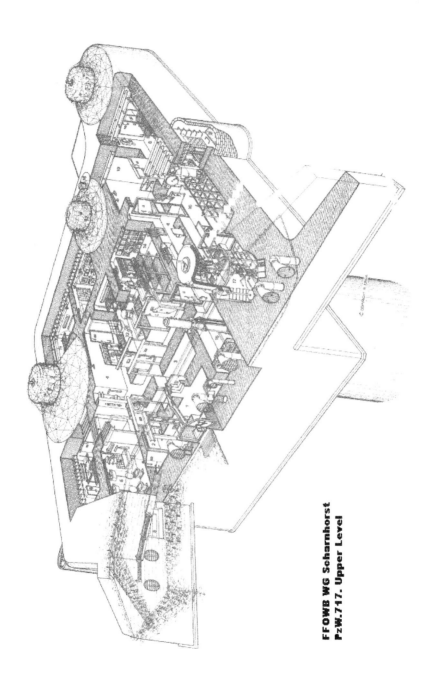

**FFOWB WG Scharnhorst
PzW.717. Upper Level**

The RAD, and later the OT, were able to provide much of the work force, but the engineer staffs were needed to direct the construction of fortifications and other defensive positions. The first engineer battalions assigned to army corps headquarters were formed in mid-1935. Battalions 41 through 47 were assigned to Army Corps I through VII. During the next two years, five more engineer battalions were formed to serve in five new corps. At mobilization, the number of engineer battalions expanded from 75 to 133, which covered every division mobilized and allowed a large number of more specialized battalions with bridging and other special equipment to be assigned to army and corps units where needed. These 133 battalions also included construction units. After the war began, the number and types of construction units also expanded. These construction units included: the construction battalion, *Baubataillon;* the fortress construction battalion, *Festungsbau-Bataillon;* the naval construction battalion, *Marine-Baubataillon;* the technical battalion, *Technisches-Bataillon,* involved in oil production, coal mining, and similar functions; the railway engineer regiment, *Kriegsgefangene-Bau und Arbeits-Bataillon;* a construction battalion of prisoners of war with German guards, *Eisenbanpionier-Regiment;* and the railway engineer construction company, *Eisenbahn Pionier-Baukompanie.* [22]

---

[22] 1. Defended entrance, gas decontamination area, 2. Main gas lock, 3. Guard room, 4. Corridor, 5. Washroom and WC, 6. Combat ready room, 7. 20P7 cloche for two MG-34 on mobile mountings, 8. Firing room for MG-08 or MG-34 with armor plate 7P7, 9. Emergency exit, 10. Command room, 11. Room for crew of observation cloche, 12. Observation Cloche 438P01, 13. CDs room, 14. Commo Room, 15. Two level emplacement for a flamethrower - FN Type B placed under an armored plate, 420P01 - on the lower level were fuel tanks, 16. Technical and storage room, 17. M-19 Automatic Mortar Cloche 424P01, 18. Armored vent, 19. Staircase to lower level

In the early 1930s, the Germans concentrated most of their efforts on preparing for defensive war, which meant developing the art of building field fortifications as well as demolitions. Many key bridges and railway embankments were prepared for demolition to delay an enemy advance; even the new fortifications were rigged for destruction. The application of explosives in demolition charges and land mines took on particular importance. But when they occupied the Czech fortifications, the German engineer units and other assault troops acquired an ideal place to experiment with methods for attacking heavy fortifications. The Czech forts were similar to those of the Maginot Line and not greatly different from the new Belgian forts built to defend the invasion route through Belgium, offering perfect conditions for experimentation. While super-artillery, like the huge rail guns,was still being developed for use against heavy fortifications, experiments showed — at the hollow charge would be quite effective against the cloches, turrets, and other armored features of the new fortifications in the West.

As the year of 1939 began, the West was battening down the hatches and rreparing for the worst. German troops marched into Czechoslovakia on March 15 ind Hitler declared a protectorate over Bohemia and Moravia while allowing Slovakia to become a puppet state. On March 19, Germany annexed Memel from Lithuania by means of a registered letter sent to the Lithuanian government. A few lays later, Hitler demanded the Polish Corridor and Danzig. In the meantime, rlans were underway for the invasion of Poland even though the army was not yet ready to begin operations. On March 31,1939, Great Britain and France offered to fully acknowledge Poland's independence. During the following months, the British attempted to broker a deal with the Soviets. By the end of May, Hitler was determined to eliminate Poland by military means. During the summer, Poland secretly mobilized during field maneuvers and doubled the size of its army. By August 23, 1939, the Germans and Soviets concluded a pact with a secret clause regarding Poland. Germany was ready to begin a limited war against Poland.

Under the guise of securing its new borders, the new protectorates, and Slovakia, Germany prepared for offensive operations. During the summer a U-boat training flottila, a torpedo boat flottila, and the equipment and personnel of two coastal batteries, and a 75-mm flak battery with four guns were moved to Memel. During this period, almost 58 percent of the annual budget was spent on the military. It had increased from over 30 percent in 1935 and equaled almost five times as many reichsmarks. However, the German economy was not yet fully committed to a war economy when the army began mobilizing in preparation for war with Poland.

War Begins

When Poland refused to accede to the German demands, the German war machine went into action on September 1, 1939, after a false start. British demands for Germany to pull back were ignored and by September 3 both France and Great Britain were dragged into a war with Germany. As the German army engaged in its first blitzkrieg campaign in Poland, the British and French responded with halfhearted assaults against the German defenses. On September 4, the British RAF sent a force of twenty-nine Blenheim and Wellington bombers against the German warships at the naval bases of Wilhelmshaven and Brunsbuttel. However, a third of the bombers failed to even find their targets and five Blenheims were shot down by the flak batteries protecting the port of Wilhelmshaven. The pocket battleship *Admiral Scheer* suffered three hits from duds and only the cruiser *Emden* was damaged when a Blenheim bomber crashed into it. Meanwhile, the Wellingtons flew against Brunsbiittel and met with as little success. This British foray showed tha: the Luftwaffe was not yet effective in blocking the air raids, but that the flak batteries of the ports and ships were quite efficient. The British Bomber Command continued seeking out German naval units early in the war and accidental! dropped a bomb on Helgoland, the first dropped on German soil in this conflict.

In the meantime, the German surface fleet did not sit idly by. Its warships set out to create the naval version of the West Wall, called the Westwall Barrage, an extension of the land fortification. Sections of the North Sea were turned into a naval minefield (referred to as a mine barrage) as the cruisers *Konigsberg. Nuremberg, Koln, Leipzig,* and *Emden,* sixteen destroyers, ten torpedo boats, and three minelayers participated in this operation between September 3-20. The mine barrage initially covered the Bight, but was extended northward during the next year. By the spring of 1941 it reached the British Shetland Islands. When the war began, the navy had only fifteen hundred of the new magnetic mines and twenty-thousand of the more conventional contact mines. The magnetic mines sat on the sea bed and were activated by a ships magnetic field, hence their name. They were mostly deployed off enemy coasts. Most of the standard contact mines were moored at depths of ten to five hundred meters.

As the Allies sought out the German fleet in its North Sea bases, they soon found that the German seaports were relatively well-fortified. By exposing their weaknesses early in the war, they even gave the Germans time to correct any deficiencies. Before the war, Helgoland had been once again turned into an island fortress with impressive coastal artillery positions and antiaircraft weapons. The Frisian Islands also had been reinforced by December 18, 1939. An experimental radar station *(Freya* type) on Wangerooge Island helped direct fighter aircraft to intercept the intruders heading for Wilhelmshaven and, combined with the flak batteries, inflicted heavy losses on the Allied bombers forces. Even though the Germans had developed radar well before the war, they still had to learn to employ it in the most effective manner. After their first disastrous foray, the British bombers gave up flying close to the German mainland, and at the end of the year, resorted to nighttime raids to reduce their losses.

On the Western Front things were a little shaky, but the situation wasn't desperate. By early September, the Germans had already laid 12,900 S-mines from a stock of 706,000 and 82,000 T-mines from a stock of 773,000. Throughout the month of September, the German armament industry produced almost three times as many S-mines and about 80 percent of the number of T-mines already planted in the West Wall. Meanwhile, the German field troops had erected additional field fortifications to support the West Wall. Only a few German divisions were positioned north of the Mosel River to garrison the West Wall where it ran along the frontier of Belgium, which was neutral. About twenty infantry divisions were situated between the Mosel and Rhine Rivers and along the Upper Rhine, defending the Franco-German border and the West Wall. Many of these divisions were not first-class units and came from the second and third waves newly mobilized, and included a few divisions of *Landwehr* troops, reservists between the age of thirty-five and forty-five. They were organized under several corps under the command of Army Group C, and eventually under three army headquarters. Of the eleven regular divisions assigned to the Western Front, six were deployed to cover the Saar region and were backed by a couple of second-wave reservist divisions. The Saar Corps with three regular army divisions, the best trained to handle a difficult situation and retrograde operations, was concentrated near the Saar Gap. The sectors along the border with Belgium consisted mostly of reservist formations of the second and third wave including *Landwehr*.

Having pledged to undertake an offensive against Germany if Poland was invaded, France launched a token offensive against the Saar region through the large gap in the Sarre Sector of the Maginot Line early in September. On September 6, 1939, troops of the French Fourth Army gathered on the border and on September 7 crossed into German territory. Fortunately for the Germans, the French attack was halfhearted. After its first encounter with the minefields of the West Wall and the deadly antipersonnel mines, the French contingent gave up its token offensive. No serious attempt was made to take Saarbrlicken, which was situated almost in the front lines. By the middle of the month, the French halted offensive operations. The delay allowed the Germans to bring reinforcements from the Polish campaign and to eventually force the French force out of German territory by mid-October.

On the Eastern Front, the OWB Fortified Front was garrisoned mainly by low category divisions, since Poland was not considered to be a serious threat. The strong offensive elements were concentrated on both sides of this fortified area. The East Wall would not play an important role again until late in the war. Before the conquest of Poland was completed, German divisions moved west to take up positions on the Western Front. After Poland was partitioned, a small number of German divisions took up position on the new frontier with the Soviet Union and the entire East Wall, which no longer served any defensive purpose, went into caretaker status until 1944. Only a small portion of the pre-war fortifications built in East Prussia faced Soviet occupied Poland, but the takeover of Lithuania and the other Baltic States in the months that followed changed their status, too. However, no massive fortifications were built along the new eastern frontier with the Soviets. Instead, a chain of border positions and a number of strongpoints mostly of field-type construction, were created. Some Regelbau, mostly of C- and D-strength, and a few B-strength positions with armored cloches were built.

During the winter of 1939-1940, which became known as the period of the Phony War, Hitler began to realize that there would be no compromise solution and that the Allies intended to continue to wage war against him. The Phony War consisted mostly of RAF leaflet raids on Germany and bombing missions against the High Seas Fleet. The territory of the Reich remained unscathed. Three German army groups took up positions from the North Sea to Switzerland and prepared a modified version of the WWI-era Schlieffen Plan, which called for an invasion of Belgium, and possibly the Netherlands, and the by-passing of the French Maginot Line. The invasion was postponed several times during the autumn and winter months and did not take place until May 1940, after the plan was modified during the winter. All of the Wehrmacht's new weapons and formations were to be deployed, except for poison gas, which remained stockpiled until the end of the war. Hitler and his generals assumed that the first phase of their massive offensive would secure them a large slice of northern France up to the old Somme battlefields of the previous war. Then they intended to consolidate their gains and prepare for a second phase. It is not clear what type of situation the Germans expected to develop, but it is possible that they may have intended to establish a trench system across the front line until they could launch a new offensive.

Field Fortifications

Most armies, including the German army, issued manuals or soldier's handbooks that included information on how to prepare various types of field fortifications and instructions on how to iestroy them. Before the war, emphasis was placed on the construction of trench systems similar to those used in World War I. Throughout the war, the Germans continued to dig trench systems, which were considered important supplements to fixed defenses. However, early in the war the Germans also introduced instructions for preparing foxholes or dugout positions, which turned out to be so useful that other armies also used them. Such individual positions for the protection of the troops in the field were important during advances into enemy territory. A simple shallow pit, called *Russenloch* Russian Hole) by the Germans and foxhole by the Americans, was enough for the individual soldier. When time allowed, these pits could be dug deep

I enough to stand in. A two-man version was also standard. Similar positions for three men were ; designed for a machine gun, others for mortars. Positions for antitank guns and light field guns included adjacent slit positions where the crew could take cover and be safe from being overrun by a tank. Even positions for light flak weapons were included in the manuals. More complex field positions could be made with logs, sandbags, if available, and tank turrets or disabled tanks whose turrets could still be used. A few positions of a more permanent nature required more time to build and were made of.concrete, steel, or large quantities of logs. They constituted machine-gun bunkers—not of the *Regelbauten* type—and communication, accommodation, and kitchen bunkers. The kitchen bunker included tables, cupboards, a place to store firewood, and a chimney.

Three observation posts *(Baumbeobachtungsstand)* in wooded areas simply consisted of convenient tree branches accessed by wooden steps nailed on the trunk. In some cases they resembled hunters' blinds. Wooden towers were also used in forests, but the most impressive observation position was a small, two-level, wooden structure built in more open areas called *wachturme* or watch tower.

The *Fliegembwehrstrum* (antiaircraft tower) was a wooden structure rising about fifteen meters above the ground with a position for a machine gun on a roof platform and crew accommodations below. Obstacles were an integral part of fixed fortifications. The *Koppelzaune* or barbed-wire fences were single and double fences with a coiled wire between them. There were special barbed-wire designs for different terrains and conditions such as snow, swamps, rocky areas, and frozen ground. *Astverhau.* or branch entanglements, were heavily used where the appropriate vegetations were available. For instance, acacia trees with their long and sharp barbs provided a natural obstacle. This type of obstacle probably dates back to the neolithic age. The *Wolfsgruben,* or wolf's pit, a more sinister device used since Roman times, consisted of a large number of circular pits containing sharpened spikes whose openings were covered with a light layer of vegetation, which gave way under the pressure of a man's foot.

The Spanish Rider or *Spanische Reiter* (the French *Chevaux de Frise* and American knife stand) were used as effective roadblocks. They consisted of a wooden frame with barbed wire wrapped around it and carrying handles on each side.

Antitank ditches, an important feature of field fortifications, were usually reinforced with logs or stakes only on the side facing the enemy and were "V" shaped. The soil from the excavation was thrown on the defenders' side whereas in most pit positions it was used to form a parapet against the enemy. In hilly terrain, a continuous tank barrier or *Panzerhindemis* was created by cutting into the slope, creating an almost vertical wall about 1.9 meters in height that could not be negotiated by tanks. Czech hedgehogs were deployed early in the war to reinforce the German fixed lines. They were anchored to the ground and linked to each other in as many as three belts. Reportedly, they could stop a 12-ton tank. Many of the concrete Czech hedgehogs were used to form roadblocks. After 1940, the Germans also adopted the Finnish idea of using a continuous line of boulders, several boulders deep, as an antitank obstacle.

Build-ip of Coastal Fortifications

Early in the war the British had discovered, to their dismay, that the island of Helgoland and the neighboring island of Dime had been refortified since the late 1930s. Subterranean positions, which had supposedly been rendered useless after World War I, were re-excavated. New artillery emplacements, set up by the end of the decade, occupied many of the positions used by the WWI-era batteries. For an island only about 2.4 kilometers long and about a kilometer at its widest point, this was a heavily fortified position, especially if one includes the naval base on its southeast end. In addition, a subterranean system of tunnels and storage areas was reopened and new ones excavated early in the war. Plans went ahead for the construction of the first U-boat bunker or pen since World War I. German propagandists touted this fortified island as the equal of British Malta.

The remainder of the North Sea and Baltic coasts went relatively unnoticed since their fortifications consisted mostly of old forts serving as munitions depots which had been modernized in the 1930s on the orders of Admiral Raeder. On the Baltic coast, six coast artillery batteries and antiaircraft defenses were scattered across the shoreline before 1940. This left the entire region weakly defended. The Kriegsmarine essentially represented the first and only important line of defense in the area. To bolster the defenses of the Baltic, Section Memel received a naval flak detachment and Sections Gotenhafen and Pillau got two each. The 3rd Naval Flak Regiment defended Swinemünde and the 1st Naval Flak Regiment at Lahoe protected the east end of the Kiel Canal.

On the other hand, the situation on the North Sea coast was much better because its positions were more concentrated. Each of the Frisian Islands, which represented a section, were home to a naval artillery detachment, a naval flak detachment, and a flotilla. Wangerooge was reinforced with an additional naval artillery detachment when the war began. Section Emden included two naval flak detachments; Section Wilhelmshaven, a flotilla and the 2nd Naval Flak Regiment; Section Wesermiinde, two naval flak detachments; and Section Cuxhaven, one flak detachment and a flotilla. The west end of the Kiel Canal was protected by Section Brunsbiittel with the 14th Naval Flak Regiment. Section Sylt, on the island off the Danish coast, had the 8th Naval Flak Regiment and three detachments of naval flak.

The naval coast artillery consisted mainly of a number of old weapons, a few of which were placed in turrets or casemates, and others that were on open pedestal-type mounts, some protected by a shield. When the war began, on the North Sea the two artillery batteries of Section Borkum included Battery Coronel with four naval 280-mm guns—two of which were old Russian weapons on open emplacements—and Battery Oldenburg with two naval 240-mm guns. Hamburg Sectior. on Norderney had Battery Hamburg with four more old 240-mm naval guns Battery Graf Spec, with four naval 280-mm guns, and Battery Friedrich August with three naval 305-mm guns, defended Wangerooge. Battery Skagerrak on Sylt had four old naval 240-mm guns, while on Helgoland, Battery Jacobson operated three old naval 170-mm guns. The heavy gun batteries of the Baltic were concentrated at four points: Kiel, with a battery of three old 170-mm naval guns an; another with three naval 280-mm guns; Fehmarn, with a battery of two naval 28C-mm guns; Swinemunde, with two four-gun batteries of 210-mm and 280-mm naval gun; and Pillau, with a battery of four 280-mm naval guns.

One of the most impressive of the older restored forts was Fort Kugelbake at Cuxhaven, originally built during the period following the Franco-Prussian War. It was rather typical of the period, with five sides, open gun positions on the two frontal faces, positions for lighter artillery pieces on the two flanks, and a surrounding ditch with caponiers. When World War I began, it mounted 280-mm guns, which were removed during the war. In 1939, a naval flak battery was installed at the old fort. It included four 88-mm antiaircraft guns, which were replaced with 105-mm antiaircraft guns with full armored shields. Strangely, even this fort served as part of the lightly defended *Luftverteidigungszone West* or Air Defense Zone West, which included sixty other flak batteries.

High Seas Fortress of Helgoland

Although Helgoland was disarmed and theoretically neutralized after World War I, Admiral Raeder had plans for restoring it as a vital base protecting the approaches to the Kriegsmarine's North Sea ports. Situated about forty kilometers north of Wangerooge Island, near the mouth of the Weser River, and about equal distance from the islands at the mouth of the Elbe River, it was ideally located for heavy coastal batteries and as a base for torpedo boats and submarines. The island was about two kilometers long running in a northwest to southeasterly direction. Its core, known as the *Oberland* or Upper Country, was virtually surrounded by cliffs that dominated most of the western coastline. A lowland section less than four hundred meters wide ran alone the eastern section of the island to the port on the east and southeast end.

Plans were made to build a pair of landing fields for aircraft nearby, on the northern end c: the island of Dune and a small harbor on its west side. A number of flak positions were set up near the center of Dune, where it barely averaged a width of four hundred meters.

After a construction period that lasted from 1935 through 1936, the first flak batteries became operational on Helgoland in 1937. Battery Schroder with three 305-mm guns was installed in the northwest end of the island in the general area of two heavy batteries destroyed after World War I. Flak Battery Nordspitze, located nearby, consisted of four 88-mm antiaircraft guns. On the other side of the Upper Country, on the southeast, stood Naval Battery Jacobson with three old 170-mm guns. Nearby, in the southeast corner of the Upper Country, was Flak Battery Flam with four 105-mm antiaircraft guns. Between the two naval gun batteries and near the western cliff side was Flak Battery Westklipe which consisted of two 105-mm antiaircraft guns. Smaller positions for 37-mm flak were also present.

The armored turrets of the guns of Battery Schroder were not completed until late in 1939. In 1940, work began on the first U-boat bunker in Germany, which, when finally completed, included three bays, one of which accommodated a floating dock to lift submarines out of the water. Beginning in 1935 through the war years, the island of Helgoland was honeycombed with jj numerous tunnels and subterranean chambers that served as magazines for weapons, storerooms for supplies, and even a hospital. Additional flak units, including heavy 128-mm anti-aircraft guns, arrived during the war and various radar positions were set up on the island to detect enemy air and naval units.

On April 18, 1945, the RAF Bomber Command targeted the island with over 950 bombers, inflicting devastating damage across the island and destroying the guns of Battery Schroder, flak positions, and more. Although the island was effectively neutralized, its underground facilities re-

mained in good condition.
Helgoland is considered to have been the most heavily defended German strongpoint on the northern end of the
Western Front. Istein, another remarkable position, was
located on the southern end of the front. The former feste
was destroyed at the end of World War I, but by 1936 the
Festwng *Pionier* plans were made for the construction of
an elaborate subterranean fortress at the site. The actual
groundbreaking did not take place until the following year,
but the grandiose plans for the rocky ridge came at a time
when the Germans were still dazzled by the massive fortifications of the Maginot Line. Like the large B-Werke that
were planned to form werkgruppen with connecting tunnels, Werkgruppe Istein was to have a two kilometer-long
gallery linking a rear entrance and service area with the
combat positions in and around the ridge. In this sense, Istein would have resembled the Maginot Line ouvrages
(forts) more than any type of werk-gruppe on the East
Wall. The plans for this fortress called for fifty combat
positions, four heavy-gun batteries, and a subterranean garage for over one hundred tanks. Some of the proposed
combat positions were to include a 75-mm gun turret, an
80-mm mortar cloche, and four unusual positions for
ejecting mine-like projectiles that would explode above the
block for close defense. The turreted gun batteries, similar
to those unfinished on the East Wall, were to include two
armored batteries, each with four 170-mm guns. The other
two batteries were to have 88-mm guns. In addition, there
would have been several infirmaries, workshops, depots,
magazines, and other facilities to maintain a fortress on
the scale of the British position at Gibraltar. The planned
garrison would have numbered 2,600 men, a contingent
larger than the one allotted to the East Wall tunnel system
and twice the size of the largest ouvrage of the Maginot
Line. In addition to such a large garrison, the fort was supposed to accommodate another one thousand men. This

may be why Hermann Goring called it the "Gibraltar of the West" during his visit in the spring of 1938. By 1939 six machine-gun casemates, three of which faced the Rhine, and an artillery observation cloche, built within the ruins of the old fort atop the ridge, were actually finished. Since the projected entrance block and gallery were not completed, the temporary access was from inside the railroad tunnel that passed through the ridge. This tunnel gave access to one of three color-coded galleries. The topmost gallery was the Red Gallery, which was connected to two of the combat casemates and extended for over two kilometers. The fort of Istein was intended to support sixteen free-standing bunkers along the Rhine. Unlike the large positions completed on the East Wall, Istein received neither machinery for elevators nor other equipment such as fortress flamethrowers and M-19 mortars. But work on Istein's two armored batteries was not even begun because by 1940 the war had passed it by.

The Propaganda Campaign

The propaganda campaign, controlled by the Reich Ministry of Informatic and Propaganda headed by Joseph Gobbels, was one of Germany's most effech weapons. In *Propaganda,* Anthony Rhodes describes how Gobbels succeeded inciting the German people toward war with his masterly manipulation of media. During the Czech Crisis of 1938 and on September 1,1939, the threat of and the actual war were not received with the same enthusiasm as in August 1914. J The Germans simply accepted the fact as a necessary evil and went forward witi their lives. During the Phony War, Gobbels managed to convince the German pi lie that Germany had to defend itself from the unjust persecution of the Allies had declared war first. In the spring of 1940, he persuaded the people Germany had invaded Denmark, Norway, and the Low Countries only to prote itself from an Allied invasion, conveniently omitting the fact that the West had been previously touted as enough protection against invasion. [23]

Throughout the war, Gobbels reassured the Germans through magazine radio, and film, and kept them fighting to the bitter end. The press, as the oldess method of disseminating information, was an excellent propaganda instrument. Gobbels also used the cinema as a place to distribute films, whose subject matte was imbued with patriotic flavor, anti-Semitic fervor, or pride in Germany's tary victories. A weekly newsreel featuring the Wehrmacht's activities was insti-j tuted after the war began to keep the public abreast of the news and heartened at the same time. The novelty of the medium left a deep impression on a public thai had not yet learned to be critical. The radio, also a new medium, had found its way into almost every German home by the end of the 1930s. Carefully controlled and orchestrated radio programs spread propaganda messages to friend and foe alike and every effort was made to drown out Allied radio signals that might provide! alternative sources of information. Thanks to Gobbels's efforts, the morale of the troops and the population was maintained at high levels, bolstering the success of the military machine.

---

[23] East Wall - Oder-Warthe-Bend Fortified Front (OWB) A. Northern Sector; B. Central Sector; C. Southern Sector

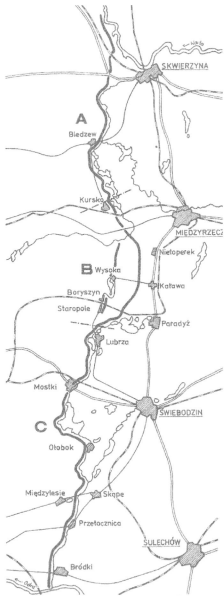

Before the war began, the propaganda ministry expertly hid the weaknesses of the Wehrmacht. Government films showed the construction of the West Wall, laborers at work, and huge supply depots of materials. Thanks to some of the most impressive camera angles, the dragon's teeth obstacles appeared to run for endle kilometers across the country side. A now classic scene shot at the testing ground" of Hillersleben reveals German troops marching into a subterranean fort with the name of *Werkgruppe Scharnhorst, Panzerwerk 1238* painted above its entrance short view of the gallery leaves the viewer with the impression that this was a for: of the same caliber as the ouvrages of the Maginot Line shown in French propaganda films. In reality, the entrance shown on the German film was only an experimental position built for testing and not part of an actual fortification. Nonetheless, this film later succeeded in convincing both friend and foe that Germany had massive forts on the West Wall, even though no such positions had actually been built. The only positions that might have embodied the film version - were the A-Werkes whose construction was canceled early in the war.

The German propaganda machine not only used the media to deceive and misinform the public in Germany and abroad. Another propaganda tool was the expertly led tours given to foreign dignitaries that created a vastly inflated impression of Germany's defenses. Thus during the Phony War, on February 22,1940, thirty military attaches from twenty-three different nations were taken to Ktistrin where they met General Alfred Jacobs, a member of the General Staff in charge of fortifications who had served as inspector of fortifications in the East between 1936 and 1938. The group—which consisted of representatives of Germany's allies, neutral European countries, and American nations—was bused to the OWB Fortified Front and taken to a fortification identified as Number 864, a block of Werkgruppe Ludendorff. Some of the attaches reported seeing a six-embrasured, well-camouflaged cloche and being told that it mounted antitank guns and machine guns. They were shown two other blocks with cloches from a distance, but were not allowed to approach them. Their guides informed them that *"dead areas"* were covered by field fortifications. Next they visited a block where they were shown the gasproof doors, the decontamination area, and pit obstacles covered by a drawbridge inside the entrance. They were led inside the block in such a way that they became confused as to what they actually saw. The drawings produced by one of the three American attaches suggests that the site consisted of three positions with a six-embrasure cloche each surrounded by barbed-wire obstacles. The bunker they actually saw was Number 867, which only had a half cloche covering the small concrete bridge over the stream. They probably failed to realize that it was linked to the main position by a tunnel. Although there is no mention that any of the visitors were allowed into the cloche, the Americans reported that it mounted machine guns and guns. A sketch of a cross section gave an estimated diameter of three meters and showed the location of a periscope in the center of the roof. Most interestingly, a notation indicates that the "ceiling of turret [was] painted in colored sectors corresponding to different fields of fire." This could indicate the attache either had a brief, unauthorized look, or he reported the guides' description. Their concept of the bunkers and tunnels appeared very confused since their illustration shows several meters of earth between the first and second levels of the positions.

The sketches made by the two American attaches left quite an impression and were incorporated in descriptions of the German military fortifications in 1941 published in the technical manuals of the U.S. Army. Soon the East Wall became confused with the West Wall. The same sketches were also reprinted as late as the 1970s as the only representation for the East Wall, since the Soviets never release: information on the topic after occupying the OWE in 1945. The 1941 visitors to the OWB were also taken to the work camp at Hochwalde. where General Jacobs was quoted as saying: "The Maginot Line and our West Wai have many points of similarity in the actual construction of tunnels, turrets entrances and gas locks . . . The French line is generally of heavier construction with less depth than our line and has much less mobility for the artillery than our system."

Jacobs also convinced his visitors that the West Wall was built in great depth. and included numerous heavy fortifications of the type they had just visited. He concluded by stating that "our Führer spares no expense and does not questior changes demanded by the latest experience." On the way to the extensive tunneL system linking many of the werkgruppen in the area, the group was told abou: the dragon's teeth supposedly concealed under a heavy blanket of snow. The visitors were then rushed into one of the blocks accessing the tunnels and informec that work was still in progress. The group most likely entered Number 766 since it was the only one with two entrances behind the tunnels. The American attaches apparently mistook the protective weapons embrasure for a third entrance. They saw some of the equipment and the rail line for an electric train in the tunnel. The guide informed them that thirty-two kilometers of track already existed and there were thirty-six exits for a garrison of three thousand men. Unlike Hitler, the attaches did not question the large number of men needed in such a position, In his report, Major William Hohenthal noted that they were also shown the film "Der Westwall' which showed German troops manning positions similar to those of the fortifications they had just visited. Apparently some of the other visitors informed the Americans that they had visited the West Wall an.d that everything their German escorts had told them was accurate. Thus the German propaganda machine scored a significant hit with this visit.

In 1939, at about the same time as the war began, Captain

Rudolf T. Kuhne from the OKH published a book titled *Der Westwall,* and subtitled *Unbezwingbare Abwehrzone von Stahl und Beton an Deutschlands Westgrenze (Invincible Defense Zone of Steel and Concrete on Germany's Western Border).* In his book, Kuhne described Germany's situation regarding fortifications in the West and quoted Articles 42,43, and 180 of the Treaty of Versailles that restricted German fortifications and demilitarized the Rhineland. He briefly described the construction of the French Maginot Line which took place while Germany was virtually defenseless. Kiihne then quite accurately described the early work by the German military engineers mentioning Fortress Pioneer Staffs and other organizations. He also included a map that showed the Army Defensive Zone stretching from the Swiss border near Basel and following the border northward to the point where the Rhine enters the Xetherlands. Behind this line, the Air Defense Zone was shown occupying most ?f the east bank of the Upper Rhine and most of the west bank of the Rhine from Karlrsruhe to the Rhine. This Air Defense Zone was largely incomplete and mythical. In actuality Luftwaffe General Kitzinger began work on Air Defense Zone •Vest in 1938. His staff adopted mostly Bl-strength army designs prior to the Limes Program and only completed about fifteen hundred concrete positions. Despite the many inaccuracies and the deliberate misinformation, Kiihne's map, in a modified form, was included in most books published on the subject for the next fifty years.

In his book, Kühne also described Hermann Goring's visit to inspect the work of the West Wall from the Dutch to the Swiss borders in June 1938, and mentioned tihat Hitler was preparing to visit the East Wall. Kuhne also commented that because of the "gigantic" nature of the building task, many more officers and technicians were required—which was not an exaggeration—and Hitler had to call upon Dr. Todt to administer this project.

According to Kühne, the heavy cloches and other armored parts were transported by ship and truck. When work began on the West Wall six thousand rail wagons arrived daily, but their number had to be increased to eight thousand, and a fleet of over fifteen thousand trucks hauled the construction material to the line while a veritable flotilla of ships plied the Rhine with the cargo. Six million tons of cement, the equivalent of one-third of Germany's yearly production, were poured during 1938 alone. Furthermore, the construction of the fortifications consumed about 695,000 cubic meters of lumber and 1 million tons of iron bars. German industry diverted steel not needed for weapons, naval vessels, and tanks for pouring into the molds to create the cloches and armored parts needed for the fortifications. Construction heavy equipment, such as compressors and concrete mixers, was brought in from all over the country. The resources of the Reich, according to Kiihne, were mobilized for this gigantic effort.

To accomplish all this work, claimed Künhe manpower of OT had to expand rapidly. In July 1938 the organization employed 35,000 men; a week later, that number increased by 10,000. On August 3 there were 77,000 workers and at the end of the month the number rose to 170,000. On September 7 the total was 170,000 men, but it expanded to 342,000 by October 6. The Fortress Engineers Staffs, on the other hand, numbered 90,000 troops. These numbers, like most of the others, are accepted as fact and there is little reason to doubt their accuracy. To ge: to the work sites and to accommodate all these men, roads had to be improved in the region and rail tracks laid down. Massive numbers of unemployed Germans found work and were housed in camps that offered all types of amenities such as libraries, sports facilities, movie theaters, and concert halls. A fleet of five thousand large buses supplied by the postal service transported these men to work. The number of buses represented 70 percent of the total the service had on hand. Although Kiihne does not mention it, most workers received a special medal, decorated with a bunker on one face, for their service on the West Wall.

According to Kühne, Hitler ordered the construction of 17,000 fortifications on the West Wall that fall, but later revised that number to 22,000. Although these numbers are quoted in most books today, it is difficult to be certain that such a large number of positions were actually completed. Kiihne provides a decent description of the terrain spanned by the West Wall and includes photos showing the construction work, the dragon's teeth, the curved steel antitank barriers, antitank walls, infantry obstacles, some of the bunkers including a few on the banks of the Rhine, and, of course, the famous fictitious Werkgruppe Scharnhorst. [24]

Also included are photos depicting flak units in the Air Defense Zone with searchlights and guns, a large air-raid

---

[24] The Leistand (Fire Control Bunker) of the tower type at MKB Waldam east Calais

shelter with a conical roof, and a small platform on top for a light flak weapon. The caption for the air-raid shelter states it can take two thousand men. Most of the photos are similar in content to those on the film clips showing soldiers marching into Werkgruppe Scharnhorst with interior shots of a gallery and a small train carrying troops. Many of these photos, including Kühne's descriptions, have continued to be used in postwar material on the West Wall.

Since little was written on the West Wall before the war and even right after the war, this book became one of the major sources of information in postwar literature, especially with regard to figures. It must be pointed out, however, that Kiihne was writing for OKH, probably under the direction of Gobbels's Propaganda Ministry, and that, therefore, many of his facts must be considered suspect at best. His description of the Air Defense Zone West, for example, is effectively over-exaggerated; so are his claims that the workers labored day and night. However, other data, like the delivery of 3 million rolls of wire, have been corroborated by other documentary sources. It is safe to assume that the numbers may be exaggerated to a limited extent, but otherwise the description is not far from accurate. However, there is obviously no mention of the friction between the military engineers and the OT or between Hitler and his generals regarding the construction plans.

After he inspected the West Wall, Hitler issued the following message dated May 20, 1939: "Soldiers and Workers of the West Front! The inspection of the West Wall has convinced me of its invincibility. The German people and I thank you all, through unrelenting work you have created in the shortest time concrete and steel defenses for Germany's security. The soldiers, West Wall workers, and Border "work force, through commitment to the National Socialist Party and the community, deserve our thanks."

The effectiveness of the German military and civilian propaganda is revealed in an American intelligence report by Major Hohenthal in May 1940 based on his experiences as a military attache in Germany. According to Hohenthal, the defenses of East Prussia consisted of little more than a series of bunkers, but the East and West Wall were modern fortified zones. However, he does not mention whether they were very different from each other. Since he was not allowed to tour the West Wall, he simply assumed that the large B-Werke of the East Wall were similar to the standard works in the West, as his German guide had informed him. He also appears to have been convinced that the East Wall actually had as much depth as the Germans claimed. In the report Hohenthal summarizes German doctrine rather accurately and mentions the emphasis on the use of fortifications as a base and support for offensive actions. He duly notes the premise that the fortified zone must be placed far enough back from the border so that the enemy cannot bombard its positions, but he seems unaware of the fact that Hitler forced the military to move the West Wall right up to the border.

Hohenthal reports some significant tactical considerations used in planning the German fortifications, pointing out that the Germans felt that air bombardment to destroy the West Wall would not be economically viable. Surprisingly, despite dramatic improvements in the effectiveness of air bombing between 1940 and 1944, the positions of the West Wall and even those of the Maginot Line proved to be remarkably impervious to air power.

Hohenthal was also struck by the emphasis placed on depth and uniformity. He notes the preference for *"steel turrets,"* i.e. cloches, for frontal fire and all-around fires and mentions that the Germans considered the revolving turrets to be impractical. However, the Germans felt the need to maintain flanking fires with machine guns and provide bunkers with sufficient ammunition. The protection of the defensive zone with antitank weapons and obstacles and camouflage were considered vital. According to Hohenthal, a certain number of batteries in the fortified zone had sufficient armor protection to withstand the heaviest enemy guns. It appears from this statement that he must have been told during his visit about the armored batteries planned for the East Wall. Hohenthal presumed that the primary mission of these German defensive zones was "to increase the striking power of the highly mobile field armies."

He went on: "The basic tactics for the German field armies are not changed by reason of the existence of German fortified zones. In fact, their mobility has bee increased because the fortified zones free them from the immobility of the ol trench system. The World War and the Civil War in Spain have demonstrated that the border of a country in defense and the lines of communication of a field arm'. in attack are always in danger of developing into a line of trenches and a costly war of attrition. Germany must avoid this, because she is weaker both economically and in man power than the probable combination of enemies she will face in war."

In the report, Hohenthal also analyzes the psychological effect of the fortifications. According to him, "The natural desire of the great majority of German people to avoid war and the assurance of their government that these fortifications were solely for the defense of the Reich reacted to gain the support of the Germar. people in this project and to build up their confidence in Adolph Hitler and his plans for the reconstruction of Germany." He also claimed that an industrial booir. took place in East Prussia, the Rhineland, and the Saar because the fortification? instilled confidence that "war would be avoided and that these industries would be safe" while providing for the increased demands of the German war machine including building the West Wall.

It must be remembered that in 1939-1940, Germany's only

possible combination of enemies included France and
Great Britain, already at war, and possibly the Netherlands
and Belgium. Hohenthal was pointing out that the Allies
and most of the democratic nations believed in the superi-
ority of their forces. Hohenthal seems to have been influ-
enced to some extent by the German propaganda line that
claimed that the Reich was forced into the war and was
merely defending itself, Included with Hohenthal's attache
report was a copy of *Signal* magazine with ar. article on
the West Wall, a product of the German propaganda machine.
Toward the end of the Polish campaign in 1939, the
commander-in-chief of the army *(OKH),* General Walter
von Brauchitsch, who had replaced, von Fritsch in 1938,
declared that: "The erection of the Western Wall, the
strongest fortification in the world, enabled us to destroy
the Polish army in the shortest possible time without being
obliged to split up the mass of our forces at various fronts
as was the case in 1914. Now that we have no enemy in the
rear, we can calmly await the future development of events
without encountering the danger of a two-front war." This
statement was widely disseminated for both German and
foreign public consumption. Other works were published
on the subject of the German fortifications, but they were
usually based on the carefully controlled data released by
German sources. One of these works was *The Maginot and
Siegfried Lines* by James Eastwood, circulated in November 1939. In this book, Eastwood compared the French
and German defensive lines and concluded that they were
both unlike any of the older fortifications because they
were built in depth. Although he did not differentiate
much between the two, he pointed out that they "are not
glorified trenches, and they cannot be captured or pierced
as were trenches in the last war," and that they were really
"fortified districts of great depth." Eastwood claimed that
the West Wall, like the Maginot Line, included "bewilder-

ing underground rassages which pass beneath their own tank traps ... and other obstacles ... lead into huge underground fortresses ..." This is an image that the Germans carefully cultivated. However, no such structures existed except, perhaps, in the East A'all. Although Eastwood downplayed German claims of the West Wall's impregnability he gave it too much credit overall. For instance, he claimed that the fort of Istein had been rebuilt since July 1938 and was equipped with long-range artillery " when, in reality, most of the work remained undone. He also alleged, probably i\ith little basis for it, that the workers were treated almost like prisoners and called for an improvement of their conditions. In addition, he implied that contractors used inferior products and that whole segments of the local population were displaced. He often used the standard German figures, but did not always quote them in the proper context. "Until July 1939," he claimed, "6 million tons of cement, 25 million cubic feet of wood, 8,000 rail truck-loads delivered daily and 3 million rolls of barbed wire used with over 332,000 workers after October 1938." He remarked that "No matter what the German Government says to the contrary, it is certain the Siegfried Line is still far from finished." However, he concluded that even though the construction continued day and night, the position was essentially strong.

The French venture into the West Wall in September 1939 did not dispel the misconceptions, but added a new preoccupation: the minefields. During the foray, the French managed to recover samples of the mines, which were eventually described in Allied military publications. The French alerted their allies and others to the "silent soldier," the German S-mine or antipersonnel mine, which was ejected several meters and then exploded spewing out 350 steel balls. They also recovered a German antitank T-mine. Both types of mines had been kept under wraps until then by the Germans who did not want the world to know about them.

In actuality the depth of the West Wall was comparable to the Maginot Line's and was not as deep as indicated on the propaganda maps. However, it contained a greater number of bunkers than the Maginot Line. The line reached its greatest depth around Aachen and between a point north of Saarbriicken and Pirmasens. The so-called Air Defense Zone West was less impressive than indicated by the propaganda and probably numbered fewer than two thousand concrete positions However, its flak batteries were distributed in depth. It is possible that many of the 22,000 positions attributed to Air Defense Zone West had been actually built as part of the West Wall prior to 1939. In his book *Der Atlantikwall,* Rudy Rolf estimates that the actual figure for the various types of structures built in the area was about fifteen thousand. The larger B-Werke and A-Werke were never built, and the "German Gibraltar" of Istein never reached the stage of completion claimed by the propaganda. An American journalist gave the West Wall the name of the "Siegfried Line," which soon stuck.

The ground weapons for air defense had come a long way since the Germans first used captured Russian guns and rebored French 75-mm guns in World War I as their first flak weapons. (Note: Some form of antiballoon gun existed before the war began.) The Reichswehr, under von Seeckt's leadership, had laid the groundwork for air power and air defense even though the Treaty of Versailles expresslv forbade German ownership of antiaircraft weapons. The Germans were able to sidestep the treaty restrictions by developing weapons abroad. Since the German company Rheinmetall had interests in the Swiss Solothurn company, it was able to develop the 37-mm Flak 18 during the 1920s. At the same time, the Swedish Bofors company, partially owned by Krupp, shared information on its latest developments with the Germans. Krupp's technicians even worked on new designs at Bofors in Sweden, which they took back to Germany in 1931. As a result of this clandestine work, the famous "88-mm" gun—Germany's main flak weapon—was produced as early as 1933.

In *On Air Defense,* James Crabtree points out that the German army began the secret creation of seven antiaircraft batteries using Krupp 75-mm guns manufactured for export. These batteries were placed in remote regions where they would not be noticed, and were expanded in 1932 when they were designated *&s Transport-Abteilungen* (transport detachments). Meanwhile, flak companies armed with machine guns were organized under the sponsorship of a sporting association known as the *Deutscher Luftsportsverband.* The Ministry of Air Transport took over the army flak battalions in 1934 and soon after a small number of flak battalions were assigned to the newly formed Luftwaffe. By late 1935, Flak Regiments 1 through 13, and 22, 23, and 25 came into existence. Most consisted of a single battalion and seven of the eighteen battalions were new formations. Many of these regiments acquired a second battalion by late 1938, and, when the number of regiments totaled over forty, a few got even a third one. The number of battalions rose to 115 by 1939 and over 840 in 1941. The main weapons for these regiments was die 88-mm Flak, which became one of the most effective dual-purpose weapons of the war since it was also used as an antitank weapon by its crews. For lower altitudes, 20-mm and 37-mm guns were used. The Luftwaffe assigned about 75,000 men to flak and supporting units, which operated about 2,600 heavy weapons and ?,700 other guns, and 3,000 searchlights in the spring of 1939. In 1938, as preparations for the invasion of Czechoslovakia went ahead, the *Luftverteidigungszone West* (Air Defense Zone West) was created behind the West Wall. In his book *Phoenix Triumphant, E.* R. Hooton observed that General Kitizinger was put in charge of this zone, which was twenty to one hundred kilometers in depth and contained thirteen hundred flak guns under the command of *Festungsflakartillerie III.* Most of the aircraft were stationed in the East, so the defenses in the West had to rely mainly on flak, searchlights, and barrage balloons. The few aircraft serving as night-fighters relied on searchlights to find their prey. To solidify the Air Defense Zone West, Kitizinger made plans to build permanent defensive structures in the zone, but little work was accomplished until 1939. Small defensive commands vrere set up around Berlin, Leipzig, Stettin, Hamburg, and Düsseldorf.

The army also maintained several flak units after 1940 for the protection of the Held forces, since most Luftwaffe flak units were assigned to secure sites in the interior and only a few were deployed in the Air Defense Zone West of the West Wall. The army flak units totaled about thirty battalions, which increased in number and were still equipped and supplied by the Luftwaffe.

According to John Kreis, author of *Air Warfare and Air Base Air Defense,* a directive entitled "The Conduct of Air Operations," published in Air Field Manual No. 16 in 1935, explained the role of the Luftwaffe and established the procedure for Luftwaffe cooperation with the other services. The directive called for first strikes against the enemy's air forces to protect the Luftwaffe, its bases, and aircraft. Control of the sky was the key to victory and combat against strong fighter forces was not encouraged; the preferred method was to destroy their bases. This policy was effective in the first years of the war, but when Germany went on the defensive a new policy had to be adopted. Late in the war, one last desperate attempt to strike at the enemy's bases on the Western Front ended in a dismal failure. Flak units and fighter aircraft were placed under a single command when they operated in a combat zone. Luftwaffe officers were assigned to the field armies to maintain cooperation.

To protect German airfields and sites from air attack, the

flak units could be replaced or supported by fighter air-craft units composed of twin engine Me 110s, *with* limited uses, and the single engine Me 109, which dominated the skies early in the war. The radars of the Luftwaffe that went into operation in 1939 helped detect approaching air-craft and direct flak units. When the British switched to nighttime bombing missions, the Germans were unable to stop them because they had no adequate nightfighters and no effective ground defenses except for flak and search-light units in major cities and bases. E. R. Hooton, author of *Eagle in Flames* says that at the end of 1942, 30 percent of the heavy flak batteries had no target acquisition equip-ment and less than 30 percent had radar fire control. In 1940, the number of flak batteries rose from 756 to 1,182, only 174 of which were heavy batteries. The majority of these units were stationed outside Germany. Hooton ob-serves that the Reich's antiaircraft gun shield was too weak and had to be replaced by aircraft.

In the summer of 1940, after the fall of France, Colonel (later General) Joseph Kammhuber was given the mission of establishing the night defenses of the Reich. During the next two years, he established what the British called the *"Kammhuber Line,"* which began with two lines of search-lights and flak. The searchlights backed by flak were with-drawn from some cities to help create a real line that ex-tended along Germany's northwestern border toward Aa-chen. When enemy raiders crossed the line, the search-lights would illuminate them so that night-fighter aircraft, such as the Me-109, could find and engage them. Although Kammhuber had little knowledge about radar, he was as-sisted by Lieutenant Hermann Diehl, who had developed the technique for intercepting incoming bombers by using the Freya radar in late 1939. In October 1940, six of the first Wiirzburg Riese (FuMG 65) radar units were put under his control to protect the Ruhr. This type of radar was used to detect enemy aircraft and also to guide German fighters to them. Kammhuber also received the assistance of Captain Wolfgang Flack, who had been using the Würzburg units for night interception since April 1940. In January 1941, the searchlight belt extended from Hamburg to Liege and was fully supported by nightfighters. According to James Crabtree, author of *On Air Defense,* the Wiirzburg radars with a limited range of thirty-two kilometers—this range was later doubled—were placed in front of the belt of searchlights and used in defensive boxes known as *Himmelbett* because of their shape. The boxes included a long-range Freya radar set, a control center, two Wiirzburg tracking radars, and a nightfighter on patrol. The Himmelbett system, created during the last half of 1941, was eventually expanded in depth and more nightfighter units were added.

According to E. R. Hooton, the Kammhuber Line first began as a line of searchlights operated by the 1st and 2nd Flak Searchlight Brigades in 1940. By early 1941 it formed a belt manned by six searchlight regiments consisting of seventeen battalion-size zones extending from Liibeck to Liege and two battalion zones protecting Kiel. By March 1941, Kammhuber setup a dozen nightfighter bases, the larges: of which was near Venlo. In 1942, the new Mammut and Wasserman radars allowed longer-range detection of enemy aircraft. Also at this time the nightfight-ers were equipped with their own radar mounted on Bf-llOs. The Kammhube Line of 1941 to early 1942 grew into two belts, the largest of which extended fror the Baltic Sea to Alsace, largely on Reich territory. It included nine sections wit twenty-one control stations.

A second line was formed on occupied territory, from the Pas de Calais area into Denmark up to the Skaggerak. [25]

Since the Himmelbett system provided only one nightfighter per box, the British found in the summer of 1942 that the best way to overcome it was to overwhelm it with massive bomber formations. General Kammhuber countered the British move in 1943 by resorting to the employment of more nightfighters and radar units. However, even though new methods were devised before the end of the year, the increasing numbers of Allied aircraft began to weaken the German defenses. The Kammhuber Line increased in width, reaching a depth of 150 to 2(X kilometers and consisting of over two hundred radar stations in 1943 and 1944.

The deficiency of nightfighters was not made up until late 1940 through 1941 when aircraft equipped with radar were developed, allowing the Germans to intercept Allied bombers at night. In early 1939, the Luftwaffe included seven *Nachtjagdversuchsstaffeln* (nightfighter squadrons) consisting of Ar-68s and Me 109s. The Ar-68 was an older biplane first built in 1933 and still in service early in the war with limited daytime uses. Soon after the war began, these planes participated in experiments for night interception. A nightfighter division was forme in May 1940. Soon even "heavy" nightfighters, such as the modified Do-1 bomber, were modified so bombardier's nose position were replaced with five! machine guns. The first airborne radar

---

[25] Messerschmitt Bf 110F-2 II/ZG 76 Zerstörer Gruppen operating in Defense of the Reich 1943

units, the Liechtenstein sets, were tested on the Do-17 Z-10. During the summer of 1941, Do-215s, improved versions of the Do-17, replaced the Do-17 Z-10. On the night of August 8-9, 1941, a Do-21 equipped with the FuG 202 B/C radar shot down a British bomber. Nightfighter with airborne radar were now able to mount successful night interceptions to defend the Reich. By 1942, these aircraft were replaced with more advanced models and types mounting airborne radar. Thus radar, which was first developed to direct gun fire, was adapted to search for aircraft. However, work on more effective radar units ceased early in the war and did not resume until Germany was subjected to heavy Allied bombing raids after 1942.

The equipment used in air defense included the following:
Searchlights or *Scheinwerfer* (sizes 110-cm and 200-cm)
The 110-cm and 200-cm were the same as those used on warships in World War I and had ranges of 4,000 and 5,500 meters respectively.
60-cm *Flakscheinwerfer* range of 3,600 meters (for light flak)
150-cm *Flakscheimverfer 35* range of 10,000 meters (for heavy flak)
150-cm *Flakscheimverfer 37* range of 12,000 meters (for heavy flak)
200-cm *Flakscheinwerfer 40* range of 12,000 meters (for heavy flak)
Trumpet Sound Detector or *Richtungshorer* (RHH)—
range for detecting aircraft sounds was from 5 km to 12 km depending on the weather.
Radar units for antiaircraft defense:
FuMG 39 *Kurpfalz* Range of 10 to 25 km (20 supplied to Ruhr and Channel coast)
FuMG 62 *Wiirzburg*   Range 32 to 40 km
FuMG 65 *Wiirzburg-Riese* (Giant)   Range 50 to 70 km
Mammut Range   300 km
Wasserman Range   190 km

Radar units for air warning:
Freya   Range 80 km
Airborne radar for nightfighters:
FuG 202 *Lichtenstein BC*   Range 200 to 5,000 km
The searchlights were necessary for the most primitive
night defense. Those used in the Great War had too short a
range and not as much intensity. A new 200-cm searchlight entered service after 1940, when greater ranges were
needed. Sound detectors were used in most major armed
forces with limited success. The Germans concluded that
they were good at determining direction, but little else.
Range-finders came in several types, including fire control
systems, which were useful in directing the antiaircraft
guns and the main batteries of warships and coastal artillery. Most of these radars were improved or replaced after
1942. In addition, when the Allies began using radar to
guide their own bomber formations to their targets, the
Germans had to develop jamming devices. Several radars
with ranges of over 150 kilometers also came into service.

Passive air Defences

To protect airfields, transportation centers, bridges, factories, and other key targets from air attack, the Germans
used various methods of camouflage. Early in the war
these methods were rather crude and not as effective as
those used to disguise fortifications and facilities from the
ground. Targets that were easily identifiable, like bridges
and industrial areas, were protected with a barrage of balloons to prevent low altitude attacks. Many of these key
targets were also protected by flak and, when possible, aircraft from nearby airfields.
Airfield camouflage was difficult early in the war because
the straight lines of the runways gave away their location.
In some cases, the edges of concrete runways were soft-
ened to make them blend with nearby fields. Hangars and

other buildings were difficult to hide because of the shadows they cast on the ground. However, various types of netting proved quite successful. Decoy airfields sometimes deceived Allied bombers, but they had to be maintained so they looked real and they had to be equipped with dummy aircraft, oil tanks, hangars, and even some type of camouflage. However, the lack of access roads usually gave them away as decoys. Late in the war, the Allies effectively struck at any airfield that might be active and the Germans resorted to painting simulated craters on the runways, but they failed to deceive the Allies. Another solution was to disperse aircraft into wooded areas near airfields with revetments, but the telltale trail gave away their location. The Luftwaffe finally resorted to using sections of the auto-bahns as runways and hiding aircraft off the road.

Many of the methods used for disguising airfields were used to hide factories. Early in the war roofs were painted with dazzle designs, but this soon made them easier targets. Roy M. Stanley, author of *To Fool A Glass Eye,* claims that when attempts to disguise the Skoda Works near Pilsen failed, the Germans built a complete dummy site, including a replica of a prison the bombers used to guide them to the target. The actual prison was well camouflaged to remove it as a marker for the bomber pilots. The Germans's subterfuge was relatively successful.

Disguising targets of any type in a city was more difficult. In Hamburg paint was used to disguise railway patterns. Where its key Lombards Bridge separated the inner from the outer basin, the inner basin was disguised and a decoy bridge was built across the outer basin. However, fire bombing destroyed much of Hamburg's camouflage, including the decoy bridge. Stanley also mentions a new ball-bearing plant, built at Schweinfurt after the earlier destructive raids, that was made of reinforced concrete and whose roof was covered with camouflage nets and debris to give the impression it was a pile of rubble.

One of the most successful defensive methods was the use of smoke generators. By the fall of 1942, the number of sites protected by these devices increased dramatically. The number, size, and type of smoke generators varied according to the size of the target to be obscured. A small site needed as few as ten, while a port city might require over three hundred. However, the effectiveness of smoke generators greatly depended on the weather. On some days a smokescreen could be highly effective, and on others it barely concealed anything. According to Stanley, conditions at Brest were usually ideal for blanketing the city, but at Kiel conditions were not always as favorable. At Brest, the navy's 4th Marine Nebelabteilung operated the smoke generators. Similar units served in other ports in France and elsewhere. It may be assumed that the army and Luftwaffe assigned their own special units to operate smoke generators to protect cities and airfields. According to the American Strategic Bombing Survey, Leuna, Germany's largest synthetic oil plant, was protected by a highly effective smokescreen and the heaviest flak concentration in Europe. When it underwent twenty-two air attacks between May and December 1944, production was greatly reduced and almost stopped at times, but it was quickly restored because the smoke and the weather prevented the Allied bombers from obliterating the site.

When the Allies started using radar directions, the smoke generators lost much of their effectiveness and the Germans resorted to the corner reflector, a device probably made of some kind of metal, which, when floated in sufficient numbers on a body of water, such as a river or basin, changed the shape of the coastline on the radar screens. However, no amount of corner reflectors could deceive the bombardiers on a clear day.

Air Raid Protection

Aircraft technology had made such dramatic strides during this period that it was no longer enough to protect only frontline troops. It now became necessary to safeguard rear-area troops, headquarters, bases, industry, and the civilian population in the interior of the country as well. In Germany bunkers were designed for the rear area, some even built before World War II when the possibility of aerial bombardment was already taken into consideration. The first modest steps were taken in 1934, when air-raid sirens were installed in Berlin to warn the population, but few shelters were actually built. In 1935 plans were made to handle damage from potential air raids and a few shelters were built, but no significant steps were taken to protect the civilian population. It was not until August 1939 that the government required the construction of shelters for all new buildings. When the war began, trenches were dug in parks and a few more safety measures were taken.

In 1934 the architect Leo Winkel received his first patent for air-raid shelters and air-raid shelter towers in the form of "ant hills." He continued developing additional designs during the next decade. After he formed his own company, Winkel sold his designs to the Wehrmacht, the national railroad system, and the aircraft industry before and early in the war. Of particular interest is the *Luftschutzturme,* or "air-raid tower" developed both for military and civil defense, which caught the interest of the Luftwaffe's leadership in 1937. One of his most popular models was a tower designed to hold five hundred men. The *Luftschutztiirme* was adopted by *Deutschen Reichsbah,* the German National Railroad, because it could be placed in the limited space available in congested rai-lyards. A total of seventeen of these towers were built during the war by the railroad. The aircraft and some related industries ordered twenty-nine towers, seven of which were built for the *Focke-Wulf Flug-*

zeugbau GmbH at Bremen. More towers were erected for aluminum and steel factories and even for Daimler-Benz. The Wehrmacht ordered thirty-four *Luftschutztürme,* four of which were earmarked for the Wehrmacht command post at Potsdam and the remaining nineteen for its newly completed OKH command headquarters at Zossen.

Soon, Winkel had a competitor, the engineer Paul Zombeck, who proposed a new type of tower. By 1939, several towers were either under construction and/or completed. One of the most interesting designs was the Dietel tower, which looked like a large mushroom and consisted of four levels for the personnel, and an upper floor that projected over the tower walls where the machinery, such as ventilators and fans, was installed. On top of the conical roof was a platform that could mount a light flak weapon and searchlight. Only a couple of these towers were built in the Air Defense Zone West, and one for the Kriegsmarine at Wilhelmshaven. Eventually, different types of towers were erected throughout Germany, the largest of which could accommodate a few hundred to a thousand people.

The *Luftschutzturme* were equipped with gas locks and some basic facilities. Most had round or conical roofs. However, Winkel's "ant hill," with its rocket-like shape, probably had the best bomb-deflecting capability and was the most imitated. Most *Luftschutztürme* were erected during the war, after Hitler authorized an emergency program in 1940 and the civil defense effort could begin in earnest. They held the largest number of occupants and required less space than most of the other large shelters.

Other types of air-raid shelters, or *Luftschutze,* such as the air protection tunnel and more simple ground and underground shelters were also designed. Until 1940, the tunnel and modified building basement were the most common types available for civil defense. In 1940 Hitler authorized the emergency construction of bunkers for 5 percent of the population of seventy cities. The work force that had once been engaged in building the West Wall was now free to tackle other projects By July 1941 the government produced pamphlets establishing minimum standards for shelters.

These pamphlets included:
I. General layout and planning:
Classification: detached and attached; they should normally be multistory above-ground structures; below-ground bunkers should be small and only used in special cases. Types of concrete thickness:
A. 3.00 meters for 750 or more occupants
B. 2.50 meters for 300 to 750 occupants
C. 2.00 meters for less than 300 occupants
Should contain the following rooms: Entry (gas lock, stairs, etc.), guard rooms, wardens office, first aid, separate rooms, halls, lavatories (male and female separate), wash rooms, and rooms for machinery and equipment.
II.   Structural Design: Outside walls and roof to have reinforcing steel; Brunswick method for spacing of steel beams; German standard for Portland cement or blast furnace cement; minimum of two gas locks.
III.   Ventilation, Heating and Cooling: for protection against gas and to maintain livable conditions.
IV.   Water Supply and Sewage: requirements for water supply given including use of wells if possible and water lines to be two meters below ground. All water pipes to be code painted.
V.   Electrical Supply and Fittings: Shelters with capacity of up to 300 people will use batteries; shelters with capacity of 300 or more and hospital shelters will use emergency generators; connection to outside power grid (two separate connections preferred); transformer stations needed for larger shelters and they should be in bomb-proof positions; shelters for over 300 people will include radio receiving and transmitting equipment.

VI.   Signs and Furnishings—This included information on marking rooms, entrances, etc., fire extinguishing apparatus, locks for doors, painting.
VII. Hospital Shelters
VIII. Underground Shelters

Civil Defense and Military Air-Raid Bunkers

Standard designs for air-raid shelters came into use probably after 1941, although no official documentation seems to exist for this before 1944. The use of *Luftschutzturme* or air-raid towers was Ignited because they were large, tall, and expensive. Most of the air-raid shelters were in the form of bunkers below ground although some standard above-ground types were used. The amount of concrete used in reinforced concrete bunkers has been given as:

Personnel Capacity	Total Volume of Concrete
500 to 600	1,800 cubic meters
1,000 to 1,200	3,300 cubic meters
2,000 to 2,400	5,000 cubic meters
4,000 to 4,800	8,800 cubic meters

In 1940 German inspectors discovered that many bunkers were inferior because they were constructed with concrete that was weak in cement content. It was not until March 1944 that research dictated that a standard blast furnace :ement was required, but the number of days for curing to reach maximum strength was not specified.

The thickness of the roof was as critical as that of the walls. German research came up with die following standards based on tests:

Roof Thickness
1.40 meters 2.00 meters 2.50 meters
Resists
500 Ib (230 kg) bomb 1,000 Ib (460 kg) bomb 2,000 Ib (920 kg) bomb

The wall thickness generally was designed proportionally

to that of the roof and lighter. The method developed at Brunswick University
became the standard for the placement of steel beams in the roof and walls.

The foundation type was described as a free-floating mat-type reinforced concrete slab. This type of foundation allowed the bunker to "rock" when there was a direct hit or near miss. In some cases a deep foundation was used with the walls extended downward into the ground.

The bunkers were linked to outside power sources and had gasoline or diesel motors for emergency use. Like in most combat bunkers, the wiring was attached on the exposed walls. Some of the more interesting features included electric motors to operate the sewage and water pumps and the heating and cooling systems. Gas filters were an important component for full protection. When possible a well was included, but the bunkers were usually linked to the city water system. A few large bunkers included electric elevators. The interior features were basically Spartan-like, possibly even more so than military bunkers. They were intended for shelter against air raids and not for comfort or long-term occupation.

The location of air-raid shelters in relation to the people they protected also had some standards to follow. A distance of five hundred meters was considered the maximum average distance that a person should need to travel to reach a bunker during an air raid, but in some cases this was allowed to be doubled to one thousand meters, although that was a considerable distance for a person to cover once the airraid warning was sounded. [26]

The German administrators were just as efficient in designing air-raid shelters as they were in planning combat bunkers, but their efforts in the case of civil defense came

---

[26] Source: *U.S. Strategic Bombing Survey:* Report No. 22, Public Air-Raid Shelters in Germany, 1945.

just a little late.

The capacity of the various types of shelters varied according to type. Cellars sheltered fifty to one hundred; tunnels, one hundred to five hundred; anc bunkers, five hundred to four thousand. Some large bunkers were designed tc accommodate as many as eight thousand people, and a few rare examples up tc eighteen thousand. During one raid on Hamburg, sixty thousand supposedly crammed into a bunker meant for eighteen thousand people.

The first bunkers were designed to resist 500-lb (230-kg) bombs, but by 1942 shelters had to resist 1,000-lb (460-kg) bombs, and soon after 2,000-lb (920-kg bombs. By 1945, based on an interview with Professor Theolor Kristen, the American Strategic Bombing Survey concluded that enough shelters had beer built in Germany to protect about 15 percent of the population of most cities and towns and up to 75 percent if they were overcrowded. The professor had worked on testing the best methods for reinforced concrete construction for these shelters as early as 1937.

The final design for the civil defense bunkers was approved by the government. The air-raid protection program was assigned to General Lindner of the Civil Defense Department of the Air Ministry, and therefore it was under the auspices of the Luftwaffe. According to Lindner, the policy for building shelters was highly debated. He disapproved of the large air-raid bunkers that were finally approved because he thought they were bad for morale and because obtaining the construction materials would be difficult since they were needed elsewhere. Instead he preferred to improve and strengthen cellar shelters.

During the first years of the war, bunkers built in residential districts were often designed to blend architecturally with their surroundings. Their bombproof slab was covered by a tile roof and concrete walls were covered with a stone or brick veneer. Sometimes trompe-l'oeil windows and doors were also painted on the walls. Late in the war, some of these bunkers were painted to match surrounding bombed-out buildings. However, it was probably unnecessary to camouflage these air-raid shelters because they were of little interest to Allied bombers. At best, the camouflage may have prevented them from being mistaken for military positions.

One positive point about the German air-raid shelters was that even though their construction began late, they were probably the most modern and effective air-raid shelters of the war. Some of them would probably have withstood an atomic attack better than shelters built in other countries at the time. Of course, one reported disadvantage was that during an incendiary raid, which created a firestorm, even the best of these bunkers turned into an oven, virtually roasting their occupants alive.

Flak Towers

In August 1940, Hitler authorized the construction of special "high bunkers" or *"Flak Türme"* that served as civil defense shelters or positions for heavy flak. These flak towers were the largest air-raid shelters and antiaircraft gun positions built in Germany or anywhere else at the time. They were designed by Albert Speer and built by the OT. In Berlin, Hamburg, and Vienna they were built in pairs; one mounted the antiaircraft guns and the other the fire-control equipment. Of the first four that were built, three were in Berlin and one in Hamburg. After the initial design was modified, two more were erected in Hamburg and two in Vienna. The towers in Vienna as well as those in Bremen were not built until the fall of 1942.

Michael Feodrowitz, author of *The Flak Towers,* gives the following specifications for the towers: Square with sides of 60 meters length for the flak tower and 30 or 40 meters for the fire control tower (these dimensions became larger in Hamburg); height 25 meters, although one set of towers in Berlin and Hamburg rose to 39 meters; distance between gun tower and command tower between 300 and 500 meters; four corner-turret positions for heavy flak (initially twin-mounted 105-mm naval guns planned for); light flak on the fire-control towers.

One of the best known flak towers was the Berlin Zoo Tower, completed in April 1941. This huge structure consisted of seven levels, including a basement. It was designed to hold eight thousand people, but reportedly could accommodate more than three times that number. It had its own water supply, power generators, and kitchens. One of its levels was used to safeguard art treasures from Berlin museums, another was a hospital, which included operating rooms. Flak crews totaling about three hundred men were quartered near the top. Heavy antiaircraft guns were mounted on the roof, in each of the four open concrete turrets. According to some sources, 88-mm guns, 20-mm and 37-mm Flak were used initially and more guns were placed on the lower terrace, below the large guns. However, according to Hans Sakkers, the guns used on the tower were heavier that 88-mm, and were replaced a year later with 128-mm flak guns on twin mounts.

Heavy armored cupolas covering the ammunition elevators were located next to each of the gun positions and the turret positions. A range finder was placed in a pit in the center. The gun tower was linked to the fire-control tower by tunnels carrying the communications cables. The fire-control tower, also a command center, served as the headquarters for the 1st Flak Division and mounted a Würzburg Giant radar on its roof.

The three sets of flak towers in Berlin were laid out to form a triangle to protect the area in between. A similar triangular layout was planned for Hamburg Vienna, and Bremen. Work in Hamburg did not begin until the fall of 1942. The sets of flak towers at Hamburg were not identical and the third was never completed. The Heiligengeistfeld Tower, identified as Flak Tower IV, was similar to those in Berlin and could accommodate as many as eighteen thousand civilians. The Wilhelmsburg Tower, or Flak Tower V, belonged to the second generation of towers and was characterized by large flak turrets on each corner, that made it look like a massive medieval keep. Only the inner part of these positions was open, like a hole in a donut, to give maximum protection to the crew and ammunition. The ammunition elevators were never completed. In the center of the position was a rolling crane. In Vienna sets of towers were built at Arenberg Park Stiftskaserne, and Augarten, forming a triangle that protected the cultural district of the city. Most of the work was done by foreign laborers and RAD. The last tower was begun and completed in the first half of 1944. Stiftskaserne and Augarten towers differed from the Arenberg tower in design.

Both consisted of sixteen sides and had a diameter of forty-three meters. The four heavy antiaircraft gun positions on the roof were located within the circumference of the tower. The circular gun turrets were fitted with an armored roof with an opening that allowed the guns to fire and change elevation, while affording protection for the entire gun crew. A gallery below the roof housed eight positions for smaller flak weapons. Like the towers in Berlin, the towers in Vienna included all the standard features necessary for independent operations.

There were also smaller structures inside and outside of the Reich that were sometimes erroneously called flak towers, but they should not to be confused with the massive structures built in Berlin, Hamburg, and Vienna. These smaller structures served primarily as shelters, but may also have mounted some light flak on their roofs. A pair of these smaller towers was located near the East Wall.

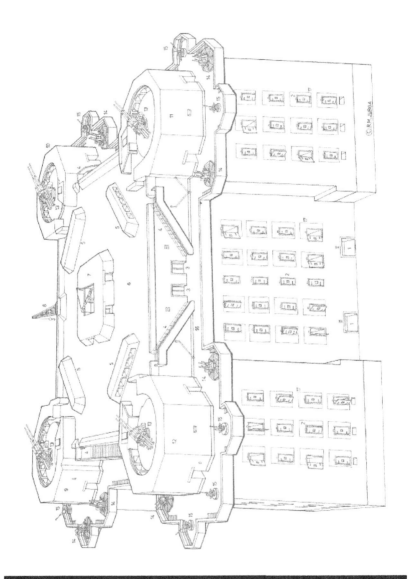

Flak Tower IV Heiligengeistfeld, Hamburg

Flak Tower IV Heiligengeistfeld, Hamburg
1.Entrance
2.Armored shutters
3.Exit to lower combat platform
4.Concrete stairs
5.Ammunition storage
6.Main combat platform
7.Command post and range finder
8.Crane for equipment
9.Gun tower
10.Gun tower
11.Gun tower
12.Gun tower
13.120-mm twin flak
14.Light 20-mm Flak 38
15.Light 20-mm Flak 38
16.Access to combat platform
17. Outline painted on windows as camouflage

One housed a radio tower and the other mounted light antiaircraft weapons on its roof. Outside of Angers, France, a pair of such towers near the German naval barracks also mounted light weapons on their roofs. A number of bunkers, not as high as these towers, were also built for mounting a flak weapon. These structures can be seen in many of the Atlantic Wall positions and in some of the coastal fortresses.

Construction

The flak towers that Hitler ordered in the fall of 1940 were designed by Albert Speer and built by the OT as priority projects. In the vicinity of these gun towers stood a command or fire-control tower. The huge gun towers also served as air-raid shelters for thousands of civilians and proved to be virtually bombproof and almost impossible to demolish after the war. They were intended to mount 128-mm flak guns on their roofs, even though these weapons were not initially ready for service.

The flak towers were built and completed together with their fire-control towers as follows:

Berlin

I Zoo Tower: Completed April 1941, initially mounted 105-mm guns.
II Friedrichshain Tower: Completed October 1941; mounted 105-mm flak guns
III The Humboldthain Tower: Completed April 1942; mounted 105-mm flak guns.
Between September 1942 and February 1943, 12 new 128-mm guns arrived with the Zoo Tower being the first of the three Berlin towers to be rearmed.

Hamburg

IV Heiligengeistfeld Tower: Completed in October 1942, mounted twin 128-mm flak guns.
V Wilhelmsburg Tower: Completed in October 1942.

Vienna

VIII Arenberg Park Tower: Completed October 1943, initially mounted 105-mm flak which was replaced by twin 128-mm flak in January 1944.
VI   Stiftskaserne Tower: Completed September 1943, mounted 128-mm flak.
VII   Augarten Tower. Completed 1944, mounted 128-mm flak.
*It was once believed that the Berlin Zoo Tower may have been first armed with 88-mm guns but that apparently was not the case.
Source: *The Flak Tower* by Michael Foedrowitz, 1998. *Flaktürm:Berlin-Hamburg-Wien* by Hans Sakkers, 1998. *Weapons of the Third Reich* by Terry Gander and Peter Chamberlain, 1979.
Command and Control: Protecting the Leadership

Germany's leaders not only were interested in sheltering their troops from air raids and heavy-caliber ordinance, but in assuring their own safety. Thus the Wehrmacht considered building large bunkers for a major headquarters complex and government officials and high-ranking members of the Nazi Party also decided they needed secure shelters. Hitler too got on the bandwagon since his primary headquarters, located at the Chancellery of the Reich, offered only modest personal protection against air attack. In 1936 a bunker for the Flihrer's protection was built in the garden of the Chancellery. In January 1938, Hitler asked Albert Speer, the inspector general of buildings, to rebuild the Chancellery as a part of his grandiose plans for rebuilding Berlin. The new Chancellery of the Reich, which must have been given the same priority level as the West Wall, was completed m time to meet the deadline of January 1939. It included reinforced cellars and was linked to the bunker in the garden by a tunnel when the war began. (This was not Hitler's famous Berlin bunker, that would be built during the war.)

Albert Speer wrote in his memoirs that Hitler "wherever he went, issued orders for building bunkers for his personal protection." In so doing he created a series of bunkers and underground headquarters that tied up thousands of workers needed for other projects. As the Polish campaign began, so did work on the firs: command sites for Hitler in the West. One of the first was *Adlerhorst,* "Eagle's Nest," at Bad Nauheim on the Western Front, where a mansion was converted tc include bunkers and a massive communications system. However, claiming that his headquarters should not be so lavish, Hitler opted for another site. *Felsennest,* or "Mountain Nest," was located on a hill a few hundred meters from the town of Rodert in the Eifel. A small bunker was completed for Hitler while he traveled in his command train "Amerika" after the Polish campaign. Hitler moved into the site in time to oversee the launching of his offensive in the West in May.

The bunkers for Hitler's personal use and protection became known as the *Führerbunkers.* The bunker complexes were fenced in and well-guarded, included accommodations, usually wooden structures for staff, escort troops, and specialists, and were linked to the outside world by a communications system. In addition, there were airfields nearby, and, whenever possible, access to the railroad for the Fuhrer's train. The next bunker built for him was at the Belgian village of Bruly-dePesche in late May 1940 as the German army swept to the English Channel. This site, called *Wolfsschlucht* or "Wolf's Gorge," was the place where Hitler oversaw the final operations of the conquest of France and made plans for the invasion of England. Another position for Hitler was established in the Black Forest, near the Upper Rhine, at the site known as Tannenberg, which had two bunkers and the usual array of wooden structures.

The most famous of Hitler's campaign headquarters sites

was the *Wolfsschanze,* or "Wolf's Lair," located near Ras-
tenburg in the lake region of East Prussia and built in secret during 1940. Hitler chose to locate this site in a
wooded, swampy region to prevent an attack by special
troops. He moved into this complex on June 24,1941, two
days after invading the Soviet Union. The initial construction took olace between 1940 and 1941, and consisted of
concrete and brick buildings and some wooden structures.
In addition to a chain-link fence, barbed wire, and minefields, gun emplacements were added. Between 1942 and
1943, a second phase of construction at this site saw the
erection of additional wooden buildings for staff and liai-
son officers from the Luftwaffe and Kriegsmarine. Accommodations for guests and a movie theater were also added.
These structures were soon reinforced with brick and concrete, particularly in 1944, when a barracks for the SS Escort Detachment and other units and additional amenities
were added. When it was completed in 1944, the Wolf's
Lair became the best protected and largest of the Fiihrer's
headquarters but retained the Spartan quality demanded
by Hitler.
In addition to the bunker command posts, Hitler had at
his disposal several residences, including the Chancellery
and his famous chalet known as Berghof that was located
at Berchtesgaden on the eighteen-hundred-meter-high
mountain of Obersalzberg. So many of his devoted fol-
lowers flocked to the site of the chalet that a security fence
and barbed wire had to be installed not only to keep out
the fans but also would-be assassins. According to Albert
Speer, Martin Bormann, the man in charge of developing
this site, spent a fortune on labor and expansion, con-
stantly blasting into the rock. During the late 1930s, additional buildings were erected on the site to house visitors,
the SS guard, Goring, Bormann, Gobbels, and Speer. Before and during the entire war Bormann diverted valuable
labor resources to continue building new facilities and

underground bunkers at the site, despite Speer's efforts to stop it in 1942, The bunkers for Hitler and his top officials at Berghof were elaborate affairs, far removed from the original Spartan plans. After arriving up the mountain along the last of the road's hairpin turns, an elevator was added to carry passengers up the last 110 meters to the top. According to Peter Hoffmann, author of *Hitler's Personal Security,* Goring's bunker at the site had three-meter-thick walls and roofs. A total of seventy-nine additional underground positions were built in the mountain. Theoretically, this would have been Hitler's hideout in the Alpine or National Redoubt, which was never completed.

According to Albert Speer, in addition to the *Führerbunkers,* Hitler approved the construction of shelters on the outskirts of major cities for the protection of the *Gauleiters* (senior Nazi area commanders) because they were important in maintaining control of the civilian population. The *Gaue,* or Nazi Party administrative areas, became Reich Defense Districts in 1942 with headquarters in forty-two cities. Each of the gauleiters was to receive his own special air-raid bunker. Even Goring built himself a vast complex of underground installations at his Karinhall residence and at a castle near Nuremberg. Thus the Nazi leadership was probably the best protected political group in Europe, or perhaps the world.

Hitler also had at his disposal a mobile command post on a special train called the *Filhrersonderzug,* or "Führer Special" with the code name of *Amerika.* Equipped with two special flak cars and cars for a staff and SS escort, the train served as Hitler's command post during the Polish campaign of 1939 and the Balkans campaign of 1941. Special tunnels were built for its protection in Poland, just before the Russian campaign. Other German military and political leaders also had similar trains, which should not be confused with the armored trains that were used during the war.

The command headquarters for all three branches of the armed forces were located in Berlin or on the outskirts during the mid-1930s. The *Oberkommando der 'Wehrmacht* was in Berlin since it was under Hitler's direct control; the *Oberkommando der Kriegsmarine* was located nearby; and Goring's *Oberkommando der Luftwaffe* was southwest of Berlin near Potsdam. The army moved its *Oberkommando der Heeres* south of Berlin to Zossen but also maintained another headquarters communications site at Ohrdruf, In 1937, a large subterranean communications bunker codenamed "Zeppelin" was built at Zossen with an above-ground concrete entrance concealed in a large house. The ceilings of the underground bunker consisted of 3.0 meters of concrete covered by a layer of several meters of earth. The structure consisted of two levels, was over one hundred meters long, and about fifty meters wide. The lower level housed the engine room, water pumps, several shower rooms, and toilets. The telephone exchange and other offices were located on the upper level. Like the headquarters communications centers of the other services, the Zeppelin bunker was connected to a large number of communications lines and equipment to maintain contact with virtually all fighting fronts. The bunker housed a wide variety of state-of-the-art equipment, from telephones to teletype machines for sending coded messages. Early in the war two other bunker complexes codenamed "Maybach" were built about a kilometer from the Zeppelin. A dozen concrete buildings disguised as homes contained facilities for the General Staff in Maybach I and duplicate facilities were available in the underground works. The tunnel system also connected to Zeppelin.

All these subterranean works were fully equipped with wells, diesel engines, and filtering systems for gas protection. Zeppelin and Maybach I were ready in time for the war, while Maybach II was not. As noted previously, several Winkel air-raid towers were also built on these sites. In addition, another OKH command complex was built near Frankfurt on the Main at Giessem. This site also included a large subterranean communications bunker initially codenamed Giesela. Two smaller above-ground command bunker groups, similar to Maybach, named Hansa I and Hansa II, were built nearby in the fall of 1939. These command complexes probably were the best protected in all of Europe.

Armored Trains

Armored trains served in the German army until the end of the war. Early in the war they were used in offensive operations, but later they also served as defensive units. Seven of these trains—numbered 1 to 7—were being readied in September 1939. Four more trains—numbered 21 to 24— were available for the Western campaign and over thirty more were added between then and mid-1944, by which time they were used mainly for defensive purposes. Many were captured Czech and Polish trains, and, later, Russian units as well.

By the end of 1942, most of the trains were used for internal security, i.e. protecting the rail lines from Russian partisans. Special light scout trains, more lightly armed than the others, were used effectively in the Balkans to secure the rail lines. Captured enemy armored vehicles were also adapted for use on the rails, adding to the number of rolling forts.

The locomotives and various wagons for the crew and weapons were covered with armor. In many cases the locomotive was not placed in the lead, but rather in the center of the train. Some wagons mounted guns, others were adapted for carrying tanks on armored flat cars, others still carried troops. The tanks could quickly be unloaded to pursue the enemy. Most trains also included a special command car with communications equipment. Artillery cars were special armored wagons that transported a variety of weapons, including, more often than not, a turret-mounted gun. The flak car was either a flatbed wagon that mounted the weapons, or an armored wagon with a hatch in the roof that opened for a pair of 20-mm guns. Some of the special trains, created in mid-1943, included light scout cars that mounted machine guns or heavy scout cars that mounted a tank turret from a Panzer III or IV with a

75-mm gun.

These trains continued to serve until the end of the war, carrying out a wide variety of functions from patrolling the coast of the French Riviera to helping tear up track on the Eastern Front during the retreat. As long as the rail lines remained intact, they could fill in gaps in the line.

German Expansion 1939-1942

The Polish campaign was virtually over in one month, and late in September 1939 the Wehrmacht repositioned its forces in the West. The Polish state was partitioned with the Soviets, and a German occupation force was left in the Germar -occupied territory. During the fall and winter of 1939-1940, the German arrrr readied to strike several times, but each time the offensive was called off for various reasons. At the time, the world's attention was focused on the Franco-Germar frontier where the two greatest fortification lines in the West faced each other German operations at sea had limited success during this period as U-boats and surface raiders failed to cut the British life lines. In addition, the loss of the pocket battleship *Graf Spec* in 1939 represented a setback for the Kriegsmarine. If victor, was to be achieved, it had to be on land, not at sea. In the meantime, the Allied armies stood on the defensive, but received no cooperation from Belgium, wh: refused them access to its territory, fearing German reprisal.

While waiting to go on the offensive, the Germans reinforced and extended the West Wall. The French, on the other hand, merely readied for defensive operations The Winter War between the Finns and Soviets put considerable strain on the future relations between the Allies and the Soviet Union. The success of the Mannerheim Line in delaying the Soviet advance did not go unnoticed by the Germans. The Finnish fortifications were of the type more suited to Hitler's idea of a defensive line since they were not intended to be hiding places from which the troops could fight. The Germans also found the Finnish use of boulders as antitank obstacles a practical alternative when not enough concrete and metal obstacles could be manufactured.

The Germans returned to the offensive in the spring of 1940 with a combined air-land-sea campaign against Denmark and Norway. Denmark quickly surrendered, most of Norway was overrun that April, and the Allies were forced north to Narvik. The occupation of Denmark gave Germany control of the key straits in and out of the Baltic, helped keep the Kiel Canal from becoming a vulnerable bottleneck, and facilitated access to the North Sea for surface raiders and U-boats. This blitzkrieg campaign temporarily crippled the Kriegsmarine's surface fleet but the vital ore routes along the Norwegian coast and from Sweden to Narvik were secured, insuring the uninterrupted flow of raw materials for the Germar. war industries. The Norwegian coast also offered excellent bases for the German fleet. The only drawback was that the entire Norwegian coast would have to be defended if Britain and France were not soon taken out of the picture.

As the war raged on in northern Norway, the Germans launched Case Yellow in May. The offensive in the West began with the invasion of Belgium, Luxembourg, and the Netherlands. Airborne units took Fort Eben Emael, the lynch pin of the Belgian fortified front facing Germany. In the meantime, two divisions were parachuted and landed in the Netherlands, opening the Dutch fortress from the inside. Within days, the Netherlands surrendered, followed by Belgium a little later. By the end of May, the German troops had passed through the Ardennes and trapped the British Expeditionary Force and a French army in the area around Dunkirk. After the remnants of this force were evacuated, the Germans prepared for their final offensive in the West, Case Red. The Allied lines stretched from the Maginot Line to the Somme Front. The Germans started moving in June and within weeks most of France was overrun and the remaining British troops evacuated. Hitler's ally, Italy, entered the conflict in the last days of the campaign, but scored no significant victories. At the beginning of July 1940, Great Britain was left to face Germany alone. The entry of Italy in the war complicated the situation and extended the theaters of war into East Africa and North Africa, where the Italians battled the British for several months, achieving no significant success. During the summer of 1940, Hitler ordered preparations for Operation Sea Lion, which involved the invasion of England. However, he continued to negotiate with the British because the German economy was not yet ready for a prolonged war, despite the fact that it had begun to absorb the resources of the conquered territories. Hitler was convinced that victory over the British would end the war.

Hopes of Franco's Fascist Spain joining the Axis powers failed to materialize. However, Germany extracted promises of continued economic cooperation not only from Spain, but also from Sweden and Switzerland. Without trade with these nations, the German war machine may not have been able to operate as long as it did. During the latter half of 1940, plans were made to take Gibraltar in order to secure Germany's strategic position, but without Spanish help that proved impossible. In November 1940, Hitler ordered his staff to make plans for the occupation of the Spanish Canary Islands and the Portuguese Cape Verde Islands, considered vital in the protection of the approaches to Vichy-controlled French Northwest Africa and the prevention of a cross-oceanic invasion. The Portuguese Azores also offered an excellent advanced post. The German occupation plans were canceled in December 1940 and revised in May 1941 to include the occupation of Spain, who refused to get involved. However, President Roosevelt warned Hitler against such a move, and since Germany's surface fleet was not large enough to tackle the British or American navies, one can speculate how much this may have contributed to the invasion plans being shelved once more.

Hitler's ambition to dominate all of Western Europe by the end of 1940 came t; naught because the British could not be brought to their knees. The failure to occupy Great Britain forced Hitler to return to his original goals and redirect his force; towards the East, leaving an undefeated enemy at his rear. In the spring of 1941,; political crisis in Yugoslavia gave Hitler an excuse to enter the Balkans and force the other states in the area into the Axis. At the same time, he sent an army southward to help the Italians in their unsuccessful war against the Greeks. The Britisr countered by sending troops from North Africa to Greece, but the move stripper their North African army, which led to a double disaster. The first units of the Afrika Korps under Rommel arrived in Libya to bolster the Italians and quick?, struck at the weakened British Eighth Army, driving it back to the Egyptian frontier. In Greece, the Greeks and British were also defeated and forced to retreat to the island of Crete, which fell to an assault by German airborne and air-land divisions. The Germans and the Italians were able to setup a defensive position in the Aegean, using these islands as bases and exerting pressure on Turkey, a supplier of chromium to the Axis Powers. In spite of these successes, final victory in North-Africa never materialized when the Germans failed to take Egypt and turn the Mediterranean into an Axis sea.

During the North Africa campaign, the Germans built extensive fortified positions at certain fortified Libyan cities and in the desert. They relied heavily or. minefields and their own system of desert field fortifications. During the battle of El Alamein in 1942, the Germans and the Italians laid out an extensive system of minefields across their front in the desert. In this theater where battle operations were usually fluid and mobile warfare dominant, fixed defensive positions were still needed.

After the Balkan campaign in April and May 1941, the German forces moved back to the Eastern frontier to prepare for the invasion of the Soviet Union. The Soviets, who were busily fortifying their new border with the Reich with the Molotov Line, did not realize that the Germans were not building a major fortified position like the East and West Wall. On June 22,1941, the Germans, after assembling one of the largest invasion forces seen in Europe, moved against the U.S.S.R. However, they faced a Soviet force of almost equal size if not actually much greater.

As the Axis invasion went forward, in the West construction proceeded to protect vital harbors and installations from the Spanish border in southern France to Cape North in Norway because Germany was still at war with Great Britain. These defenses eventually formed the famous Atlantic Wall. The U-boats were finally beginning to have some effect on the British shipping lines, although the surface fleet was still inefficient. The battleships *Gneisenau* and *Scharnhorst,* assigned to the Atlantic for raiding purposes, arrived at the French base at Brest where the *Scharnhorst* was damaged in March 1941. The new battleship *Bismarck,* escorted by the cruiser *Prince Eugene,* made its way to Norwegian bases and sailed out into the Atlantic in May 1941, only to be hunted down and destroyed. Its escort escaped to Brest where the RAF bombed it. In February 1942, all three ships made their famous "Channel Dash" to escape back to Germany and more secure ports. Only the pocket battleship *Admiral Scheer* had a successful Atlantic cruise. After this unpropitious beginning, the German surface fleet was content to remain in the Baltic, where it was in the least danger, and, to a more limited degree, to patrol the Norwegian coast, threatening Allied convoys to Murmansk. Since the Atlantic became the domain of the U-boats, they needed concrete shelters on the French coast where they could be secure while being serviced. The first U-boat pens or bunkers were built on the French Atlantic coast.

In 1942 the Germans launched their last major offensive operations against the Allies. After Rommel's offensive in North Africa was stopped at El Alamein, the Germans were forced to retreat and go on the defensive, using whatever type of fortifications were available. The ill-fated offensive on the Eastern Front ended with the defeat at Stalingrad during the winter of 1942-1943, which led to the collapse of the front along the Caucasus where the Germans had hoped to take over the valuable oil centers. From that point on, Germany had to take up the defensive. In addition, the United States was drawn into the war after the Japanese attacked the American base of Pearl Harbor in the Pacific and Hitler declared war. As a result, the entire Atlantic coast from Norway to French North Africa became more vulnerable, since the Americans soon drastically increased the number of Allied divisions in the West. By November 1942, the cross-ocean invasion came closer to reality as the Germans hastened to create an Atlantic Wall.

Border Defenses on the German-Soviet Border 1939-1941

The following positions were created on the new border between Germany and the U.S.S.R. after the conquest of Poland. Most of the positions were basically for security and many positions were not completed because of the invasion of the Soviet Union on June 22,1941:

The Narew-Pisa Position

About 60 km. long. Independent positions with a 10 km non-fortified interval.
Strongpoints *(Stützpunkte):*
-Zbojna: 3 Grüppenunterstand (shelters), 1 MG-Schartenstand (heavy machine-gun bunker)
-Pieklik: 1 Grüppenunterstand. 2 MG-Schar-tenstand
-Turocel: 3 Grüppenunterstand, 1 MG-Schar-tenstand
-Koziol: 2 Grüppenunterstand, 1 MG-Schar-tenstand
-Gehsen (Jeze): 1 "armored work" with a 6-embrasure cloche (20P7), 1 MG-Schartenstand with an infantry observation cloche, 1 shelter for infantry and antitank gun
-Johannisburg (Pisz): 9 Grüppenunterstand, 2 MG-Schar-

tenstand, 1 artillery observation post, 1 Regelbau 107a for 2 machine guns, 1 antitank gun and MG bunker

Masurias Border and Suwatki Observation Positions

About 150 km. long. Bunkers of C and D strength. Strongpoints:

-Schwiddern (Swidry): 2 Grüppenunterstand, 1 "armored work" with 6-embrasure cloche (20P7), 3 MG-Schartenstand, 1 artillery observation post, 7 C- and D-type bunkers

-Schrfenrade (Prostki): 1 Grüppenunterstand, 1 "armored work" with a 3-embrasure half cloche, 1 MG-Schartenstand, 1 artillery observation post, 7 C- and D-type bunkers

-Grenzwacht (Zawady): 2 Grüppenunterstand, 1 "armored work" with 6-embrasure cloche (20P7), 2 MG-Schartenstand, 2 artillery observation posts, 5 C- and D-type bunkers

-Raczki: 2 "armored works" with 3-embrasure half cloches, 2 MG-Schartenstand, 1 artillery observation post, 7 C- and D-type bunkers

-Deutscheck (Bakalarzewo): 1 Grüppenunterstand, 1 "armored work" with a 6-embrasure cloche (20P7), 1 MG-Schartenstand, 6 other C-and D-type bunkers.

-Filipowo: 1 Grüppenunterstand, 1 "armoir: work" with 6-embrasure cloche (20P7), "_ "armored work" with 3-embrasure half cloche, 3 MG-Schartenstand, 1 artillery observation post, 5 other C- and D-type bunkers

Gumbinen-Grenzstellung

About 50 km. long with 56 bunkers B(neu) category and many C- and D-type bunkers. Most at the heavy bunkers (4 with 20P7 cloche, 2 with 3-embrasure half cloche, 1 PAK (antitank bunke: near Schirwindt, opposite Naumiestis (PoliA name Wladyslawow)—now in Russia, opposi:- Lithuanian Border.

17 Grüppenunterstand, 12 "armored work" with 6-embra-

sure cloche (20P7), 14 "armored work" with 3-embrasure half cloches, 9 army tank bunkers, 4 artillery observation posts.

San-Vistula-Narew Line.

About 430 km. long. [27]

Galicia Border Position (120 km. long): 38 coirbat positions, 695 field bunkers (made with wood and earth, for 2-3 men), 1 observation post, 12 bunkers for PAK and infantry, 2 permanent works.

San Position and Bridgehead Krzeszow (100 km. long): 58 combat positions, 1,392 field bunkers (made with wood and earth, for 2-3 men), 930 observation posts, 92 shelters, permanent work

Bridgehead Annopol and Pulawy-Deblin km. long): 33 combat positions, 719 field bunkers (made with wood and earth, for 2-r men), 124 observation posts, 78 shelters, permanent works.

Bridgehead Warsaw: 65 combat positions, 747 field bunkers (made with wood and earth, flk 2-3 men), 34 observation posts, 68 shelters, 17 or 20 permanent works [10 MG-Schartenstand Regelbau 105 with armored plate 7P7, 4 observation posts with flanking-fbr .emplacements-Regelbau 120 a-, 1 observation post, 2 shelters-Regelbau 101 V Jaroslaw Chorzepa [28]

Command Trains and Railroad Command Posts

When the war began, Hitler had no headquarters complex on the Polish front and had to content himself with his Chancellery in Berlin. Whenever he left Berlin, he was protected by a special unit, the *Fiihrer Begleit Kommando* or Escort Command, which came from Himmler's SS. Another bodyguard unit, the *Ftihrer Begleit Batallion* or

---

[27] Armored train of the standard BP42 Type.

[28] Sources: *Die deutschen Landesbefestigungen r Osten 1919-1945,* by K. Burk, 1993. Also fide examination by Jaroslaw Chorzepa.

Fuhrer's Escort Battalion, was commanded by General Erwin Rommel and came from the special Berlin *Wachregi-
ment* or Guard Regiment, which became the Gross
Deutschland Regiment in June 1939. Added to this were
antiaircraft units taken from Regiment General Goring.
When Rommel was given the command of the new 7th
Panzer Division after the Polish campaign, he was replaced
by Lieutenant Colonel Kurt Thomas. Since Hitler had risen
to power, he was also protected by troops from the Nazi
Party's private army, the SS; more specifically, from the
Leibstandarte SS 'Adolf Hitler/ the Adolf Hitler Bodyguard Regiment, who formed guard units at the Chancellery and his headquarters. The escort units traveled with
him whenever possible. Hitler traveled in one of his special
Mercedes cars for short trips or flew on longer trips. When
Germany was at war, Hitler usually took his entourage
with him on a special train.

For the Polish campaign, he departed Berlin on September
3 in his special command train, which allowed him to
move to wherever he felt he was needed. The wagons and
special cars with new all-steel coaches were provided by
the National Railroad and were built especially for Hitler
between 1937 and 1939. According to Peter Hoffmann,
there were two types of trains known as *Führersonderzug*
or Führer Special: the peacetime version without flak cars
and the fully armed wartime version. His wartime train,
code-named *"Amerika,"* consisted of two locomotives, an
armored flak car with a 20-mm gun, a baggage and engine
car, a Pullman, a conference car, an escort car for SS men,
a dining car, two sleeping cars, a bath car, a dining car, two
personnel cars, the press chief's car, a baggage car, a baggage and power car, and a second flak car. Hitler's personal car was the Pullman.

Other special trains were also used and given codenames,
which were changed in early 1943: Hitler's *Amerika* became the *Brandenburg;* Goring's *Asien,* the *Pommern;*

Keitel's *Afrika,* the *Braunschweig;* Ribbentrop's *Westfalen* remained unchanged; Himmler's *Heinrich* became the *Steiermark;* the Wehrmacht's *Atlas* became *Franken I* and *II* (two trains).

During the Balkan campaign, Hitler used his special train as a command headquarters and took up position at Monichkirchen, Austria, about seventy kilometers southwest of Vienna. The OKH set up their headquarters in a special train called *Atlas* further north at Wiener Neustadt. Since tunnels were the most convenient places for the trains to hide from air attacks, Hitler and his staff made sure there were some nearby during the Balkan campaign. [29]

For the Russian campaign, two sets of special tunnels were built on the Polish plain late in the spring of 1940 and were ready for use by 1941. The construction of the four tunnels involved several thousand workers of Organization Todt. According to Robert Jurga, only one of them was covered with earth. One set, known as *Anlage Mitte* or In-

---

[29] A croatinan narrow gauge armored train, consisting of four armored cars, of which the inner two have two machine guns turrets, and the outside ones a French tank turret with a 4.7mm tank gun

stallation Center, was located near Tomaszow Mazowiecki and consisted of a dome-type bunker at the village of Jelen and the other at Konewka. The other set was in the south, in more hilly terrain that still did not have enough relief to necessitate a railway tunnel. *Anlage Stid,* or Installation South, was located west of Przemysl near Rzeszow. A third above-ground tunnel was actually another dome-like bunker at Stepina and a fourth tunnel was built into a small ridge at Strzyzow.

These tunnels, specifically built to accommodate the Fiihrer's train, were about four hundred meters long on the average and were secured with a set of heavy armored doors. At Strzyzow, the train could pass through both ends so there were two sets of armored doors. At Stepina the tunnel was 382.6 meters long and 14.4 meters wide with a vaulted ceiling 8.76 meters high. It was built on a rail spur running parallel to a low ridge for added protection. Auxiliary buildings built along the ridge to support the tunnel included a large power house and an underground gallery for the power cables connected to the tunnel. A road passed between these structures and the tunnel and at either side of the tunnel complex a *Gruppenstand* (squad-size bunker) was built for security. These additional structures, except for the power houses, were not found at the tunnel at Strzyzow.

The tunnels in Poland were built for Hitler's sole use and protection, but he only used those in Installation South once, two months after the beginning of the Russian campaign. He arrived at the tunnel of Strzyzow on his special trair *Amerika,* on August 27,1941, to meet with Ben;: Mussolini. From there, the two leaders went to the facilities at Stepina, where Hitler had tea in : house near the dome tunnel bunker. (Curiously. Hitler insisted on having a tea house within :: near all his headquarters complexes). After the meeting, Hitler and Mussolini flew off from & nearby airfield for an inspection of the souther front in the Ukraine. [30]

West Wall at War

When the war began, minefields and additional fortifications were added to the West Wall. The strongest sections
were located at Aachen and the Trier-Saarbriicken area
where there were switch lines thanks to Hitler's insistence
on moving the line to the border.

More than two hundred different types and design varia-
tions were developed during the construction of the West
Wall between 1937 and 1940. Light constructions with Bl,
C and D strength were used from late 1936 during the Fortress Engineer phase until the beginning of the Limes Program in 1938. A new generation of designs, known as *Bl-
Neu,* was developed for the Limes Program. They used
more concrete and were about .5 meters thick in the walls
and 1.5 meters in the roof instead of 1 meter. The Limes
bunkers had more irregular floor plans but more regular
shapes than previous ones. In the past, the final form of a
bunker was determined by the layout of the interior
rooms, which were designed first. When the Limes
bunkers were built, the form of a bunker was created first,
and the interior rooms were made to fit inside. During the
Aachen-Saar phase of construction in 1939, the 100 Series
appeared following the same design pattern as the Limes
bunkers, but were of A and B strength, ie. a minimum of
two meters of concrete. One of these new models accommodated fortress-type weapons such as the Czech 47-mm
antitank gun and others the German M-19 automatic mortar. The 100 Series was followed by the 400 and 500 Series, which required less armor. A number of the 500 Series
appeared on the West Wall in 1939.

---

[30] Sources: "Guide to Hitler's Headquarters by R. Raiber in *After
the Battle # 19,1977. Hitler* ; *Personal Security* by Peter Hoffmann, The MIT Press: 1979.

Years of retreat 1942 to 1944

As the year 1943 dawned, the Wehrmacht faced defeat on all fronts. The German Afrika Korps and its Italian allies had already begun the long retreat across Libya, no longer able to check the British Eighth Army. The Anglo-American invasion of French North Africa in November 1942 had sealed the fate of the Axis forces in North Africa. Although Hitler rushed additional units to secure Tunisia, the situation was still precarious. The island fortress of Malta, which the Axis forces were never able to neutralize or capture, continued to threaten the supply line to North Africa. The invasion of Vichy's "neutral" North African colonies triggered the German occupation of Vichy France, giving Germany a Mediterranean coastline that had to be defended.

In the 1930s, Italian Air Marshal Italo Balbo had fortified the port of Tobruk in Libya where the Italian navy had built a major base with shelters and storage depots tunneled into the headland. Balbo turned the place into a veritable fortress by creating a belt of defenses that both British and Axis troops eventually had to face. The line extended about thirteen kilometers to the east of the port and fourteen kilometers to the west, forming a semicircle spanning forty-five kilometers. The west flank, which touched the sea, consisted of fortifications that occupied the inside of Wadi Sehal for up to seven kilometers. On the east flank, Wadi Zeitum formed part of the defenses for a shorter distance. Numerous antitank-gun and machine-gun positions were set up as strongpoints along two lines, one behind the other. The strongpoints, called "nests" by the Germans, were surrounded by trenches and may have consisted of a couple of machine-gun positions and/or antitank-gun position set up in deep open pits. The entire complex was surrounded by wire obstacles and was supposedly linked by underground passages to other strongpoints. It is possible that these small open circular positions gave rise to the term "Tobruk," the name used by the Allies to refer to the German *Ringstände*. Once camouflaged, these positions were not visible from the ground especially since most of the defenses were on an open, level plateau that deni the enemy cover. In addition, many sections of the perimeter included antitank ditches and barbed wire, forming the main belt of defenses. The first line of fortified positions was linked by a man-made antitank ditch, except on the coast flanks where a wadi served that purpose. These positions were further reinforo with barbedwire obstacles. The second line of positions was not linked to a continuous antitank ditch or wire obstacles, but it was reinforced with minefields. To the rear of this belt there were emplacements for heavy artillery and additional fortifications, including the forts of Parrone, Arienti, Solaro, and Pilastrino. In 1940, the Italians failed to hold Tobruk, but the British-Australian forces did much better in 1941, especially thanks to the extensive use of mines, which were largely removed when they failed to successfully hold the fortress in 1942.

By January 1943 the Axis forces were retreating from Tripoli. The Germans took up positions on the old French Mareth Line in Tunisia in an attempt to stop the advancing Eighth Army in February 1943. The Italian high command and General Giovanni Messe, commanding the Italian First Army, had decided to use the positions of the Mareth Line. Its fortifications, built by the French, were designed for. flanking fire and the main positions were similar to the interval casemates of the Maginot Line of the STG type. In most instances, the positions were little more than light blockhouses some of which mounted antitank weapons and others only machine guns. However, the Italian Armistice Commission had disarmed the entire line and removed most of its obstacles in 1940, so all the armament had to be replaced. The Italians began to refortify and put some depth in the line during January and February 1943. Rommel had no choice but to defend it against his better judgment. Besides the Italian fortifications built at Tobruk and a few other towns, this was the only major fortified position available to the Axis Powers in North Africa. The British Eighth Army attacked the Mareth Line on March 16, but, due to adverse weather conditions, were repelled by the Axis forces until March 22. A German counterattack by the 15th Panzer Division managed to push back the British troops. Another counterattack on March 23 failed as New Zealander troops breached the front further south. Additional skirmishes took place between March 23 and March 26. Finally, on March 24, General Jurgen von Arnim, commander of Axis forces in Tunisia, ordered Messe to withdraw because the overall situation in Tunisia was deteriorating.

British and American forces moved into Tunisia from the west as the Eighth Army reached the Tunisian frontier. In February the Americans suffered a setback at the hands of Rommel in the battle of the Kasserine Pass. In March, the Allies resumed the offensive against the Mareth Line, driving the Axis forces back by the end of the month after outflanking the position. The Axis forces retreated to the Wadi Akarit position, a much smaller and easily defended line with the sea on one side and a dry salt lake on the other. This had been Rommel's first choice, instead of the Mareth Line, but there had been little time to prepare this position during the retreat from the Mareth Line. The wadi was used as an antitank ditch and the troops dug an antitank ditch beyond and planted minefields in front. Once again, the mine proved to be a valuable element in fortifications, but the depleted German-Italian army was not able to hold the position beyond April 7, the day after the British assault began. By mid-May the Axis forces were forced back towards Tunis and a quarter of a million men soon surrendered in Tunisia. The Axis investment in troops during the final months of the campaign was questionable since it only managed to turn the battlefields into testing grounds where green American troops underwent the baptism of fire. The Germans had already lost another quarter of a million men in February when the last of their troops had surrendered at Stalingrad. As the campaign in North Africa reached the point of capitulation, the Germans were still counterattacking in southern Russia.

By May 1943, the U-boats had virtually lost the battle of the Atlantic. The British lifeline to America and its colonies was secure. Beginning in 1942, American reinforcements arrived by the shipload in the British Isles and the Allies began an air offensive with limited success. By 1943 the bombing intensified to a point that:: began to affect Germany's ability to fight the war. The massive bombing carr.-paigns that pre-war theorists had predicted had not been possible prior to this time but finally began to materialize after mid-1942.

Meanwhile, the Soviets called for a "Second Front" against Germany in the West. The Germans were not oblivious to this fact and since the first command; raids against the Atlantic coastline had taken steps to secure it. In 1942 work bega on the Atlantic Wall to fend off a potential invasion and avoid a "Second Front,* which could seriously tax the Wehrmacht. The African theater had been a mere sideshow, which drew off few resources from the Wehrmacht. In mid-1943, the Allied invasion of Sicily and the Italian mainland opened a new front that was more than a sideshow. Although the terrain on the Italian Peninsula favored the defenders more than the invaders, the war on that front placed heavier demands on the Wehrmacht than the war in the desert.

The Atlantic Wall

U-Boat Bunkers

In 1941, the British stepped up their commando raids on the Atlantic coast an;: the construction of U-boat bunkers or pens to protect the U-boats from British ar attack. The ambitious program involved building huge submarine pens at the kev French ports of Brest, Lorient, St. Nazaire, La Pallice, and Bordeaux. The urgency of building these pens was driven home by the fact that by September 1940, after only one year at war, twenty-eight U-boats (46 percent of the submarine fleet) had beer sunk. [31]

A shorter and safer journey to port or better protected bases in France were needed. Similar shelters were built at the German North Sea ports of Hamburg and Kiel and the Norwegian port of Trondheim. The German navy also built pens for minesweepers (R-boats) and torpedo boats (S-boats) along the channel coast at Cherbourg, Le Havre,

---

[31] UBoat bunker Bordeaux France

Boulogne, Dunkirk, Ostend, Ijmuiden, Amsterdam, and Rotterdam. Work on most of these pens began in 1941 and was completed in 1942 Additional roof reinforcement on the U-boat bunkers was added later, to counter heavier Allied bombs. The first two pens were actually built at Helgoland called Nordsee III, and Hamburg between 1940 and 1941. In 1942, another submarine bunker—which was not completed—was begun at Trondheim as was another bunker at Kiel. Additional bunkers were under construction in 1943 at Bremen and, after the occupation of Vichy France, at Marseilles. Additional bunkers at Hamburg and Wilhelmshaven never got beyond the planning stages. Altogether, enough pens were built to shelter over 170 U-boats.

Some of the pens in the German ports were planned as repair facilities and others as construction sites for U-boats. In 1944, several large bunkers for twenty-four and thirty-five U-boats were planned for the Baltic coast at Gotenhafen, Swinemünde, and Rügan. The first U-boat bunkers built in 1940 and 1941 consisted of several cells—called boxes by the Germans and pens by the English. Most pens normally held one or two submarines. In most cases one of the bunkers at each installation also contained one or more dry pens where the U-boats could be serviced like in dry dock, and they entered on their own power.

However, at Lorient the submarines had to be maneuvered on a trolley, pulled out of the water, and then delivered to a set of dry pens. Armored doors were used to close the pens. Some of the U-boat bunkers had their own internal power source and torpedo storage rooms. In others, power generators and magazines were located in nearby bunkers. The largest U-boat complex was built at Lorient and consisted of three sets of clunkers called Keroman I, II, and III. Only Keroman III allowed direct access by water, like most U-boat bunkers. Additions were [32] planned for Keroman I and II but never materialized.

At Keroman I, which contained five dry pens, the submarine entered through a gate into a slip way where it was maneuvered onto a trolley, which was winched up the slip way onto a track-mounted platform and rolled into one of the Keroman I pens or one of the seven Keroman II pens. Adjacent to these positions was another open-air slip way where the U-boat was pulled out of the water onto a round table from where it was taken into one of the two dome bunkers for a single U-boat. Closer to the city of Lorient, on the Scorff River, was the Scorff Bunker with two pens. Except for Keroman III, all of these positions were begun and completed in 1941.

Submarine Pens

Submarine pens were Type-A works, which meant they

---

[32] The completed U-Boat bunker complex at Brest. In the background is the Ecole Navale which has been painted with a disruptive-pattern camouflage

had reinforced concrete roofs 3.0 to 3.5 meters thick. Their thickness was increased to 7.0 meters in some cases because of new more powerful Allied bombs. Power generators and torpedo stores were located either in the U-ooat bunker or in nearby bunkers. There was also a command center. Antiaircraft gun positions, well protected in open concrete bunkers, were placed on top of some of the submarine nstallations.The entrances for men and supplies were closed with heavy armored doors. [33]

Some of these pens were located on rivers or in port basins controlled by locks. At St. Nazaire, after the British commando raid of 1942, a new fortified lock was begun but never completed. At La Pallice, another fortified lock was ready by 1944. There the submarine traveled through a concrete box-like structure, similar to a pen, that contained the lock. The most unusual location for submarine pens was at Bordeaux where they were sited well up the Garonne River, at a great distance from Allied fighter-bomber bases in Great Britain.

Bunkers for the construction of U-boats and known as U-Boat Factory Bunkers. At a conference held with Hitler from May 4-6, 1944, Donitz mentioned there was no ad-

---

[33] UBoat bunker St Nazaire France

equate protection in the shipyards and places where submarines were under construction. In Hamburg tirteen submarines were assembled each month, with each submarine taking two months to be assembled which meant about thirty submarines were always under construction and vulnerable to air attack. The factory bunkers planned for Bremen were to be ready in the spring of 1945 and initial work had begun for similar bunkers in Hamburg which were to be completed in 1946. Nothing was planned for Danzig.

Associated with some of the U-boat bunkers were *Schleusenbunker* or bunkers protecting locks into basins of the ports where the U-boat bunkers were located. [34]These structures were built in several ports in response to the commando raid on St. Nazaire. Except at Dunkirk, the protected locks were enclosed in the bunker which had armored doors at both encs Bordeaux, La Pallice, St. Nazaire, Dunkirk (tv.: bunkers for the locks). [35]

---

[34] UBoat bunker Brest France

[35] Source: *Die deutschen Ubootbunker* urar *Bunkerwerften* by Sonke Neitzel, 1991. *Gerrr.i-LJ-Boat Bunkers: Yesterday and Today* by Kail-1 Heinz and Michael Schmeelke, 1999. "U-Bca Bases" by Jean Paul Pallud, *After the Batte 1987.*

Beginnings of the Atlantic Wall

The initial work on the Atlantic Wall began in late summer of 1941 when the Kriegsmarine and the Luftwaffe set up defenses at key ports and airfields to protect their bases for Operation Sea Lion from air raids and possible naval bombardment. In addition, the army brought up heavy batteries to the Pas de Calais area in accordance with Fiihrer Directive No. 16 of July 16, 1940, which ordered not only the neutralizing of the British RAF and the clearing of mine-free zones for the crossing, but also "Strong forces of coastal artillery must command and protect the forward coastal area. It is the task of the navy to coordinate the setting up of coastal artillery—both naval and military . . . and generally direct its fire. The greatest possible number of extra-heavy guns will be brought into position as soon is possible in order to cover the crossing and to shield the flanks against enemy action from the sea. For this purpose railway guns will also be used, reinforced by all available captured weapon, and will be sited on railway turntables. Those batteries intended only to deal with targets on the English mainland, the *K5* and *K12,* will not be included. Apart from this the existing extra heavy platform gun batteries are to be enclosed in concrete opposite the Straits of Dover in such a manner that they will withstand the heaviest air attacks and will permanently, in all conditions, command the Straits of Dover with the limits of their range. The technical work will be the responsibility of the Organization Todt."

At a conference on July 21, 1940, Hitler stressed the need for the use of heavy artillery on the coast to protect minefields and keep the supply lines open to an invasion force landing in England. He also demanded to know how long it would take to emplace the heavy guns. The navy and army struggled to gather all available resources along the Channel in preparation for the invasion. On July 15 at another Führer conference, the navy reported that the batteries would be emplaced and ready on the Straits of Dover by August 15, but that the heavy 380-mm gun battery would not be ready for action before mid-September. The gun casemates with overhead protection would have to be built later, after new *Regelbau* were developed for them. Admiral Raeder demanded that the batteries be ready as soon as possible to protect his minesweepers. The 280-mm Battery Kurfurst was actually ready at the beginning of August, but the participants in this discussion were concerned about British reconnaissance aircraft detecting the placement of these guns. However, they concluded that once the guns began firing it would make no difference since their locations would be revealed.

In August 1940, in accordance with Hitler's directive, sixty-two heavy and medium army batteries, twenty of which came from the navy, were moved into position. The 210-mm rail guns were among the first to arrive in August, and were followed by 280-mm rail guns. Positions with turntables were created to increase their area of coverage. The heaviest guns were intended to engage the British positions at Dover while the remainder would deny access to the English Channel and prevent possible British interference with a German invasion force. As the Battle of Britain raged in September 1940, construction began on the first three concrete dome bunkers for the heavy rail guns. The K-type 280-mm railway guns could move on their railroad carriage into these dome bunkers, sometimes called cathedral bunkers. Once inside the armored doors, the concrete shelter provided all the protection needed as long as the guns were not in the firing position. These bunkers were large enough to house the two 280-mm guns and the locomotive of one battery. One of these dome bunkers was situated on the northwest side of Calais, about one kilometer from the coast. Another one was at Vallee [36] Heureuse, about four kilometers east of Marquise, almost halfway between Calais and Boulogne, about six kilometers from the coast. A third one was at about one kilometer north of Wimereux, five kilometers north of Boulogne, near the coast. A fourth even larger bunker for a railroad gun battery was built later, not far from the first dome bunker near Calais.

Since the big K-type rail guns were too large for their own carriage to mount a turntable, curved sections of track were used for aiming. After 1936 the Vogele turntable was adopted. It consisted of a platform on which the gun car was mounted and which revolved around a circular track for aiming the gun. This made it possible for the gun to cover *a.* full 360 degrees. The Vogele turntable was transported with each gun and assembled at the firing site. Nine railway artillery regiments totaling sixteen batteries were available in the summer of 1940. Some of them were stationed on the Channel coast during the autumn of 1940. The navy also had one of the two 150-mm rail-gun batteries known as *Batterie Gneisenau.* This naval battery was the subject of many propaganda features, including a wartime postage stamp. It is possible that about half the rail-gun batteries eventually took up position in the Pas de Calais during 1940 and early 1941. However, most were withdrawn to participate in Operation Barbarossa against the Soviet Union in mid-1941.

---

[36] The protected lock at St Nazaire is still in remarkably good condition as shown in this photo.

Hitler's initial directive for the invasion of England clarified the role of the army and navy in regard to artillery fire directed against enemy naval targets. The Kriegsmarine was put in charge. Many of its heavy batteries were naval batteries brought up from positions on the West Wall and from the German coastal defenses, so their operational control did not seem to be a problem. However, the navy did not have enough coastal artillery units and personnel, so the army eventually took over. In 1940, the army formed its own coastal artillery branch. All the army units on the Channel from the area around Cherbourg to the Dutch border were placed under Army Artillery Command 104. The problem arose after 1941 when the question was no longer if the navy should direct the firing of all these artillery batteries at naval targets, but which service was best suited to command them in the face of an invasion force. The solution left some gray areas, but essentially the navy was given the assignment of directing fire against naval targets, the army the task of directing the fire of all the coastal artillery against an invasion force once it landed.

This still left the problem of when priority would shift from firing at enemy ships to firing on troops landing on the beaches.

In 1940 as the rail guns moved in, the heavy naval artillery was readied for transfer from German coastal positions to the Channel, and batteries from the West Wall were also moved to the Atlantic Wall. Some of the first concrete mounts for these heavy guns were completed during the month of November. Most of these weapons included armored shields, which were either placed in huge casemates later or mounted on concrete emplacements. Work on some of the gun casemates such as Battery Friedrich August was begun as early as August. The heavy naval guns were mounted in turrets and some were placed in concrete casemates with their turrets. The turrets of Battery Grosser Kurfiirst were mounted on their own concrete bunker with no overhead concrete cover. Various types of bunkers, such as defensive posts and munitions bunkers, had to be built to support these positions. Most of the gun casemates for the heavy batteries were completed in 1941. The largest gun position in the Pas de Calais, Battery Schleswig Holstein (renamed Lindemann), with three 406-mm naval guns intended for the new class "H" battleships that were never built, did not arrive until 1941. Its heavy pieces were not installed and ready to fire until the fall of 1941 and its huge gun casemates were not completed until 1942.

While preparations for the invasion of England went ahead, construction on battery positions in northern Norway began before September 1940 and ended before the close of the year. Naval batteries were also moved into Norway from the German coastal defenses and made ready for action during 1941. It was clear that a chain of positions would have to be created to defend the coast after Operation Sea Lion was canceled.

Building the Atlantic Wall: 1942 to January 1944

After Hitler canceled the invasion plans in 1940, the batteries that were setup ir the Pas de Calais for the invasion of England were given a new role in the sprine of 1941. From that point on, they were given the order to challenge British shipping in the Channel and bombard the Dover area. The building of the Atlanc: Wall had begun in 1941 in response to British commando raids that began in 194t and were stepped up in 1941 with the strike against the Loften Islands in northe Norway early in March. Other raids followed along the occupied coast of Frar and even in North Africa. The British operations infuriated Hitler causing him issue a special Commando Order calling for the execution of any raiders tal prisoner. In December 1941, the commandos returned to the Loften Islands, while a larger commando force struck at Vaagso in southern Norway. This was the firs: attempt to take a defended port and the raid proved too successful. Hitler concluded that the Norwegian coast would be the "Zone of Destiny" and ordered the country to be heavily fortified and garrisoned.

In February, a successful commando raid at Bruneval allowed the British t: examine the components of the Wurzburg radar. In March 1942, a large-scale commando raid took place at St. Nazaire, a well-defended position. The target was the Normandy Dock, the only one considered large enough for the battleship *Tirpi:z* to use for repairs should it breakout into the Atlantic. A secondary objective was the submarine pens, mainly the locks to the basin that allowed access to the pens. Even though over half of the 611-man assault force from Number 2 Commando and the naval personnel who transported them were lost, the mission succeeded in crippling its main objective.

Atlantic Wall 1942-1944

The raid at Vaagso apparently weighed heavy on Hitler. He concluded that ir the British established a bridgehead in Norway, they would disrupt iron ore shipments from Sweden through Narvik. This had been his reason for invading Norway in 1940. An order issued from Hitler's headquarters on December 14, 1941, called for the continued con-

struction of light fortifications along the coas: and permanent strongpoints in the most endangered areas. The long-
range coastal, batteries at points where the enemy might
attempt to establish bridgeheads were to be reinforced.
That meant that building had to proceed at important harbors used for shipping, mainly in the Norwegian fjords,
and all military and industrial targets in the coastal regions. The chief of the Luftwaffe was to provide the
antiaircraft defenses in the coastal regions, and, if possible, flak batteries to be used against enemy landing craft in
cooperation with the army and naval forces in the area.
Norway was assigned first priority: Regardless of any
measures taken in the past, the fortification of Norway's
geographical position, its climatic conditions, and its poor
transportation system which renders the employment of
mobile reserves and the bringing up of reinforcements
more difficult. All these factors also limit the effective employment of strong air forces against an enemy near the
coast. Fjords reaching deep into the interior cutting vital
communication lines, especially in the North, as well as
important targets in remote areas are a constant incentive
to the enemy to stage raids.

In addition to an impregnable defense against enemy landings, it is of the utmost importance to safeguard the sea entrances of protected waterways and to increase the number
of emergency hideouts. A lengthy interruption of coastal
shipping by the enemy's superior naval forces would have
serious consequences in Norway at this time. For this reason, the improvement of land routes in Norway is equally
as important as the construction of fortifications.

Thus the priority for work on fortifications was:
1. Norway
2. French-Belgian coastline:
a. British Channel Islands
b. From the Seine to the Scheldt Rivers

c. Atlantic coast from Brest to Quiberon in Brittany
d. Gironde Estuary
e. Normandy and Brittany
3. The Dutch coast and the coast of Northern Jutland—only Jammer Bay
was considered suitable for amphibious operations.
4. Helgoland Bay and the Dutch coast behind the West Frisian Islands.

Navigation was considered very difficult except in some of the Frisian Islands where it was believed that raiding could take place. Since the Kriegsmarine and Hitler considered the Baltic to be secure because its entrance was guarded by positions in occupied Denmark, they decided to dismantle the coast artillery positions on the German Baltic coast and send them to the projected Atlantic Wall. No additional work was intended on the Baltic coast. The idea was to erect new fortifications along the Atlantic coast thereby reducing the number of troops needed to defend it. However, this turned out to be overly optimistic thinking.

When Germany declared war against the United States, it became obvious that the British armed forces would soon receive massive reinforcements. During a conference on January 22, 1942, Hitler informed Vice Admiral Fricke, the chief of for the Naval Staff, that he was convinced that the British and their new ally would attack northern Norway, somewhere between Trondheim and Kirkenes. He ever seemed convinced that such an action would push the Swedes into the Alliec camp. The army and Luftwaffe were instructed to reinforce their positions in Norway and the Kriegsmarine was to be ready to meet an Allied fleet at sea. Except for the S-boats in the Channel, Hitler wanted every available vessel sent to Norway and agreed to the construction of additional naval ships. Heavy artillery including captured French weapons, were to be shipped to Norway.

In February, the navy reported to Hitler that its forces in Norway were still weak but that new minefields were being laid and the situation was improving. Plans were made to move cruisers, the battleship *Tirpitz,* the battlecruiser *Scharnhorst,* and additional naval units north. All these actions further confirmed Hitler's commitment to the orders of December 14,1941, concerning his priorities.

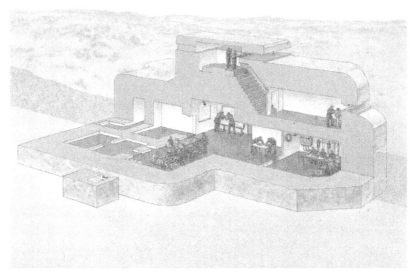

On March 23, 1942, several days before the St. Nazaire raid, Fiihrer Directive Number 40 officially called for the creation of the Atlantic Wall. [37]This directive included a few important points about coastal defenses that Hitler insisted upon: In defending the coast—and this includes coastal waters within the range of medium coastal artillery—the responsibility for the planning and impli-mentation of defensive measures must ... lie ... in the hands of a single commander. Enemy forces which have landed must be destroyed or thrown back into the sea by immediate counterattack. All personnel bearing arms— irrespective to which branch of the Armed Forces or to which non-service organization they may belong—will be employed for this.

---

[37] Ml 78 Fire Control Post. Seezielbatterie Heerrenduin, WN 81, Ijmuiden,The Netherlands

The enemy must be prevented from securing a foothold on all islands which could present a threat to the mainland or coastal shipping.

The distribution of forces and the extension of defensive works must be so carried out that our strong defense points are situated in those sectors most likely to be chosen by the enemy for landings. Other coastal sectors which may be threatened by small-scale surprise attacks will be defended by a series of strongpoints, supported if possible by the coastal batteries. Less threatened sectors will be kept under observation.

Kriegsmarine coastal gun batteries included a fire control post *(Leitstand)* to identify, track, and designate targets for the battery. Three-story posts like this one had a rangefinder post on the top, an observation deck in the front, and working space on the lower level. The rangefinder post could use a variety of stereoscopic range finders, usually warship types mounted on sockets. The observation deck had variety of fixed observation devices for target tracking, usually a pedestal-mounted optical sight for determining bearing with the data passed electrically to the computing room below.

Although the two observation decks were the most obvious features of such a bunker, the heart of the operation was in the chambers located at the base of the bunker. These compartments mimicked the fire control on a warship, but due to the fixed position of the battery, the firing computations were less elaborate than on a moving warship. The computing room received data from the observation decks above which were entered into the fire direction computer *(Rechenschleber)* and then integrated with bearing data from an adjacent bearing computer *(Klemgerat)* obtained from the battery's small Pel/stand bunker located some distance away. The adjacent plotting room maintained data on the targets, usually with range and deflection plotting boards. Once the target's range, bearing, and speed were determined, a firing solution was computed and passed to the individual guns via a special switchboard *(Schaltkasten)*. The fire control bunker was the battery's communication hub having radio and telephone links to higher headquarters as well as to other battery posts. The M178 configuration shown here was first constructed in April 1943 and was not especially common, with one each in Norway and the Netherlands and two in France. However, the general features were fairly typical.

Fortified areas and strongpoints will be defended to the last man. They must never be forced to surrender from lack of ammuniton, rations, or water. The directive went into details such as which commander was responsible for the defense of each region, including the Black Sea and Mediterranean Sea. The directive also established the pattern for setting up of the defenses.

On April 13,1942, in response to the raid on St. Nazaire, Hitler ordered the most important naval bases, including all the submarines bases, to be heavily defended to prevent another raid. As a result, until late 1943 most fortifications were concentrated around the ports.

The months that followed were busy with preparations. The greatest effort and concentration of forces was seen in Norway, where the *Scharnhorst* had moved after the famous "Channel Dash" from Brest. The *Gneisenau* was not as lucky since it suffered additional damage from Allied bombing while being repaired at Kiel. One of its gun turrets was so badly wrecked by a bomb that repair work was soon abandoned. Its main battery turrets were removed and one of its turrets was sent to form a battery position on the island of Wangerooge, whose heavy guns had been sent to the Channel coast in 1940. The other turret of the *Gneisenau* was sent to form a battery position in Norway. The guns of the damaged turret were sent to the Netherlands for installation in individual positions.

Hitler had two great obsessions when it came to the defense of the West: protecting his "Zone of Destiny" in Norway and devoting an excessive amount of effort to turn the British Channel Islands into an "impregnable fortress." Both of these commitments eventually immobilized a large number of troops before, during, and for many months after the Allied landings in Normandy in June 1944. [38]

When the war ended, the Norwegian coastline was as heavily defended as Western Europe's and over a hundred thousand men remained committed to its defense. The Channel Islands covered a smaller area, but were as heavily defended, if not more, than any other position of the Atlantic Wall with *a* full-strength army division committed there until the end of the war. Even a month after the invasion of the U.S.S.R., Hitler in Directive Number 33, which concerned the Eastern Front, ended noting that all branches of the armed forces must be aware of the threat of British attacks against the Channel Islands and the Nor-

---

[38] Rommel tours the Atlantic Wall in 1944. The German field marshal harboured grave doubts as to the effectiveness of the fortifications

wegian coast.

Soon after German troops occupied the Channel Islands in 1940, Hitler haz decided to transform them into an advance base for the invasion of England. Not long after, in 1941, he resolved that these islands had to be turned into "the strongest sea fortresses in the world," according to General Max Joseph Pemsel chief of staff of the Seventh Army. A full-strength division and the OT, the 319th Infantry Division, and technical units from the army, navy, and Luftwaffe were dispatched to the islands during the summer of 1941.

At the same time, massive reinforcements were sent to Norway and new coastal defense positions were built mainly in early 1942 in response to the earlier commando raids. From 1940 through 1941 Army Group D under Field Marshal Erwin von Witzleben stationed only a small number of divisions in the Netherlands, Belgium, and occupied France. In the spring of 1942, Field Marshal Gerd von Rundstedt took command as the number of divisions began to increase in the area. However, many of these units were sent there primarily to rest and rebuild after taking heavy losses in the Russian campaign. Under von Rundsted: the construction of the Atlantic Wall began in earnest.

During August 1942, British commandos joined by the 2nd Canadian Division attempted the largest raid of all. They attacked the defended port of Dieppe, which was protected by a number of coastal guns. The Canadian division landed between Pourville and Puys along the coastal front of Dieppe while Number 4 Commando assaulted positions and the coast defense battery to the west. Number 3 Commando attempted to land to the east, to attack the coastal defense batten-near Berneval. The Canadians found it impossible to break through the heavily defended beachfront of Dieppe and suffered heavy losses. The experience they gained, however, was critical to the action of June 6, 1944.

Meanwhile, the German people were informed of a great victory at Dieppe that proved that the Atlantic Wall would be able to repel any invasion in the West. In his report on "Preparations for Invasion" for the U.S. Army Historical Service, General Pemsel summarized the results of the raid: "It surprised us that precisely at that time the strongly fortified town of Dieppe had been selected as a target for this attack . . . Dieppe was played up by German propagandists as a great success . . . The German public opinion and through self deception in OKW there arose an utterly fallacious conception of the defensive strength of Atlantic Wall." [39]

Construction work in 1941 had been devoted mainly to the building of positions for coastal batteries and U-boat pens. Most of the concrete poured in 1941 went into U-boat pens and the second largest amount to Luftwaffe airfields and iTjtallations. Actual construction work on the Atlantic Wall began in 1942, when rurther hopes of any offensive in the West waned. Meanwhile, prospects of a victory in the East were dimming, the situation in North Africa offered great possibilities throughout the summer, and a major offensive on the economic regions in southern Russia was in the works.

Since before the war, the inspector general of Land Defense West was responsible for the construction of fortifications in the West. As work on the West Wall was abandoned and minefields were removed in August 1940, the inspector general moved his headquarters from Wiesbaden to Metz. Once again, the army engineers had to rely on the OT and the RAD for the bulk of the construction. A number of *Bautruppen* or army construction troops were also available.

Late in 1941, the OT formed *Einsatzgruppen,* (operations groups) to handle various regions. The Einsatzgruppe West setup offices in Paris to direct construction in the Netherlands, Belgium, and occupied France. In military

---

[39] German bunkers at Longues-sur-Mer in France

terms this was the equivalent of a corps-sized unit with brigade-size units, known as *Oberbauleitung,* under its command. The oberbauleitung included regiment-type units,
known as *Baukitung* or construction command, of about
three thousand men. The building sites and camps, which
were further broken down, came under authority of the
bauleitung. In addition to Einsatzgruppe West in Paris
under the leadership of Karl Weis, Einsatzgruppe Wiking
was set up in Oslo to direct construction in Norway. Transportation was provided by the *NSKK (Nationalsozialis-
tisches Kraftfahrkorps/* National Socialist Motor Corps).
In Einsatzgruppe West several command staffs were
formed to group several oberbauleitung together for work
on various fronts. These *Einsatz* were actually in operation
in late 1940 before the einsatzgruppe was created. Einsatz
Westkiiste initially worked on the U-boat pens; Einsatz Ka-
nalkiiste on the Channel Islands and coastal batteries; and
Einsatz Luftwaffe on airfield construction and later V-
sites.

By comparison, Einsatzgruppe Wiking had four einsatz
(including one in Denmark) but employed fewer workers
than Einsatzgruppe West in mid-1943. Serious personnel
shortages began in 1943 when the American bomber force
was able to undertake massive bombing efforts against the
Reich and the OT was forced to withdraw men from
abroad to effect repairs in Germany. The bombing missions not only caused a shortage of manpower on the
Western Front, but also a shortage of materials, which
were needed at home. As a result, the quality of concrete
began to decrease, but by then most of the massive construction projects, such as the U-boat pens, had been completed.

The first oberbauleitungs for the construction of the U-
boat pens were set up at Brest, Lorient, St. Nazaire, La Rochelle, and Bordeaux and organized under Einsatz West-
küste. Other oberbauleitungs were placed under the direc-

tion Einsatz Kanalküste with headquarters at St. Malo on the Channel Island of Alderney, and in the vicinity of the coast between Pas de Calais, and the Netherlands where their number gradually increased after the invasion of England was canceled. By the end of 1942, there was a total of four oberbauleitur covering this section of the coastline: one near Rouen, one near Dunkirk, one Belgium, and one in the Netherlands. More oberbauleitung were added in 1942 and 1943, including one at Marseilles for the construction of the Süd Wall.

Between May 1942 and December 1943, construction on the Atlantic Wall finally became a priority. By April 1943 seven times as much concrete was poured the Atlantic Wall as in May 1942 during which time it had already doubled March 1942. This represented an increase from about 25,000 cubic meters of concrete to 50,000 in March and 110,000 in May 1942 rising to 780,000 in April 1943 followed by a steady decline to about 300,000 in December 1943. The U-boat pens and associated installations consumed an almost constant 80,000 to 130,000 cubic meters each month during this time period. The army complained, not without reason, that priority was given to the naval installations. Indeed, most of the OT workers were directed to the naval bases, even on the Channel coast from three mouth of the Seine to the Netherlands.

The OT was expected to work closely with the military in the west as it ha; done on the West Wall. OKW's General of Pioniers und Festung issued an order on June 17,1942, explaining the division of responsibility between the army engineers and the OT. The army engineers would do the initial reconnaissance work, select the sites, and design the installations. They would also prepare the blueprints for the OT. The fortress engineers would also be responsible for the delivery of all armored parts and their installation, the installation of all electrical wiring, mechanical equipment, weapons, and optical equipment. In addition, army would be responsible for supervising guards at the construction proj« even though the guards would be drawn from members of the OT. The OT woul; be responsible for the actual construction, according to plans supplied by the fortress engineers. During the building phase, the army engineers reserved the right to point out any errors in construction and supervise the construction Although the army would take care of installing mechanical parts, the civilians would complete work on the interior, including water supply and ventilation. The acquisition of materials and transportation, except for the armored parts, woul" also be their responsibility.

Additional responsibilities for the OT included the construction of wire obsta- cles, clearing fields of fire and, if there was enough available personnel, digging antitank ditches in the event of an immediate threat. The OT was also responsible for camouflage, which took many forms from providing hooks on the bunkers for the attachment of camouflage nets to adding wooden roofs and painted windows to exposed positions in order to make them look like churches or other buildings that would blend in with the surroundings. In many cases, as in the West Wall, bunkers were painted with appropriate colors or designs to blend into the terrain. Another technique involved giving the concrete a rough shape instead of the normal smooth face created by the wooden forms on its exposed faces. In Norway a number of positions were built into the rock (cavern-type constructions) which proved excellent camouflage. In France, there are fewer examples of this type, but the gun battery casemates below Fort Roule at Cherbourg are a good example.

The assault on Dieppe in August 1942 spurred Hitler to augment the number of positions on the Atlantic Wall. He ordered the OT, now under the directorship of Albert Speer, to complete fifteen thousand positions before the summer of 1943. The chief engineers of the OT replied that only 40 percent of this number could be finished in such a short time. By December 1942, about five thousand structures had been completed and by June 1943 the number reached eight thousand, only a little over 50 percent of what Hitler had demanded. For the remainder of 1943, the amount of concrete poured for coastal fortifications decreased as the amount for U-boat pens increased. In addition, by the end of 1943 concrete was being diverted to the construction of V-weapons sites. Thus, the construction campaign on the Atlantic Wall in 1943 was not impressive, but was not totally out of line for OB West's strategy, which was different from the OKW.

The construction of the Atlantic Wall was not done haphazardly. Von Rund-stedt's staff at OB West issued an order in May 1942 based on Hitler's Directive Number 40, which established the organization of the coastal defenses as follows: defense zone *(Verteidigungsbereiche)*, followed by strongpoint group *(Stiltzpunktgrupperi)*, strongpoint *(Stützpunkt)*, and resistance nest *(Widerstandnester)*.

Each of the fifteen defense zones in Western Europe were centered around a key point. In France, where the main part of the Atlantic Wall was formed, the key points were Royan, La Pallice-La Rochelle, St. Nazaire, Lorient, Brest, St. Malo, Le Havre, Boulogne, Calais, and Dunkirk. In 1942, the Belgian coast represented a gap between defensive zones. Ostend served as the key point defense zone in Belgium. The Dutch coastal defense zones included Vlissingen (which encompassed the islands of the Scheldt Estuary), Hoek van Holland, Ijmuiden, and Den Helder. By January 1944, Hitler, finding the situation bleak on all fronts, decided to restructure the defenses once again. He designated certain defense zones as *Festung* (fortresses). Thus in the months that followed, Gironde Slid, Gironde Nord (Royan), St. Nazaire, Lorient, Brest, St. Malo, the British Channel Islands Cherbourg, Le Havre, Boulogne, Dunkirk, Walchern Island (Vlissingen), Hoek var Holland, and Ijmuiden were redesignated as festung. Calais and La Pallice-La Rochelle may also have been made into fortresses, but they do not appear as such on all German maps. Later in 1944, Hitler began naming many of the positions he wanted defended to the last man as festung, which included Calais and La Rochelle. Alan Wilt, author of *The Atlantic Wall,* does not identify Walchern Mar.; as a fortress, but claims that the British Channel Islands, Calais, and La Rochet were promoted to fortress status in a directive issued by OKW on March 3, 19— Walchern Island may not have been actually assigned this status until about the time it was attacked.

In Germany the main defense zones were on the island positions of Borkum, Norderney, Wangerooge, Helgoland, and Sylt. In Denmark they were on the Jutland Peninsula at Fano, Hanstholm, and Frederikshavn. In the case of Norway there was even greater separation of these defensive zones then elsewhere on the Atlantic Wall because of the terrain. They were located at Oslo, Kristiansund Stavanger, Bergen, Trondheim, Narvik and Kirkenes. Positions with heavy artillerv in northern Jutland and southern Norway were used to close the Skaggerak.

The gaps between the defense zones could be covered by a strongpoint grour strongpoint, and/or resistance nest since the terrain was considered too restrictive in a large area for a full defense zone. The area between the mouth of the Sormr.r and the Belgian border consisted mostly of defense zones adjacent to one another while in places like Norway large gaps were found between defensive zones Actually, even along the heavily defended section of French coast, there were sectors between defense zones that were only defended by small positions. Most of the artillery batteries, either located inside defense zones or between them generally formed their own strongpoint.

There is some confusion regarding German fortified points and sectors of the coastline. Both defense zones and festung referred to a heavy concentration of fortifications consisting of strongpoints and resistance nests in one specific place Inside the OB West command the defense zones and fortresses were normallv given place-name designations. Outside the OB West command, the zone usuallv received the same designation as the defending division. The strongpoints and resistance nests were usually given number or letter designations such as *Stp 'a Stp '253,'* or *Wn '246,'* or a name such as *Stp Blucher* or *Wn Oleander.* The entire coast, on the other hand, was divided up into sectors that contained the *Verteidigungsbereiche, Festung, Stützpunktgruppen,* any other types of fortification and even undefended portions of the coastline. The actual coastline was divided into *Ktisten Verteidigung Abschnitt* or coast defense sectors marked on maps as KVA in the area commanded by OB West. Some KVAs with long coastlines were further subdivided into *Kusten Verteidigung Gruppe* or KVGs. The KVA of the Pas de Calais region were so short and with so few breaks in the terrain that they were simply divided into numbered sectors. In the KVA of Normandy, Brittany, and the Atlantic Coast, the KVAs were subdivided into *Kusten Verteidigung Unter Gruppe* (KVUG) or coast defense subgroup. The KVA (when not divided into KVUG) and the KVUG were divided into sectors, usually named after a town, and subsectors with numbers and sometimes names. Beginning at the Franco-Spanish border, the KVAs were F, E-2, E-l (the mouth of the Gironde), D (just south of the Loire estuary), C-2, C-l, B (northwestern Brittany), A-2, and A-l which ended near the juncture of Brittany and Cotentin Peninsulas. Moving eastward through Normandy it began with J-2, J-l, H-2, H-l, G (at the mouth of the Somme), F, E-2, E-l, D-2, D-l, C (from Boulogne to Calais), B (ending on the Franco-Belgian border), A-3, A-2, and A-l which was on Walchern Island.

Thus every section of the coastline under the command of OB West in Western Europe was identified as part of a KVG and subdivided into sectors. Within the sectors were found the actual fortifications from the simple resistance nest to strongpoint group and the festung with its own variety of fortifications. [40]

The strongpoint group consisted of two or more strongpoints, which were either infantry or artillery strongpoints. The infantry strongpoint consisted of several infantry positions with heavy weapons, and the artillery strongpoint consisted of a battery of artillery or antiaircraft weapons. The strongpoint included concrete works for various types

---

[40] Feldmarshall Erwin Rommel, the Desert Fox in the Atlantic Wall

of weapons, munitions, command posts, and/or troop shelters. Larger strongpoints could include more specialized types of bunkers for medical facilities, communications, or other specialized functions. The strongpoint were designed for all-around defense, were protected with barbed-wire obstacles and minefields where necessary, and supplied with communications and fighting trenches. Normally they were occupied by a platoon supplemented with reserve elements, but company-size formations were not uncommon. These positions maintained enough supplies to operate for about two weeks. The strongpoint group with two or more formations generally accommodated a battalion-size force. The strongpoint group held enough supplies to maintain its strong-points for four weeks. A festung was to have food and supply stocks to support all of its positions for three months. Some of these positions in the Normandy area that were identified after the battle by the U.S. Army can give the reader an idea of the nature of these German fortifications:

Strongpoint Group—Infantry position on the coast that protected the beach and beach exit leading to Vierville-sur-Mer. It consisted of an 88-mm gun casemate, a 75-mm gun casemate, a 50-mm antitank gun casemate, three To-bruk (Ringstand) mortar emplacements, two field positions for mortars, two machine-gun bunkers, three To-bruks for machine guns, one concrete machine-gun emplacement, and ten field positions for machine guns. In addition to mines and wire, this group included an antitank wall that barred the exit.

Strongpoint—Infantry position on the coast protecting the beach and road leading up the ravine to Colleville-sur-Mer. It consisted of a Renault tank turret emplaced on a concrete position (probably a ringstand), two field positions for 75-mm guns, four concrete mortar emplacements, a field position for a machine gun, a field position for an antiaircraft weapon, six stationary flamethrowers, and the usual array of mines and wire protection.

Strongpoint—Artillery position in the vicinity of Le Beau-vais covering the beaches and sea approaches. It included five concrete emplacements for 155-mm guns, six field emplacements for 75-mm or 155-mm guns, an observation post, two concrete mortar positions, seven Tobruks for machine guns, and a searchlight.

From these examples it can be seen that the strongpoints and strongpom: groups varied in size and number of positions. Most strongpoints usually included several *Ringstande,* mostly for observation and machine guns, but some for mortars and other weapons. In some cases a Strongpoint might be an observation position with a bunker mounting a cloche. The artillery strongpoints were formed around gun batteries with weapons of 75-mm or larger. Positions with a single casemate for a 75-mm or 88-mm weapon usually served as antitank guns. The old French Renault tank turrets, usually mounting a 37-mm gun, were commonlv employed on a *Ringstand-type* emplacement.

The smallest defensive position, the *Widerstandnester* (resistance nest), could be found alone or as part of a defense zone or fortress. In some cases strongpoints included these positions. These resistance nests, also called "defense posts" by the Americans, were infantry positions normally garrisoned by a unit smaller than a platoon consisting of one or two squads with enough supplies to hold out for one week. They included at least one antitank gun, several machine-gun and mortar positions, and, usually a few concrete bunkers. They were set up for all-around defense with barbed wire, minefields, and trenches.

There were several types of resistance nest. In the area of Colleville-sur-Mer, one of these resistance nests was an infantry position on the coast supplementing the defenses of a strongpoint defending the beach and a road leading up the ravine ro the town. It included a single field position for a 75-mm gun and another for a machine gun. The resistance nest covering a road leading up a ravine to St. Laurent-sur-Mer was an infantry position that included a field position for an 88-mm gun, a casemate for a 50-mm antitank gun, and a machine-gun bunker. An antitank ditch also led to this position. At Le Beauvais, the resistance nest was an artillery observation post and fire-control position for a battery of 155-mm guns. It consisted of the observation position and two Tobruks for machine guns.

The strongpoints and resistance nests were set up on the hedgehog system favored by the Germans from the time of the West Wall and also used during defensive operations on the Russian Front. This system, known in German as *Igel,* "vas based on setting up defensive positions with all-around defenses within supporting range of adjacent positions.

Knowledge of the physical makeup of the coastline is important to understanding the types of defenses the Germans needed to create. The Atlantic coastline from the Spanish border to the base of the Brittany Peninsula is a low region with long stretches of sandy beaches interspersed with headlands, which were ideal for setting up strongpoints because of their elevation, which was enough to make a seaward assault difficult but not so high as to make defense ineffective. Some of the key points for defense were the mouth of the Gironde, to deny the use of the port of Bordeaux, if, by any chance it was taken. Further up the coast were several islands that made it possible to cover the mainland and the port of La Rochelle with the submarine pens at La Pallice. Further north the Loire estuary controlled access to the ports of St. Nazaire and Nantes. The raid on St. Nazaire proved it to be too weakly defended. This entire stretch of coastline, which was placed under the command of the First Army in 1944, was probably the most vulnerable to an amphibious landing, but its distance from Allied bases in Great Britain limited the ability of the Anglo-American invaders to logistically support a great invasion force. The possibility of taking a seaport in this area was not very good without an invasion force that could be quickly reinforced and brought to a strength of at least ten full divisions in a short time. Thus no one expected an invasion to take place in this region.

Brittany was always considered target worthy by both sides. The German commander of the Seventh Army was forced by OKW to maintain a larger force there than in Normandy because it was home to the major submarine bases of Brest and Lorient and allowed easy access to St. Nazaire. The coastline of the peninsula with its many rocky outcrops would be difficult to attack, but required a minimum of defensive measures. Although there were some long stretches of beaches on the northern and south-ern sides of the peninsula, the south side was too far away from Great Britain for a large invasion to succeed and the north side had only the small and well-defended port of St. Malo. The fortress of St. Malo was protected on both flanks by terrain that lacked sufficient beaches and access for an invasion force. In addition, the German-occupied Channel Islands offered a limited threat to any invader try-ing to take St. Malo with the intent of using it as a major base of operations. At the west end of the peninsula was Brest, a highly desirable port tha: offered an invader the possibility of maintaining his operations, but it was heavily defended and offered few landing places of even modest size.

The region of Normandy up to the mouth of the Seine was unwelcoming for an invading force except for the port of Cherbourg, which was turned into a fortress and was not directly assailable. The Cotentin Peninsula of Normandy includes variable terrain with long stretches of sandy beach on the east side, but mostly cliffs and more formida-ble headlands on the north and west coast with only a few bays with small sandy beaches. The coast on the east side of the peninsula was relatively level but dominated by the cliffs of the Calvados coast, which extend to th; east of Arromanches where they disappear into more level ground with long wi beaches up to the mouth of the Orne River. Across the Orne and to the mouth c: the Seine the terrain again becomes less hospitable, being sandwiched betwi two rivers with the nearest major port on the other side of the Seine. This stretch also contains sandy beaches and a few small fishing ports, but offers little else. German Seventh Army defended Brittany and Normandy up to the Orne River where the Fifteenth Army took over, covering the remainder of the French coasr up to the Scheldt Estuary in the Netherlands. [41]

The French coast between Le Havre and the Somme River is dotted with large and small ports such as Le Havre, Fecamp, St. Valery, Dieppe, and Le Treport, but is dominated by chalk cliffs which break where small ports and stretches of beacr are nestled. Between Le Treport and the mouth of

---

[41] German turret at Omaha Beach

the Somme, the coast is dominated by dunes which grow larger on the north side of the Bay of the Somme. The dune coast continues to the Netherlands with either dunes reaching down to the sea or beaches or with dunes behind them. The only major break on this lor.r stretch of coast is located between Boulogne and Calais where the ground rises to form cliffs at several points, mainly in the area around Cap Griz Nez. Here lay the shortest cross-Channel invasion route with the ports of Boulogne, Calais, ar: Dunkirk which would have been easily assailable if they had not been heavil defended. Actually, the area between the Somme estuary and the Belgian border was the most heavily defended area in France with festung and defense zones because it was the closest point to Great Britain than anywhere else on the Atlantic Wall and it offered the most direct route for an invasion force to push on toward Germany.

The Dutch coast was similar to the Calais coast, open all the way to the Frisian Islands, which offered some degree of protection. The Dutch coast did not have any significant ports except the inland ports, which could not be used without complete control of the access waterways to the sea.

In addition, the terrain behind the coast was as important as the terrain on the coast itself. It varies from region to region, but in the Pas des Calais area it is largely open. In Normandy, west of the Orne and in the Cotentin Peninsula, the only major problem were hedgerows similar to those found across the Channel in England, but somewhat taller. Brittany is hilly and the region behind the Atlantic coast of western France is largely open, but more heavily wooded to the south. In 1944, Rommel introduced the use of flooding to certain lowland regions behind the coast, creating some serious obstacles behind the beaches of the Cotentin Peninsula and the Calvados coast. The same was done along some of the river mouths. In the Netherlands, the islands presented a serious obstacle. In addition, Walchern and many other parts of the country could be heavily flooded by opening the dikes.

The German coast, protected by the well-defended Frisian Islands, limited the prospects of an invasion reaching a satisfactory port on the rivers of the German North Sea coast. The Jutland Peninsula also offered many possible invasion beaches, but the most desirable area with a port was covered by the defenses of the island of Sylt.

In Norway the defender held all the advantages. Supplies from a beachhead were not expected to be sufficient to support an invasion force. An assault force had to quickly take a port and clear the access to it since most Norwegian ports are located on the fjords. The numerous islands along the coast were just as much a problem for the defender as an invader because of their sheer number.

A significant development in 1943, as far as strategic planning was concerned, was the creation of positions up to fifteen kilometers behind the coastal defenses ordered by OB West under Field Marshal von Rundstedt. Until then, the coastal defenses generally had no more depth than three to five kilometers in the most heavily defended sectors. Von Rundstedt did not agree with Hitler who expected the enemy to be destroyed at the landing site either by defeating him before he achieved a foothold or, failing that, by launching an immediate counterattack. The old field marshal did not believe the initial invasion would be smashed at the beachhead and felt that reserve mobile forces should be able to concentrate and defeat the enemy after he moved inland. To do this he wanted to create a secondary position, which consisted mainly of support points and strongpoints that could be used to contain the enemy and allow time for an effective counteroffensive. Insufficient manpower was assigned to the building of this secondary position and its construction proceeded very slowly.

When Field Marshall Rommel returned from Africa, he

was assigned as commander of Army Group B, which eventually took command of operations in northern Italy after the fall of Mussolini. Because of a disagreement with Albert Kesselring, the commander of German forces in Italy Rommel was reassigned to inspect the Atlantic Wall defenses late in 1943. Before his inspection, Rommel, who had apparently been taken in by German propaganda, was disappointed to see that the defenses from Denmark to France were little more than an incomplete and uncoordinated barrier that was far from being formidable in most areas. After completing his inspection and working out the initial disagreement he had with von Rundstedt over strategy, Rommel's Army Group B was assigned command of the French, Belgian, and Dutch coast and all the forces, except reserves, north of the Loire River. Army Group G was later created to command the remainder of the forces and fortifications south of the Loire and both groups came under OB West. Rommel and von Rundstedt soon worked out their differences. Rommel had been given this command mainly because he agreed with Hitler's idea of defeating the invasion immediately at the beaches. The idea of a strong reserve force for defeating the Allies inland was abandoned, but a partial compromise kept most of the armored and mobile formations far enough back from the coast to attempt a large massed counterattack.

Work on the Atlantic Wall took a new direction under Rommel. The gaps between the defense zones were to be better covered and if these included possible invasion sites they would also be more heavily defended. Although the major construction work on massive concrete structures, such as submarine pens, had almost come to an end in the West, the amount of labor from the OT and RAD and the availability of materials for concrete constructions were severely curtailed for two reasons. First, the Allied bombing campaign continued to intensify in 1944, inflicting so much damage that additional labor and material resources were needed at home for repairs and maintenance of the infrastructure, leaving fewer resources for the West. Second, Allied air attacks against transportation lines and communication centers prevented the few available resources from reaching the West in a timely manner. In addition, much of the concrete available for fortifications was earmarked for the construction of special installations for the new V-weapons. Despite these handicaps, Rommel was able to push construction to highs not seen since mid-1943. Rommel did not object to the construction of the V-weapons installations because he believed that these weapons might give the Germans the advantage in the defense of the West. However, at least one of subordinates, the commander of the Seventh Army, did not agree. According General Pemsel, the Seventh Army commander believed that construction of weapon sites in Normandy would only attract the attention of the Allies wh would want to remove the threat. Rommel was initially convinced that the Allies would land in the Pas De Calais area because of its proximity to Great Britain. He considered the sectors between Boulogne and the Somme estuary and both *sid~* of Calais as the most favorable for the Allies, whose air power and long-ran.:-guns would be most effective there. This area also included many V-weapon sits built in 1943, which constituted a prime target for the Allied air forces. Based cr this reasoning, Rommel asked for two reserve divisions to be placed near tin defenses between Boulogne and the Somme for an immediate counterattack.

Rommel also introduced his own ideas on developing beach obstacles whicr were to be covered by weapons fire to turn every beach into a deadly place. He put a premium on laying minefields and booby trapping obstacles. He wrote that hi had been deeply impressed by his experience with the Gazala Line in Libya ir 1942, where the British had set up antitank and antipersonnel mines in lar; defended minefields supported by machine guns and antitank weapons. After that, he had created his own minefield barriers along the El Alamein fror: Rommel was convinced that this insidious weapon would even the odds for th-defender. According to General Wilhelm Meise, Rommel's chief engineer for Armv Group B, the first stage of Rommel's plan consisted of creating a one-thousanc-meters-deep strip along the coast and another on the land front with ten mines pe-meter, a total of 20 million mines for France. To complete a parallel strip approximately eight thousand meters inland with the same number of mines per meter would have taken another 200 million mines. B. H. Liddel Hart, author of *The Rommel Papers,* points out that in France, Rommel used captured explosives that had been in storage.

Rommel complained that the number of antitank weapons and machine guns at the time he took over were not sufficient to cover the coast. He also wanted more obstacles placed along the coast and in the water. He believed that adding more obstacles and creating new types of obstacles, would be to the German advantage at such a late date because the Allies may not have time to prepare for mese additions to the beaches. He wanted underwater obstacles to destroy the approaching assault craft and vehicles in the water. These obstacles were to include stakes driven into the sea floor with an antitank mine atop, concrete tetrahedrons with either sharp blades or an antitank mine, and captured antitank obstacles from Belgium, France, and Czechoslovakia. He also designed the so-called "nutcracker mine," which consisted of a stake projecting into a concrete casing that held a heavy artillery round. When the stake was hit by a landing craft it .should act as a trigger and detonate the shell below. These underwater obstacles were to be deployed in four belts, but only two belts were completed in some areas. The first was at a depth of about two meters at mean high tide and the second was also at about two meters depth at half tide and a twelve-foot tide.

Work on the remaining two belts was only nearing construction when the invasion came. They included a belt at
about two meters depth at low tide and the other was at a
depth of about four meters at low tide. Since the invasion
took place at low tide, these two belts might have proved
effective. According to the War Diary of Army Group B,
517,000 of these obstacles were installed by May 13,1944.
Of this total 31,000 had an attached mine.

Inland the most forbidding obstacles created by Rommel
included flooded low-.ving areas and the "Rommel aspara-
gus" to hinder airborne landings. These obstacles consisted of stakes about three meters high, driven into the
ground in open areas and spaced about thirty meters
apart, some of which had shells attached at the top. Wire
linked the posts to each other, created an additional obstacle and could also detonate the shell. However, the captured shells did not arrive until shortly before the invasion
so work was never completed. In regions like Norway the
terrain did not require such draconian changes.

The Fortifications of the Atlantic Wall

During the initial construction of the Atlantic Wall some of
the last Re designed for the West Wall were initially used.
However, the size and type of tifications and constructions
on the Atlantic Wall required new Regelbau. Luftwaffe and
Kriegsmarine had their own construction bunker types,
most of which were similar to the army's since the *Festungpioniere* were generally considered the highest authority. By 1944, Organization Todt had set up two oper-
atrr^ commands for construction in the West and the
North. Einsatzgruppe West, headquartered in Paris in
1941, was in charge of about fifteen work commands, including several that were added in 1942 after the occupation of Vichy France. Einsatzgruppe Wiking, formed in the
summer of 1941 at Oslo, handled operations in Norway

and Denmark and was in charge of about twelve work commands, .m inspector of Land Fortifications West was the military authority for fortificar: -r in the West and the inspector of Land Fortifications North was created as the need arose to fortify Norway.

The Luftwaffe first began work on its own fortifications when General Kir Kitzinger was put in charge of creating the Air Defense Zone West behind the V.w Wall in 1938. Having served as an army engineer, Kitzinger relied on army design of Bl strength developed before the Limes program. After 1939 the Luftwaffe modified its designs for its own purposes and prefixed them with an "L" to designate their origin. The navy also developed its own bunker designs, which were prefixed with M (for naval), S (for special, associated with large coastal bunker.-Fl (Flak), and V (Medical, Command, or Radar). The 100 Series bunkers were introduced after 1939 and led to other types, which were eventually used in the Atlantic Wall. The 200 Series, consisting mostly of flak positions, began to appear in 1941 Many bunkers of the 200 Series were designed for the navy and served as redirection positions, gun casemates, and flak bunkers. The 300 Series, which came into use in 1943, included additional naval and flak bunkers and were soon followed by the 400 and *500* Series, which required less armor. The 600 Series, developed specifically for the Atlantic Wall, was considered the most modern and economical. Most of the 400 Series and some of the *500* Series designs were produce: for the Luftwaffe. Although some of the 400 and *500* Series bunkers date back to 1939 and 1940, most began to appear in 1942 while the *500* Series appeared mair-ly in 1939. The 600 Series was put into service in 1942 and soon became one of the dominant types on the Atlantic Wall, especially after 1943 when it began replacing earlier, weaker bunkers.

A special type of reinforced field fortifications known as the *Verstärkt Feldmassig,* abbreviated VF, also began to appear on the Atlantic Wall and elsewhere from 1942 until the end of the war. The VF included troop shelters, machine-gun and antitank bunkers, and positions that were the forerunners of the concrete *Ringstande*. The concrete ringstande were called *Tobruk's* by the Allies because they resembled a similar type of position built by the Italians in Libya. They were often found on bunkers and consisted of an open ring position in the roof of a concrete structure and were large enough for two men to stand in and fire their weapons. The openings of the Ringstande varied in size, depending on the weapon it mounted, which could be as small as a light machine gun or as big as an antitank gun. One of the most ubiquitous types was the VF 58c, two hundred of which were built in Norway and seventeen hundred in Denmark. Permanent concrete Ringstande became part of many new standard bunker designs, especially troop shelters. However, after 1943 they were built of reinforced concrete as separate positions similar to the VF Ringstande.

The Ringstande of Tobruks

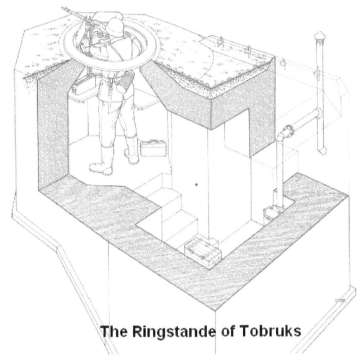

The Ringstande of Tobruks

The forerunner of the German *Ringstande,* an open-pit type position, first appeared in drawings dated March and April 1941 and formed part of the report submitted in November 1941 by the commission responsible for developing weapons for fortifications for the *Festungpioniere.* Traditionally it has been assumed this was an idea based on somewhat similar Italian positions built in Libya at Tobruk and Bardia. This may be correct, but certain factors may also mean it is not. The first German troops arrived in Libya early in 1941 and they did not encounter these fortifications until later in the year. It is not known if the Italian military shared their fortification design plans with the Germans at that time or earlier, but it is possible.The commission responsible for this 1941 report had studied the problem not just of weapons, but also of improving fortifications and making them more economical and less vulnerable at a time when rapid expansion of defenses into the conquered territories was necessary. The observation cloche and weapons cloche, the *Beobachtungsglocken* and the *Sechss-chartenturm,* were expensive to produce, especially at a time when weapons and armored vehicles had priority. The commission's report found, possibly after observing what German direct fire artillery weapons had done to the cloches of some Maginot Line casemates, that armored domes were easily targeted and vulnerable.

One proposal was to place the 441P01 artillery observation cupola with horizontal observation slits and a periscope in a lower position exposing less of the steel cupola. Another proposal was to place this type of cupola almost level to the ground so that only the periscope could be used. The one item that offered the best possibility and was eventually adopted was the ringstande which in the drawings was identified as the *Offener Beobachter* or open observation position. These positions were initially independent and belonged to a category known as *Verstarkt Feldmiifiig* (VF) or reinforced field works. As early as 1940 this type of position was already found in the West Wall as the VF 51 and VF 51a. Another report in November 1942 applied the name *Ringstande* and gave them an octagonal shape. In 1943 the designs no longer just included these positions as reinforced field works, but also as regular construction types. Both the VF types and the permanent concrete types included not just observation positions, but positions for heavy weapons. These open positions were basically small concrete positions with a circular opening in the roof where an observer could stand upright with only his head and shoulders exposed. It offered 360 degrees of unobstructed observation. Access to this position was from stairs at a side entrance.

In 1942 when Hitler finally called for the creation of an Atlantic Wall, this new design offered an inexpensive alternative to the use of steel cupolas and allowed for more rapid construction of combat positions. In November 1942, *neue Bauformen* or new forms of construction, were introduced as *Regelbauten 600 ff* based on the commission's report of 1941. They included the Ringstande which served as an observers position. The circular position was later modified to a hexagonal or octagonal shape incorporated into the wing walls.

The Allied forces that first encountered these positions found them reminiscent of similar types used in the Tobruk perimeter belt of defenses and apparently coined the term "Tobruk" for them, especially since these positions, like many of those at Tobruk, were virtually level with the ground and without overhead cover.

By May 1943 these Ringstande were built as small independent fortifications and were no longer only found attached to the 600-type bunkers. Some of these positions were not only used for machine guns, but also for a mortar. Source: Research by Martin Biiren and the report "Entwicklungsbericht der Waffenkommission Fest" of November 1941.

Types of Bunkers

The estimated fifteen thousand structures built on the Atlantic Wall can be classified into several types, some of which were more numerous than others. Beginning in 1942, Type 134 and Type 607 Munitions Bunkers were built in the West and Denmark and a few Type 607s in Norway. Type 134 *Munitionsunterstand I* consisted of two ammunition rooms, each with its own entrance which opened into a tunnel with two exits. Type 607 *Munitionsunterstand II* was designed for heavy artillery and, though larger than the Type 134, its plan was equally simple. It included a cartridge room and a shell room that had two entrances opening into a gallery on either side that led to the exit. Type 641 *Munitionsunterstand III* was similar to the Type 607, but larger. It included a ringstande and two large rooms, one of which held two hundred to five hundred cartridges and the other about two hundred shells. Only three Type 641 bunkers were actually built, all in northern France. There were other types of munitions bunker, but they were built in smaller numbers. Naval Type F1246 was a large depot type bunker for flak ammunition. Some of the heavy artillery batteries had their own special kind of ammunition depot and even smaller weapons were provided with such positions.

Flak bunkers such as the Luftwaffe L401, L409 and L409A were also numerous compared to other types. The L401 *Geschiltzstand* was a bunker with a roof emplacement for either an 88-mm or a 105-mm flak gun. It included two entrances that led to a gas lock that opened to the crews quarters. A second room held the ammunition. L409 was similar to L401, but it had only one entrance, was slightly smaller, and mounted a 37-mm flak gun on its roof. L409A was more complex and could mount either a 20-mm or 37-mm flak gun on a smaller roof position. It had a gas lock, two entrances covered by an interior crenel, and a small storage room between the ammunition room and crews quarters. There were other types of flak bunkers with positions on the roof for the weapon. Some had more complex interior designs.

The largest single class of bunkers consisted of troop shelters. They included Types 501, 502, 621, and 668. Type 501 *Gruppenunterstand,* referred to in English sources as a squad shelter, accommodated about ten men. It included a single entrance protected by an interior crenel. Its standard "T" or "L" shaped entrance led to a gas lock which gave access to the crew quarters. Type 502 *Doppelgruppenunterstand* or double squad shelter held up to twenty men and had two entrances, each covered by an interior crenel, that led to a gas lock giving access to the quarters. It also had a periscope room. Both Type 501 and 502 had a stairway access in each entrance and were first used on the West Wall in 1939. Type 502 had a latrine in the corner of the outer entrance way. The troop chambers were furnished with a pair of double bunks and pair of triple bunks, a table and chairs, closets, and rifle racks. Type 621, a one-squad shelter, was built in large numbers from Norway to the Atlantic coast of France beginning in 1943. It was similar to Type 502 with its two entrances, but had only one room for ten men. On one of its exterior wing walls it included a Ringstand accessed only from the outside. Type 622 *Doppelgruppenunterstand* was similar to Type 621 and was also built in large numbers. Each of its two chambers included three triple bunks, a ventilator, and accessories for the men. In the gas lock there was a periscope. The entire position, except for the rear wall and access to the Ringstand was covered with earth. Type 668 *Kleinstunterstand fiir 6 Mann,* a small bunker for six men, was a smaller version of Type 501 and was also widely used from 1943. It included two triple bunks and could accommodate a maximum of eighteen men if necessary. There was a number of other 600 Series type, but they were built in fewer numbers. The Kriegs-marine developed its own special types like Type M151 *Mannschaftsunterstand,* which provided quarters for twenty-four men, two NCOs, and one officer. Its two entrances, located on two different sides, were covered by an interior crenel in the men's quarters (one in each room) and turned into gas locks. The Luftwaffe also developed its own designs for bunkers, including the large L435A, but few of these designs were actually built.

The infantry and artillery type combat bunkers, which included machine gun and antitank bunkers, were also built in large numbers. These included Types 515 and 630 machine-gun bunkers, Types 600 and 667 antitank gun bunkers, and Types 611, 612, 669, and 680 artillery bunkers. The older Type 105 machine-gun casemates from 1939 required a large armored embrasured shield for the machine gun and an observation cloche making it too complex to be economical. Type 515, also from 1939, which was heavily used, was smaller than Type 105 and required the armored wall shield. Type 630 *Schartenstand mitt Panzerplatte,* a large machine-gun bunker with many defensive features, also required the large armored shield for the machine gun and included a Ringstand. It was built in large numbers in the West. Type 632 was almost identical to Type 630, but instead of the armored shield it had an embrasured concrete wall for the machine gun, making it more economical. However, only about a dozen bunkers of this type were built. Several additional types of machine-gun bunkers were built, but less extensively. Type 600 bunkers mounting a 50-mm tank gun on their roof had an interior similar to the L409's. Type 667, which mounted the same 50-mm weapon in a small casemate, was built in even larger numbers than Type 600. Types 653 and 654 were larger bunkers with crew quarters, gas locks, a Ringstand and a casemate position for a 50-mm gun. Few of these two types were actually built.

Type 611 *Geschutzschartenstand,* a casemate designed for field guns, included an opening in the rear which allowed access to the gun and a corridor that led to the gun chamber. On one side of this chamber were rooms for the shells and cartridges and on the other side was a protected entrance with gas lock. The wing wall included a Ringstand. Almost a hundred Type 611 bunkers were built in northern France. Type 669 was a simple embrasured bunker for a field gun giving only a sixty degree field of fire. Type 612, a smaller version of Type 669, was designed for an assault gun. It was built in large numbers on the Channel and Atlantic coast. Type 680, similar to Type 612 in size and shape, was designed for a 75-mm antitank gun. A larger version, Type 677, was designed for an 88-mm antitank gun and Type 703 was developed for a newer 88-mm antitank gun. Six hundred and twenty-five bunkers were built to shelter the 75-mm antitank gun, and seven hundred for the 88-mm gun.

Types 139, 631, 631b, and 642 were large casemates for the Czech 47-mm "Fortress" antitank gun, but they were not built in large numbers. A smaller casemate position, Type 676, similar but larger than the Type 667 for 50-mm tank guns, was built in small numbers from Norway to the French Atlantic coast.

Several non-movable turrets or cloche positions were designed for use on the Atlantic Wall. A number of Type 634 bunkers with quarters for the garrison similar to a squad shelter with additional features and a six-embrasure cloche were built in Northern France and Denmark. Other types of bunkers with the six-embrasure cloche and the three-embrasure half cloche were built in smaller numbers. Fewer than one hundred Type 633, designed for the M-19 automatic mortar position in a cloche, were actually built. Other types of more specialized bunkers like the combat headquarters were built in smaller numbers only because they served a specific need. They included bunkers for communications, radar, weapons storage, and observation and command posts.

The *Nachrichtenstande* or communications bunkers, though built in small numbers, were quite important. Just over a dozen Type 617 bunkers, which included a switchboard for telephones, were built in northern France. Type 618 included a radio room, a telephone exchange, the standard two entrances defended by a weapons crenel, gas locks, and a Ringstand. In the large naval bases in western France seven large Type V142 bunkers with radio, telegraph, and telephone facilities were built for the navy.

Special communications bunkers for radar were also built.

The L480 bunker for the Wassermann S radar built for the Luftwaffe in several positions in northern France, the Netherlands, and Denmark. This large bunker over twenty-seven meters in length and twelve meters wide housed equipment necessary for the radar. The L486 was a slightly larger bunker also used as a radar installation. The navy had four Type V143 bunkers, large positions built on the Channel coast for the Mammut radar system in 1942. The Luftwaffe's Mammut radar bunker was even larger than the navy's. Several Type V174 bunkers, which included a radar tower almost fourteen meters high, were built in Denmark in 1944. Several large Type L479 bunkers with two levels for control of night fighters were built for the Luftwaffe in northern France and several L487s were built in the Netherlands and Denmark.

Several types of bunkers were developed to serve as depots for storing weapons. The most common was Type 504 with a garage for and antitank gun and troop quarters. This type was replaced by 600 series types in 1942, which included Types 601, 604, 605, and 629 all of which had troop quarters and the standard protection, including a Ringstand. Type 629 could take many types of antitank guns, including all 76.2 mm weapons and 200-mm flak guns. It included quarters for six men with two triple bunks, a room for ammunition and equipment storage, and a pair of Ringstande on each wing. Type 605 had two garages. A few types, such as Type 701, were designed as a garage with no facilities. Type 602 consisted of a troop shelter and a garage for a tank. Type 603 was an even larger version with two tank bays that could shelter a Panzer II, III or IV or an armored vehicle with an assault gun. These bays could also accommodate two Panzer I tanks or two armored ammunition trailers instead of the larger vehicles. A lower level included a room for twelve men with four triple bunks. Only a few of these were built.

Type 608 was a combat headquarters bunker for a battalion or regimental staff with quarters, work space, communications rooms, a Ringstand, and two entrances covered by an exterior and interior crenels. The rooms included a large central office that gave access to a number of other rooms and one of the gas locks, the radio room, a planning room, a signal room, the adjutant's room, the commander's room, a small ready room, and the ventilator room. Most of the staff had to be quartered in nearby shelters. Slightly over one hundred Type 608 bunkers were built in all sections of the Atlantic Wall. Another one hundred Type 610 smaller headquarters bunker for a company or battery were also built in the same area.

Other observation and command bunker types included the infantry bunkers, such as Type 666, a bunker with a small observation cloche. About thirty Type 666 were built in Denmark and very few elsewhere. Type 120, an artillery observation bunker, included a small observation cloche. The fire control center of coastal batteries usually contained a command post such as Type 636, which was found along the Atlantic Coast from the Spanish border to Norway. Type 636 included a position for a range finder on its roof, quarters for the garrison, a communications center, and an observation room. A total of seventy Type 636 command bunkers were actually built. Type 637 was a small bunker with crew quarters, a Ringstand, and a range finder for army coastal batteries. Over thirty bunkers of this type were built in France.

More specialized battery fire-control positions or *Leitstande* included Types M120 and M132 for the navy's 170-mm gun coastal gun batteries. These bunker types had a large working area and quarters. M132 had two levels below the observation cloche and range finder room. Type S100, another large fire direction center intended for heavy artillery batteries, had two levels and mounted a range finder in an armored dome. Type M178 had a concrete covered range finder room to the rear of and above the observation room. The two-level Type S414 was similarly arranged, but had a second observation room below the first. Few of this type were built since there was only a small number of large coastal batteries. Type M157 had a similar arrangement of observation positions and range finder position and was used for medium and heavy batteries. Type 162a and the smaller M262 were built in larger numbers, reaching a total of a little less than fifty. They served as fire control positions for light naval batteries, were smaller than the others, and contained an observation room and with a range finder position with its own concrete roof centered above it. Some of the more spectacular types included multi-level tower and positions for a range finder and/or an observation position. The four-level Type S49 predominated on the Atlantic coast. The S448 with a twenty-seven meter high tower and a range finder in an armored dome built on a large bunker, was found mostly in the Netherlands. The Type FL250 command post for flak was an extremely large bunker with a twenty meters high tower.

There were also supporting bunkers for machinery, searchlights, power engines to provide power for a strongpoint, and so on. Types 606, L411, and L411A had a garage for a 60-cm searchlight and facilities for the crew and Type F1277 had a garage for a 150-cm searchlight. There were also kitchen bunkers such as Type 645 and water bunkers with water tanks and even wells such as Types 646, 658, and 675. Medical bunkers or dressing stations were also common, especially the large Type 118 and the smaller Type 638.

The bunkers were generally used in groups such as resistance nests and strong-points in coastal positions. A coastal battery, normally part of a strongpoint, had the largest groupings of concrete structures. Although the number of guns varied, most batteries consisted of four, each of which normally had its own casemate and associated fire-control bunker. Troop shelters were located behind the gun casemates, unless these were large enough to include quarters for the troops. Flak bunkers and searchlight positions were also associated with the larger batteries. Infantry bunkers were placed around the entire position to protect it from close assault.

In the Atlantic Wall the coastal batteries formed the core of the German defensive positions because they could reply to the ships supporting an amphibious invasion or even a raid. The number of batteries deployed by 1944 was as follows:

Norway:225 batteries with approximately 1,000 weapons of 100-mm or larger. Of these 12 batteries had 42 weapons of 240-mm or higher.

Denmark:70 batteries with 293 guns. Two batteries with 380-mm guns.

Helgoland Bay: 22 batteries with 78 guns of over 150-mm. Of these 4 batteries with 12 guns over 240-mm.

French coast: 343 batteries with 1,348 guns of 150-mm or larger. On the Atlantic Wall, 495 artillery casemates or other emplacements were built by 1944 for heavy artillery of 150-mm and more in the area of the Fifteenth Army, about two hundred in the Seventh Army area, and sixty-five in the First Army area. These batteries included over two dozen different caliber weapons that ranged from 75-mm to 406-mm, a fair proportion of which were captured French, Russian, Czech, British, Yugoslavian, and Dutch. Some of these weapons included flak and large railroad guns. Most of these batteries were army formations because there was not enough naval personnel to man so many. The army coastal battalions were the *Heereskusten Artillerie Abteilung* (HKAA), and the naval coast artillery battalions were the *Matrosenartillerie-Abteilung* (MAA). There were also army coastal artillery regiments (HKAR).

In addition to the artillery and flak batteries, the Germans built a number of radar positions to sound the alarm in

time to man and ready the guns along the coast. The Wiirzburg Riese (Giant) radar, a large circular dish, had the ability to detect nightfighters while the original Wiirzburg
could only detect aircraft and direct flak batteries weapons. The Seetakt radars detected approaching ships and
helped direct the fire of artillery batteries. The Mammut,
Wassermann, and Freya were used to detect approaching
enemy aircraft at great distances.

Most of the medium and heavy artillery in Norway was
concentrated around areas designated as fortresses. In
1944, there were 183 artillery pieces of 100-mm or 130-
mm, 114 of 150-mm or 155-mm, 5 of 170-mm, and 44 of
210-mm or larger.

The super heavy artillery batteries included the following:
Kiberg with 3 x 280-mm SKL/45 Trondenes I with 4 x
406-mm SKC/34 in single gun turrets

Lodingen with 4 x 305-mm L/30 Bofor

Engeloy I with 3 406-mm SKC/34 in naval turrets

Oerlandet with 3 x 280-mm SKC/34 in naval turrets

Jusoen with 3 x 280-mm SKC/45

Fjell (Bergen) with 3 x 280-mm SKC/34 in naval turrets

Vara with 3 x 380-m SKC/34 in a turret and 1 x 305-mm
in casemate

Oscarsborg with 3 x 280-mm K L/40

Notteroy with 3 x 380-mm K M36/35f

Knatterod 2 x 280-mm Heavy Bruno rail guns.

In the far north the coastline was dotted with batteries of
105-mm and 155-mm, mainly concentrated in the fjords
around Kirkenes and Tromso. The Trondenes I Battery
with some of the heaviest guns used in coast defense was
located in Vaagsfjord near Harstad. Its four guns were
placed in single-gun turrets mounted on a pivot-like structure that was part of the special S-384 type casemate.
These large casemates, only built in Norway were over 47
meters x 36.8 meters and contained several large storage
rooms for shells and cartridges, an engine room, quarters

for the garrison, latrine and washing area, heating, ventilation equipment and two protected entrances.

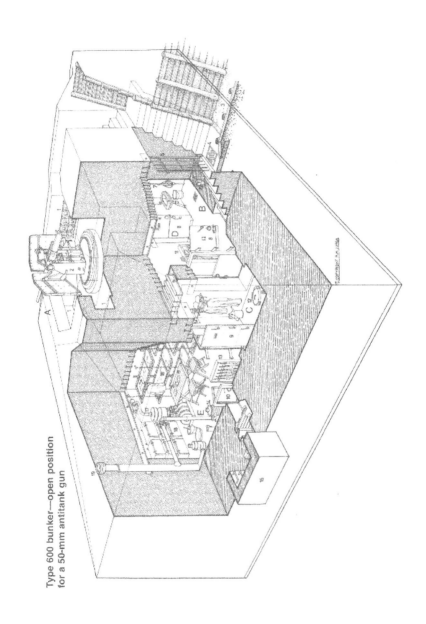

Type 600 bunker—open position for a 50-mm antitank gun

Type 600 Bunker - open position for a 50mm antitank gun
A.Open emplacement for 50-mm antitank gun
B.Entrance (ante room)
C. Decontamination niche
D.Ammunition
E.Crews quarters
1.Ready ammunition
2.50-mm antitank gun
3.Access trench
4.Well
5.Fortress grate
6.Entry point for cables into the bunker
7.Water pump
8.Double armored door type 434P01
9.Gasproof door type 1 9P7
10.Door for emergency exit 410P9
11.Stand for sappers equipment
12.Field toilet
13.Rifle rack
14.Heater Wt80K
15.Well for emergency exit
16.Triple bunks
17.Ventilator HES
18.Closet for personal equipment
19.Chimney

There were also a number of other smaller batteries, including some for flak on the same island. To the north was
the heavy battery of Andsfjord with three 210-mm Czech
guns that guarded Vaagsfjord and the approaches to Narvik. Ofotfjord, which leads to Narvik, was protected by a
number of small batteries, including two torpedo batteries
and the heavy Lodingen Battery with three 305-mm guns
located on the island of Hinnoy, near the approaches to
the fjord. Narvik itself was protected by a number of batteries with weapons of 105-mm to 240-mm guns and sev-

eral flak batteries.

Battery Dietl, located on the Vestfjord at Engeloy, included three 406-mm guns in the same type of casemates as those of Battery Trondenes I and was supported by a number of other batteries of 105-mm to 150-mm caliber dispersed around the fjord. The primary mission of these positions was to keep open the sea lanes and Narvik, which had no road connection with the town of Bodo over one hundred kilometers to the south. The sea lanes from Narvik were critical not only to the flow of iron ore from Sweden, but also to maintain communications with the German army operating in northern Finland.

Further to the south, Bodo, located at the end of the overland road on the way to Narvik, was protected by seven heavy batteries ranging from 105-mm to 210-mm guns. Further south the defenses were scattered to guard the fjords leading to Mo and Mosjoen. Heavy concentrations of artillery protected Namso, which controlled access to the road network and led to Trondheim, the largest in the region, which included a U-boat base and protected anchorage. The approaches t: the fjord leading to the city became a virtual fortress zone with numerous heavy artillery batteries, including two with guns of 280-mm. Battery Husoen, located or. the island of Tarva a few kilometers from the entrance to the fjord and away frorr. the mainland, consisted of 280-mm guns. Battery Oerlandet, protecting the entrance to the fjord leading to Trondheim, included Turret Caesar, one of three turrets removed from the battlecruiser *Gneisenau* after it was damaged at Kiel. This turret was ready for use and test-fired in September 1943.

The line of coastal batteries continued into southern Norway, thickening in the vicinity of Bergen, where the heavy Battery Fjell with three 280-mm guns was located. This battery incorporated Turret Bruno from the *Gneisenau* mounted in the same way as its sister turret at Oerlandet. The large island of Karmoy to the northwest of Stavanger harbored several batteries, one of which had 210-mm guns. A number of other batteries also protected the port of Stavanger. Egersund was also defended by several heavy batteries. The port of Kristiansund was defended by heavy batteries of 150-mm and 240-mm guns and Battery Vara consisting of three 380-mm guns, two gun turrets, and a large casemate for the third gun. These guns of a range of forty-two kilometers, in conjunction with another battery of heavy guns located at Hanstholmon, on the Danish coast and a dense minefield in a ten kilometer strip closed the Skaggerak. Battery Vara was part of a strongpoint consisting of a number of concrete structures, including troop shelters, munitions bunkers, positions for an engine room, command post, range finder, 20-mm and 88-mm flak, radar, searchlights, and bunkers for close combat.

The approaches to the Oslo fjord were heavily defended by a number of batteries, including the captured battery of 280-mm guns at the Norwegian fortress of Oscarborg located up the fjord.

Unlike the rest of the Atlantic coast, the long coastline of Norway offered many advantages to the defender since much of it lacked landing beaches or contained headlands which made an amphibious assault extremely difficult. Many of the places with conditions favorable for an invasion were too isolated to be of value because of the rough terrain inland and a limited number of roads. North of Stavenger the few beaches along the coasts and fjords were seldom more than twenty meters in length and rocky. In addition, the many skerries (single rock islands, a series of rock islands or reefs) and small islands made navigation difficult. South of Stavenger, the southeast coast was an exception since it included long sandy beaches and low terrain similar to Western Denmark. Here the Germans built numerous fortifications, including many bunkers and Ringstande with tank turrets. Beach obstacles even included dragon's teeth. In most parts of Norway artillery batteries dominated sections of the coast but in many cases large numbers of defensive positions were not required to provide adequate protection The Germans improved many of the older Norwegian battery positions and created new ones in dominant sites that remained in service throughout the twentiet century. The main objectives of an assault in the region would be the ports, but most of them were located on inland waterways, easily defended by torpedo batteries and artillery positions requiring a minimum of infantry defensive positions It did not take much to turn positions like Oslo Fjord, Bergen, Trondheim, or Narvik into veritable fortresses.

The Twentieth Mountain Army was in control of the far north with Kirkenes as the key site and was responsible for operations in the former Finnish territory of Petsamo. The XIX and LXXI Army Corps were stationed in northern Norway defending the area around Tromso and Narvik. The XXXIII Army Corps defendec central Norway from Trondheim to Kristiansund. The LXX Army Corps was in charge of southern Norway from the area around Bergen to Oslo. Norway was listed as a *wehrbezirk* or military region of the Reich. The coast of *Wehrbezirk Norwegen* or WBN was not divided into individual sectors, according to available sources instead, it had defended sectors or fortress zones and the usual assortment of strongpoints and resistance nests. As many as 403 batteries have been identified in Norway in 1944, including a railroad gun battery of two 280-mm heavy Brunos and a rail battery of four 240-mm old French guns. They were serviced by thirteen naval artillery battalions and twelve army coast artillery regiments. A line of over forty radar sites, the most common of which were the Freya and Würzburg types, formed a chain along the coastline to detect approaching aircraft and direct flak ratteries. There were also several Seetakt radars at various points on the coast to detect approaching ships and aid coast defense batteries. The total number of concrete structures built in Norway was less than 450 while in Denmark there were almost 2,000. The smaller number of positions in Norway can be attributed in part :o the nature of the terrain and in part to a shortage of materials and to weather conditions that slowed the pace of construction.

In Denmark there were a number of batteries on the island where Copenhagen is located and along the coast of Eastern Jutland, but they were not part of the main Danish defenses. The most important artillery batteries were in northern "utland, where the heavy battery of Hanstholm with four 380-mm guns and a range of fifty-four kilometers, closed the Skaggerak with the help of Battery Vara in southern Norway. The other concentrations of heavy batteries were at rrederikshavn and Esbjerg on the west coast. Near Esbjerg was another 380-mm battery with twin gun turrets mounted on a Regelbau S561. Denmark had thirty-six batteries of 100-mm guns or larger if the Baltic positions are not counted. In addition, there were about forty radar sites, a slightly smaller number than in Norway, but most of them were for aircraft detection. Like Norway, Denmark was designated a military region of the Reich named *Wehrbezirk Danemark* or WBD.

Before the war began, the German Bight and Baltic coast were defended by eighteen heavy batteries ranging in caliber from 150-mm to 305-mm guns. However most of these weapons were moved into the Atlantic Wall after the occupation of most of Western Europe. In 1944, the German Bight and Baltic coast had to be strengthened once more. Most of the weapons used this time were naval guns. The island of Helgoland had become a veritable fortress bristling with a battery of three 305-mm guns in turrets, a battery of three 170-mm guns, several lighter weapons, and five batteries of heavy naval flak. The surrounding areas of Sylt were well-defended with several medium and heavy naval batteries. In the Frisian Islands, including Wangerooge and Norderney, on the other hand, there were no batteries heavier than 150-mm except for one of 280-mm guns.

In the Netherlands certain areas were heavily defended. For instance, the *Verteidigungsbereiche* Den Helder had two batteries of 120-mm guns, one battery of French 194-mm guns, and several of 105-mm guns. The next most heavily defended area was Ijmuiden, a festung with several naval batteries of guns ranging from 120-mm to 170-mm in caliber. Another major fortress on the Dutch coast was the old fort of Hoek van Holland, which included several batteries of artillery ranging from 120-mm to three 280-mm in caliber. The northern section of this fortress, which occupied both sides of the mouth of the Nieuwe Waterweg, was protected by an antitank ditch running from the coast to the waterway.

The remaining section of the fortress occupied an island on the south side of the waterway. An old fortification stood near the mouth of the waterway. Behind the old fort, on the south section, was a strongpoint with Battery Brandenburg, which included two 240-mm guns in turrets mounted on casemates. Battery Rozenburg, located on the south side of the waterway to the rear of Battery Brandenburg, had three 280-mm guns from the turret of the battlecruiser *Gneisenau*. They were mounted individually in turrets on Regelbau S-412 casemates. The battery's strongpoint included a range finder on a tower, Regelbau S-448, almost thirty meters high since the Dutch ;oast had no high points for observation. It also had three Regelbau S-448a munitions bunkers, troops shelters, searchlight bunkers, and positions for close defense. The fortress itself included about fourteen more strongpoints and forty resistance nests. Many of the strongpoints contained an artillery battery and supporting riositions, while most of the resistance nests consisted of two to over a dozen bunkers. Most of these resistance nests included troop shelters and other bunkers for close defense which could be casemates for machine guns and/or antitank gun positions. This was how most fortresses of the Atlantic Wall were organized, but many of the others, like Ijmuiden, were centered on a port. The Netherlands were under the command of a Luftwaffe general and only technically a part of the Fifteenth Army. The coastline was divided into three *Kusten Verteidigung Abschnitt* (coast defense sector or KVA): Al, A2, and B.

Of the islands at the mouth of the Schelde and Rhine, Walchern was the most heavily defended and included a number of medium and a couple of heavy artillery batteries. On the short Belgian coast the area around Zeebriigge was heavily protected by several heavy batteries that included 155-mm, 170-mm, 203-mm, and 280-mm guns. Ostend was also the center of a *Verteidigungsbereich* defense zone which began at Walchern Island under the authority of the Fifteenth Army.

The Fifteenth Army commanded KVAs Al to A3 mainly on the Belgian coast. The Pas de Calais area between Dunkirk and Etaples was one of the most heavily defended portions of the Atlantic Wall. It included three sectors occupied by the LXXXII Army Corps: B, C, and Dl. Sector D included Fortress Dunkirk, several heavy batteries, over twenty strongpoints and over ten resistance nests. In Sector C, between Dunkirk and Boulogne, there were nine positions with dome bunkers for heavy rail guns, most of which consisted of 280-mm K-5 guns. Although the area between Calais and Gris Nez was listed as a *Verteidungsberich,* it was almost equivalent to a festung. In addition to the rail guns, it included some of the largest super heavy artillery batteries in the West. The area to the east of Calais included Battery Oldenburg with two 240-mm guns, the battery of Bastion II with three 194 mm French guns, Battery Prinz Heinrich with two 280-mm guns, and Batter." Lindemann with three 406-mm guns. In the vicinity of Gris Nez was Battery Tod: with four 380-mm guns and Battery Grosser Kurfiirst with four 280-mm guns Several batteries, mostly medium, and Battery Friedrich August with three 305-mm guns were located at festung Boulogne, which consisted of over twenty strongpoints and more than fifteen resistance nests. To the north, the fortress was anchored at the coast by three strongpoints forming the La Creche position.

Further down the coast, in the Fifteenth Army area, there were other heavily defended positions, in particular the fortress at Le Havre. In KVA El, Le Trepor: was well defended by strongpoints that included two batteries of three 170-mm guns, heavy artillery, a Seetakt radar position for detecting approaching ships and providing fire control information to the artillery batteries. Dieppe, in KVA E2, with several strongpoints and artillery batteries was also well-defended. Other small ports such as St.Valery Fecamp, and Etretat, which were not far from the major port of Le Havre, were defended by groups of strongpoints that included several medium and heavy artillery batteries. Le Havre, the major fortress in KVA F, was an easily defended position overlooking the mouth of the Seine. Its heaviest battery, the naval battery of La Corvee located at Bleville (north side of Le Havre), was to consist of three 380-mm guns mounted in Regelbau S-536 casemates. However, construction on the casemates began late so only one piece was actually mounted and the other positions were not completed. The fortress of Le Havre consisted of many strongpoints and resistance nests, including over twenty resistance nests forming *Stutzpunktgruppe Nord* and *Ost* that covered the land front. *Stutzpunktgruppe Ost* encompassed a large flooded area forming a barrier between Montvilliers and Harfleur on the east side. Most of the area on its flanks was covered by large minefields. The front of *Stutzpunktgruppe Nord* included a large minefield running eastward from Octeville across half of its length.

An antitank ditch extended from one side of the minefield to the coast. Another one covered the gap between this same minefield and the minefield of the *Ost* group. *Stutzpunktgruppe Stid* covered most of the coastline of the fortress area and the other two groups defended the remainder of the shoreline on either of its flanks. Boulogne was as heavily defended in many respects as Le Havre, the largest coastal port between the Seine and the Netherlands. Since the Germans considered the coast between Le Havre and Dunkirk as the most likely to be invaded, they made sure to secure it as well as possible. [42]

The remainder of the Fifteenth Army's command extended further into Normandy up to the Orne River. It comprised a number of strongpoints, most of which were supported by guns no larger than 155-mm. Across the Orne began the Seventh Army area, which included the remainder of Normandy and all Brittany. Although the small fishing ports of

---

[42] Fortress HKAR 180, atlantic wall - northern Denmark

the Calvados coast were defer.; most of their artillery batteries were not larger than 105-mm. The only except:: were
the batteries at Cherbourg and Battery St. Marcouf with its
Czech 21C-r guns at Crisbecq, which protected the east
coast of the Cotentin Peninsula.
The Cherbourg fortress was created because the port was
one of the largest France. Its batteries included guns ranging from 105-mm to 240-mm and each strongpoints was
heavily protected. In the city itself several vintage forts on
moles became part of the German defenses. The old forts
surrounding the city used to form an inner defense belt.
Fort Roule, on a large hill overlooking the was heavily defended and below it was a battery of 105-mm guns in caser
built into the hill. The Germans did not make any serious
effort to protect the front at Cherbourg until 1944, when
they began work on an outer belt, which to serve as the primary defense line. This belt was to follow the crest of the
rounding heights. However, only the positions of a group
on the western cc flank called *Westeck, a* group on the
eastern side called *Osteck,* and the sout approaches along
the main highway were built before the project ran out of
The western side of the Cotentin was protected by Hitler's
"Impregnable Fortress" of the Channel Island. The islands
of Guernsey, Jersey, and Alderney' been heavily fortified
since 1941. On Guernsey stood the heavy Battery Minis
four 305-mm guns and a few batteries with 210-mm howitzers and 220-mm Jersey also had 210-mm howitzer batteries and a 220-mm gun battery, but Alderney's heaviest
battery was one of 170-mm naval guns. A battery of 380
mm guns was planned for each of the islands, but the guns
never arrived and their casemates were not built. Old
French 105-mm guns were also incorporated in the defenses of the islands. A special casemate without a Regelbau number, called a *Jäger* type, was developed specifically for the Channel Islands and Denmark. By the
summer of 1944, over three hundred bunkers for artillery,

observation, fire contriv. munitions, machine guns, personnel runnel system were built on the three islands. Many kilometers of concrete antitank walls, and old granite sea walls.protected the beaches. Some bunkers were built into the sea walls and others, including observation types, were built into positions similar to old Martello towers.

The next group of heavy defenses began in Brittany near St. Malo. The bays with possible landing sites along the Breton coast were protected, but not exce^ sively. St. Malo and especially Brest and Lorient were heavily defended fortress-Brest, where the Germans used the old fortifications and added numerous strongpoints and resistance nests, was probably one of the most heavily protected fortresses in France. Lorient, one of the most important U-boat bases on the Atlantic, was also heavily defended. The mouth of the Loire was covered by a number of coast artillery batteries, and St. Nazaire, a huge naval fortress, occupied both sides of the river.

The remainder of the Atlantic coast was under the command of the First Army. La Pallice-La Rochelle was well-defended, but not considered a fortress. The *Verteidigungsbereich* included not only the area around the city and port, but also the islands of Re and Oleron. Few of the artillery batteries along the coastal front of First Army were heavier than 155-mm. The most heavily defended point was the mouth of the Gironde, which had a festung on each side to protect the great port of Bordeaux. The Fortress of Royan, *Festung Gironde Nord,* bordered on the sea and the mouth of the Gironde on one side, the Seudre River on the other side, and only a small land front on its southeast side. The western section of this peninsula was heavily wooded and the area along the Seudre was flooded. The land front consisted of a line of outposts between the Seudre River and the mouth of the Gironde that sealed off the peninsula.

Behind it, the town of Royan was encircled by fortifications, and linked to another line that cut across the peninsula. [43] A group of strongpoints at the base of a promon-
tory on the west side of the peninsula served as a final re-

---

[43] Casamate northern Jutland

doubt called la Coubre. The inland port of Bordeaux was also well-defended. The remainder of the coastline was more lightly defended although coastal batteries covered all areas that might be used by a landing force. The coastal areas of Arachon, to the southwest of Bordeaux, Bayonne, and St. Jean de Luz near the Spanish border were part of two *Verteidigungsbereiche.*

This was the Atlantic Wall in 1944. Not complete, weak in many sectors, but with enough medium and heavy artillery distributed in key locations to impede an invasion unless pre-invasion activity neutralized them. None of the major ports were left undefended from direct assault by sea and most had been prepared for all-around defense. Although a number of points afforded the possibility of a successful landing at minimal risk, no large or medium-size seaport was so vulnerable that an invasion force could take it easily and use it as a base for the necessary logistical support. However, two factors unknown to the Germans negated their advantage in controlling these ports and having the ability to demolish them before they could be captured. The first was the two artificial Allied harbors called Mulberries which allowed the Allies to support the invasion without immediately capturing a major port. The second, which the Allies did not even count on, was the ability of Allied shipping to support a large invasion force directly from the beaches even without a Mulberry.

Inside the Bunkers

German bunkers maintained some features that became standard in most Atlantic Wall positions. The entrances were "T" or "L" shaped so that fire could not be directed into the bunker from the outside. After making the turn there was usually a gas lock. In many cases there was a firing crenel on the corridor to protect the entrance and sometimes a flanking position on the exterior wall covering the entrance. Armored doors were used to close the gas locks. After 1942 many bunkers had a ringstande included for observation and light weapons. These were usually near the entrance, but entered from outside the bunker through the side.

The interior of the bunkers, like earlier ones, had instructions stenciled on the walls. Heating was available in large bunkers and a ventilation system was standard in most positions. The most effective heating unit developed was the Wt80 by the W. E. Haas & Sohn Company in 1937 that was used for central heating. It met the important requirement of being safe enough to prevent carbon dioxide from leaking. The fumes were carried away through the walls by ventilation pipes. Sufficient funds were never available to equip all troop quarters with them and bunkers with accommodations for a crew generally had only one heater per level, especially later in the war.

Smaller bunkers used a solid fuel stove. Normally only large bunkers had electrical lighting and this was with lights of 220 volts which first appeared in 1936. In 1938 some of these larger bunkers received small generators to provide power. Other types of lighting were used, such as kerosene lamps, and many bunkers had a niche to place them.

When possible, bunkers were linked by telephone lines to the group's command bunker. Several types of telephones were used. As early as 1935 bunkers included a wall-mounted fortress telephone model FS 35. It was largely replaced in 1938 with the FS 38. In 1936 the FTS 36, a desktop telephone for the bunker commander, was put into use and then replaced by the FTS 39. Many large bunkers built between 1934 and 1938 used voice tubes not much different from those used in the forts at the turn of the century.

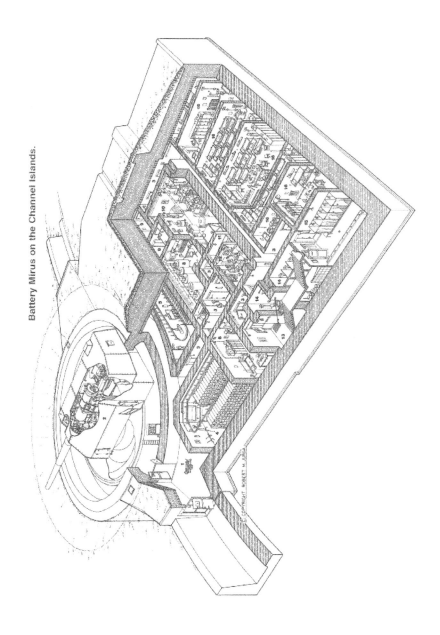

Battery Mirus on the Channel Islands.

Battery Mirus on the Channels Island
1.Entrance
2.305-mm K 14 (r) guns originally built for a Russian battleship
3.Corridor
4.Magazine for powder charges
5.Magazine for shells
6.Command Post
7.Magazine for fuses
8.Ventilator room
9.Fuel tank
10.Engine room
11.Fuel tank
12.Boiler room
13.Staircase
14.WC
15.Washroom
16.Crew quarters
17.Storage for electrical equipment
18.Officers quarters
19.Storage rooms

Other facilities were rather limited in the smaller bunkers. Ventilators were used for protection against gas. These were hand-operated, although some had their own electric motor. The main type used was the *Heeresdnheitsshutzlufter* (HES) or the Army Standard Protective Ventilator. It included a dual filter system which had to be replaced often. One of the filters simply removed dust from the air and was for normal use. The other filter was designed to protect against poison gas and was usually stored in a position where it could be quickly emplaced. The number of these units varied by the size of the bunker. There was normally at least one to cover the interior rooms and one per firing chamber. In the exposed face of the bunker there were usually two air intakes, which also came in distinctive models based on the year of production. The outside air was drawn in through a system of pipes leading to the ventilators. In addition to the filter system for gas protection, the larger bunkers were equipped with pumps that maintained an over pressure to prevent the infiltration of poison gas. This air pressure was controlled through a system of valves, but in gun rooms most embrasures could not be sealed and this system could not be used. Also, to make the anti-gas system effective all the interior doors had to be gasproof, so the Type 19P7 with airtight seals was used in many bunkers.

Latrine facilities were rather limited, but were found in certain bunkers. Some even had a urinal and a shower; metal and porcelain were used for these. Many bunkers only had a plain sink and the equivalent of a latrine bucket. A chemical portable toilet was also developed and found in many bunkers of the West Wall and Atlantic Wall although some facilities did include regular flush toilets. The portable toilets. were more like a large bucket with a lid that kept the smell inside. A can with dry earth or chemicals for covering the excrement was used with it. The bunkers that normally had these portable toilets included the squad shelters, command positions, and several types of machine gun, antitank, and antiaircraft bunkers. There were three types of special latrine bunkers with four to seven seats designed by Colonel Zimmermann of *Festungspionierkommandeur XVIII* for his sector of the Atlantic Wall. About a dozen examples can be found between the Orne River and the Netherlands in the Fifteenth Army sector. Regelbau-type hospital bunkers had regular toilets in them. Some type of water access was necessary for use in bunkers for decontamination. Larger bunkers had running water with wash troughs or basins for the troops. In some cases large bunkers had their own well and in other instances a group of bunkers would have a large water bunker to serve them.

The rooms of bunkers were rather spartan with few conveniences. Those bunkers with crew quarters included double and triple bunks for the troops. After 1936 many bunkers were equipped with metal attachments to which beds were attached suspended by chains that could be pulled up against the wall when not in use. Furniture included wooden cabinets and closets in the mid-1930s that were replaced later by metal ones, in which the troops put their personal gear. The kerosene lamps were placed in niches, hung from the ceiling, and sometimes placed on a table. Weapons racks were attached to the walls and simple tables and stools were provided for the troops. Of course, the larger the bunker the more it included; as was the case with many B- and A-types which sometimes included kitchens, latrines and many other features to make operations independent for extended periods.

When constructing bunkers the engineers had to be aware of the watertable as that determined whether it could be built into the ground or be more heavily exposed above the ground. The quality of the concrete also tended to vary late in the war as bringing in supplies became more difficult, and sometimes local aggregates had to be used which were below the standards required for the proper strength.

When completed all bunkers had to receive the proper camouflage. A number of those built in Norway and parts of Brittany were actually constructed in the rock and had natural camouflage, but this was not true for most bunkers. A good quality paint with subdued colors in brown, green, etc. were used and in some cases designs were included. During the war the Germans found that by attaching paper wads to the form boards as the concrete dried allowed for the creation of an irregular pock marked concrete surface which helped camouflage the position. Special camouflage nets were also used where needed. In those cases where the bunker was totally exposed it would be disguised as a building with painted windows, simulated wooden roof, etc. Nets would be used to conceal gun embrasures and were attached to rollers so that the net could quickly be pulled upward for firing the gun.

Each bunker was equipped with a tool kit for the crew. This included a spade, saws, hammers, wire cutters, and other items needed to maintain the site and adjacent field works. This was considered standard in the West Wall and probably most of the Atlantic Wall bunkers.

Some features that were used in various types of bunkers included the following:

19P7 *Gasture*—air tight gas doors for the interior of bunkers.

48P8 *Panzerscharte*—an armored embrasure with a sliding place to open and close it.

491P2 *Gittertür*—a grill-type gate used in outer entrances.

728P3 *Panzertür*—Armored door which had two halves— upper and lower—that could be opened separately.

The combat bunkers would be supported by field fortifications which might include machine guns placed on its flanks. For a gun bunker, these positions would be placed to the front. Communications trenches linked machine-gun bunkers with other positions in a strongpoint or resistance nest. These trenches were also camouflaged by using a chickenwire covering with various types of vegetation attached. Rifle trenches were also used in strongpoints and were linked to the communications trenches. The trench system included shelters which might be of concrete or wood.

Sources: *Jersey's German Bunkers,* by Michael Ginns, 1999. *Wyposazenie socjalne obiektow forty-fikacji niemieckiej 1933-1944* by Robert M. Jurga, 1999. *Toiletgerief in vestingwerken* by Hans Skakkers, 1999.

On the Other Fronts

Italy was a vital ally for Germany because it maintained most of the Mediterranean front while the Wehrmacht was heavily involved on the Eastern Front. The allocation of resources for defensive purposes in the West was also a drain on Germany. As the OT and RAD labored on the Atlantic defenses, only a minimum of German army divisions remained in the West. However, in mid-1943 the war unfolded far to the south while many of the Italian islands served as a buffer zone. Likewise in the eastern Mediterranean, Italian island positions protected the Greek coastline to some degree.

On July 13, when the Allies successfully invaded Sicily, Hitler finally became aware that his southern front was also threatened. He ordered the transfer of several panzer divisions to Italy, bringing to an end the Kursk offensive, despite the fact that it was about to achieve some limited success. Soon after this fateful decision, the Soviets launched a summer offensive along the German central and southern fronts in Russia, driving the Axis forces back to the Dnieper River by the end of November 1943. Reluctantly Hitler conceded that there was a need to create some type of permanent fortifications in the East.

As the Eastern Front teetered on the verge of collapse, Hitler's attention was diverted to Italy. Before the end of July, Mussolini had been arrested and his government had fallen. A more determined defense of Sicily with a greater commitment of German and Italian troops might have affected the outcome of the Allied invasion. However, the Germans had been duped by Operation Mincemeat, which involved the planting of a cadaver carrying false papers that indicated that the next target of the Allied forces would be Greece. The ploy worked so well that the 1st Panzer Division and other formations were sent to Greece and even Rommel and the staff of his Army Group B were dispatched to improve the defenses of Salonika before the Allies invaded Sicily. As a result, Sicily and the Italian Fascist government fell within a month. By September, the Italian armed forces were considered so unreliable that a number of German divisions were sent into the peninsula to bolster the defenses.

In June 1943, the Italian defenses were bolstered with the arrival of the OT whose original mission to keep the Brenner Pass open was quickly expanded to repairing damage to the Italian infrastructure. Soon the organization was directed to build fortifications in Italy in cooperation with the new Fascist government formed after the surrender of Italy in September 1943 and the rescue of Mussolini from his captors. Within a year the OT numbered six thousand Germans and over two hundred thousand Italians and foreigners working in Italy with the *Einsatzgruppe Italien* set up at Sirmione on Lake Garda in the north. Over a dozen *Oberbauleitungen* (construction commands) were eventually set up. During the next year, as the German organization grew, the Italian equivalent, *Organizzazione Paladino* (Paladino Organization), named after General Paladino, was formed. Dragon's teeth, numerous bunkers, concrete antitank walls, and antitank ditches were built along sections of the Adriatic coast. However, since the weather did not cooperate and in many cases materials were lacking, smaller positions were built. Many of the Regelbau used were of the VF 58 c type, an eight-sided Ringstand, and a few of the VF 61 a type, a Ringstand for a 50-mm fortress mortar. A ringstand for the French Renault FT 17 tank turret mounting a 37-mm gun was also used since a good number of these turrets were available. Regelbau Type 667, a small casemate for a 50-mm antitank gun, was also popular because of its simple design and small size. Type 677, a small casemate for 88-mm antitank guns, was built mainly for flanking fire.

One of the most useful positions, the portable *panzer nest,*

consisted of a four-ton portable steel machine-gun position which may have been inspired by similar designs used
by the Dutch before the war. This turret-like position was
prefabricated and hauled to the site where it was quickly
placed over a hole in the ground, obviating the need to
pour concrete. The turret could not actually rotate, but it
had all that was needed for its two occupants, including a
ventilator system run by foot power. When necessary, the
turret could be extracted and hauled to a new position.
When installed, its profile was very low. Many portable
panzer nests were employed in Italy and at the Eastern
Front where the Germans hurriedly set up a defense line
late in 1943. The Germans also built some coast artillery
casemates of the standard type on the coastline of northern Italy. These were among the largest concrete fortifications they created in the peninsula.

In September 1943 the Allied landings at Salerno, supported by smaller landings in the south near Taranto and
at Reggio Calabria on the toe of Italy, resulted in the immediate unconditional surrender of the Italian government.
Although the Italian divisions in the peninsula had to be
quickly disarmed and demobilized by the Germans, a few
Italian formations made up the nucleus for a Fascist-led
army reorganized by Mussolini in northern Italy several
months later. In fact, however, only German troops were
left to face the Allied invasion. Field Marshal Albert Kesselring commanded the *Oberkommando Slid (OB Sud),* responsible for the southern part of the peninsula. Field
Marshal Rommel, in command of Army Group B in the
northern part of the peninsula, suggested that the south
should be abandoned and a more solid defense setup in
the north. However, his ideas were rejected in October because they conflicted with Hitler's desire to hold on to the
whole peninsula. Rommel and his staff were dispatched to
inspect the Atlantic Wall and Army Group B was transferred to the West, leaving Kesselring in complete com-

mand of Italy. Kesselring was later appointed commander-in-chief southwest.

In 1943 Kesselring created defensive positions in central Italy which included the Viktor Line, the Barbara Line, and, behind them, the Gustav Line and the Hitler Line (later renamed the Senger Line). In October 1943 these lines consisted merely of field fortifications. The Gustav Line was intended to serve as the "Winter Line" and to hold the Allies as long as possible in the south. The mountainous terrain provided the defensive advantages that made up for the lack of concrete fortifications. The advanced lines allowed more time for the engineers to work on the Gustav Line.

According to W. G. F. Jackson, author of *The Battle for Italy,* who gives one of the few descriptions of the German fortification system in Italy, the Viktor Line served as a delaying position. It ran along the Volturno River then crossed the peninsula through the mountains, extending to the Adriatic just south of Termoli. It proved of little value. The Barbara Line, between the Volturno and Garigliano Rivers, was also a delaying position. It ran from Mondragone on the Tyrrhenian Sea tc Presenzano near the Volturno River, up the road leading through the most difficult part of the Apennines where it ended. The position was located five to eighteen kilometers in front of the Gustav Line. The Bernhardt Line, another advanced position located just in front of the Gustav Line, defended the approaches to the Liri Valley. The Gustav Line itself followed the Garigliano River from the coast, crossed the Liri Valley, passed through Monte Cassino along the course of the Rapido River, went over the highest sections of the Apennines past Alfedena, Roccarso, and Casoli, and followed the hills behind the Sangro River to the Adriatic Sea. The only relatively open terrain on this front was the Liri Valley near Cassino, but it was protected by the Rapido River which formed a natural obstacle, and it was heavily mined.

Only four roads passed through this position: one on each coast, one through the Liri Valley, and one through the most mountainous and easily defended section of the line. The Bernhardt or Rheinhardt Line occupied the terrain around the Mignano Pass and led to the Rapido River and Liri Valley. This was an easily defended position in front of the weakest part of the Gustav Line, used by the Germans almost as an extension of the Gustav Line since it was much stronger than the position along the Rapido in the Liri Valley. This line joined the Gustav Line near Sant'Ambrogio and continued south of Mignano, across the main road, Route 6, which was in a defile, to Monte Cesima, and then arched back, running northward parallel to the Volturno River, past Venafro, northward to Castel di Sangro where it rejoined the Gustav Line. General Hube, commander of the XIV Panzer Corps, was responsible for its defense. Since he received no aid from the army engineers, he was only able to build a number of strongpoints in depth with the material available to him. It took the Allies from October to early January to break the Bernhardt Line. Had more work been done on its defenses, it would have been even more difficult to breach. After breaking the Bernhardt Line, the American Fifth Army was able to direct its efforts at the Liri Valley and Cassino on the Gustav Line. By this time, workers from the OT had had over three months to prepare the positions on the Gustav Line.

As the OT also labored on the coast defenses, Kesselring realized that he would not be able to defend his vulnerable coastal flanks. During January 1944, when an Allied invasion force disembarked at Anzio, the Germans were taken completely by surprise simply because they could not effectively defend the Italian coastline. When the Gustav position was outflanked, the German divisions that manned it faced the threat of being cut off.

The Senger Line was also fortified during the month of December. Located only about ten kilometers behind the Gustav Line, it covered the Liri Valley, extending from Mount Cairo to St. Olivia, on Tyrrhenian Sea. It consisted of a number of strongpoints complete with obstacles, mines, and Ringstande, many of which mounted a Panther tank turret. At the time the Allies were landing at Anzio, work was still being done on these positions. If the Germans hadn't had enough time to rush in units from diverse locations to seal the bridgehead, the Gustav Line and associated positions would have been quickly turned and Rome would have fallen in short order. It was not until the Allied offensive of May 11, 1944, that the Gustav Line was finally broken and the entire front from Cassino southward virtually collapsed. German troops retrenched behind the Senger Line on May 18.

Kesselring soon realized that Rommel had been right in predicting that Allied air power would limit the ability of the Germans to depend upon mobile warfare to control the battlefield. Kesselring insisted that it was necessary to prepare a succession of defensive lines because no single line could be expected to hold out indefinitely. In his memoirs he wrote that "These fortification measures gave our strategy the greatest possible degree of freedom; it was nevertheless restricted by the air supremacy of the Allies . . ." Thus work began on other lines, including an expansion of the Senger Line across the mountains to the Tyrrhenian Sea, just east of Formia. However, although the plans were drawn, little work was actually done on this extension, called the Dora Line. When the Allies finally broke the Gustav Line in May 1944, the Dora position had few defenses.

Just a few kilometers from the Anzio beachhead was the Caesar Line or Line 'C', which extended across the peninsula. This defensive line was only in its initial stages of construction and far from completion when the Allied offensive began. It consisted mainly of field fortifications because resources had to be shared with the Senger Line, which was still being finished. The Caesar Line began between Anzio and the Tiber River, ran south of Albanoto to Valmontone, across the Apennines to Celano and Popoli, and then followed the Pescara River to the Adriatic and the coastal town of the same name. While working on these new lines, the Germans still had to contain the Anzio beachhead, and guard against any further amphibious landings on either side of the peninsula. The Caesar Line was the last defensive position before Rome. The Senger Line and its extension, the Dora Line, were penetrated after May 18 while the Allied forces at Anzio began their breakout, threatening the remainder of the German positions. The American forces coming out of Anzio were delayed on the Caesar Line for several days. At the end of May, the 36th American Division penetrated the Caesar Line about fifteen kilometers west of Valmonte, finally breaking it. Since Kesselring refused to occupy a switch line formed along the Tiber River from the sea to Tivoli because he did not want to bring the city of Rome into the battle line, the Germans began a massive withdrawal to the north.

The Germans tried to delay the Allied advance at the Viterbo Line, in front of the town of the same name. However, this position, which consisted of little more than field works and relied mainly on the terrain for defense, was quickly overrun. In June the Germans retreated behind the Trasimene Line, which also relied heavily on the terrain to impede the enemy advance. The Trasimene Line ran along the Orcia River, south of Lake Trasimene to the River Chienti and the Adriatic coast, south of Ancona. It fell by the end of June, but Kesselring's objective was only to gain time to prepare the defenses in the north. Next, German troops held the Arno Line, which ran from the city of Pisa along the Arno River across the Apennines to the Adriatic south of the coastal town of Pesaro. Like the preceding lines, the Arno Line relied only on the terrain and whatever field positions the troops could prepare in order to slow the Allied advance. During the month of July, the Germans worked on [44] Kesselring's Green Line in the Apennines, which eventually became known as the Gothic Line, and was to become his new Winter Line. The Allied invasion of Normandy convinced Kesselring that his flanks were safe from amphibious assault and no large airborne units would be available to the Allies in the south for several weeks. The OT was put to work on the new line before the advancing Allied armies could regroup and attempt a breakthrough.

The Gothic Line extended from south of the naval base at La Spezia, through the mountains north of the Arno River, to the sea south of Rimini. There was not enough time to build a heavily fortified line. The sections running through the Apennines along the ridges were formidable enough, but the coastal area near the Adriatic was not. Some positions for Panther turrets were setup. Several types of positions were available for deploying these turrets, but it is not clear how many were of the VF type—reinforced field works consisting of an excavated area with a wooden structure—and how many were on a concrete foundation.

---

[44] A number of bunkers were built on the Lido di Venezia, a strip of land that separates the Venetian Lagoon from the Adriatic Sea.

The Panther turrets evolved since they were first installed on the Hitler Line. At first they were regular Panther tank turrets, but later some turrets were specially produced with extra armor to resist heavy bombardment and were most certainly placed on concrete positions. Although some of the Panther bunkers appear to have been connected to an electrical power supply for light, the turrets were hand operated. Their low profile made them difficult targets since only the turret was above ground. They were effectively used in guarding enemy routes through defiles, roads and other possible lines of advance. Some bunkers mounted turrets from older French tanks, but they were less successful in stopping enemy armor.

At least one antitank wall that ran for about three to four kilometers and w~ about three meters high was built on the western part of the Gothic Line. Thi Germans only had time to prepare a few antitank ditches, dig trenches, lay wire obstacles, and create some small bunkers. On the eastern end of the line, some Regelbau bunkers that may have been originally part of the coast defenses were built near the shoreline.

The German Tenth and Fourteenth Armies retired behind the Gothic Line in August 1944. The Allied offensive against the line began late in August when the British Eighth Army's I Canadian Corps broke through the line near Pesaro on th; Adriatic coast. Despite the fact that the positions with Panther turrets inflictec heavy losses on the advancing tanks, the Commonwealth troops managed to breathrough. The American Fifth Army attacked on the other side of the line, eventually pushing the Germans back from their advanced position on the Arno River into the Gothic Line. In September, the Americans reached the Futa Pass; by mid-September, they had reached the II Gi-go Pass, north of Florence; and by the end of the month they penetrated the line and advanced deeper into the Apennines. By early October, the Gothic Line was smashed between Futa and the Adriatic. Only the heavy rains, mud, and flooded streams and rivers slowed the Allies's relent-less advance and gave the German frontline divisions a brief respite. As the Gothic Line broke under the onslaught of the British V Corps and the Canadian I Corps on the Adriatic sector and the Allies advanced on Rimini, Kesselr-ing prepared a final line of resistance that ran westward from Lake Comacchio along the Idice River south of Bolo-gna and into the Apennines. This final line before the Po Valley was named the Genghis Khan Line.

The Southeast Front

Winston Churchill defined the Mediterranean as the "soft underbelly," which appeared to be a contradiction since it is the most mountainous part of Europe and gave the de-fender most of the advantages. Because of the rough ter-rain, southern and southeastern Europe were the most likely theaters of a war of attrition in a major campaign. In fact, the Italian campaign became just that. In the strategic sense, however, Churchill was correct because an assault on Italy, even if it only yielded control of southern Italy, left the Balkans open to amphibious raids and air attacks and opened the French Mediterranean coast to an invasion. If Rommel's strategy of an immediate withdrawal to the northern part of the peninsula had been adopted, the situation in the Balkans may have quickly become untenable. The chance of any type of invasion of the Balkan coast was slim. Even Kesselring did not believe it possible without the conquest of Sicily, and possibly southern Italy first.

The Germans had committed a minimum of forces to the defense of the Balkans and the Aegean. The largest number of divisions assigned to the region were engaged in antiguerrilla operations against Tito's partisans in Yugoslavia. Army Group E, under General Lohr, absorbed the Twelfth Army and took control of Greece where it was responsible for coastal defense and dealing with Greek guerrillas. Army Group F, under General von Weichs, was formed in the summer of 1943 to control other units in the Balkans, including Army Group E , after its command was designated commander-in-chief southeast. The Second Army, under Army Group F, had four corps with fifteen divisions and four divisions of a Bulgarian corps in Yugoslavia and Albania to deal with the partisans. Army Group E had four corps with seven divisions (including one Bulgarian) and a two-division Bulgarian corps to occupy Greece and the Aegean Islands. In June 1943, when the Germans were tricked into believing that an invasion of Greece was imminenr the 1st Panzer Division was sent to the Balkans to take up position in the Peloponnesus; but after the invasion of Sicily it was dispatched to the Ukraine ir. August. When the surrender of Italy created a major void in September 1943, the Germans implemented Operation Konstantin to disarm Italian forces in the Balkans. When the Allies took Foggia with its huge air base in southern Italy on September 17, German units had to quickly secure the positions of the Italian units on the Dalmatian coast, prevent a major raid, and nip any show of support for the partisans from across the Adriatic. Partisan and German units alike raced to disarm the Italian garrisons. To make the situation worse, a large number of Italian troops joined the partisans in Yugoslavia and Albania. The port of Split, with it? vast amounts of supplies, was taken by the partisans and retaken by the Germans who succeeded in taking control of all the ports and population centers on the Adriatic coast by the end of October, but not before four thousand Italian soldiers of the Isonzo, Bergamo, and Zara Divisions in Dalmatia, Slovenia, and Croatia went over to the partisans. In Albania the Firenze Division defected to the enemy.

In Greece most Italian units surrendered to the Germans, but a few, including the Pinerolo Division and the Aosta Cavalry Regiment joined the guerrillas after thev were disarmed by the Greeks. On Cephalonia, where the Italians resisted the Germans, the commander and four thousand of his men were executed. The Germans quickly disarmed the Italians on Crete, but encountered some resistance on Rhodes. Some of the Italian units holding islands radioed the British for support. Thus the 5,400-man garrison of Leros was joined by over 3,200 British troops German forces attacked Leros and the Italian garrison on Samos, forcing their surrender by mid-November. The Germans were able to capture these defended, islands and incorporate them into their own defensive schemes because the Allies did not have naval, air, and land forces to spare to take full advantage of the situation. Hitler refused to abandon southern Greece or the Aegean Islands not only because he was reluctant to give up territory, but also because at the time an estimated 50 percent of Germany's oil, 60 percent of its bauxite, 100 percent of its chrome, 24 percent of its antimony, and 21 percent of its copper came from the Balkans. Thus every fortified island and the Greek coast had to be defended by order of the Fiihrer. Major campaigns against the guerrillas and partisans were aborted as preparations were made to defend the coast.

Hitler's Directive Number 40 of March 23, 1942, gave instructions on coastal defense, including the Balkans and Aegean under the jurisdiction of the OB Siidos: (Command of Armed Forces Southeast). Like the commanders of other regions OB Südost gave full local power to the generals commanding army divisions assigned to coastal defense. The only exception was Crete, which was designated a fortress and whose commander was to appoint his own subordinates. The Peloponnesus, Crete, and the Dodecanese Island, except Mytilene and Chios, were to be fortified. The Germans were responsible for fortifying the western part of Crete since they shared the occupation of the island with the Italians, who fortified the eastern third of Crete and the Dodecanese Islands with the assistance of the *Festungpionier* of *Kustenverteidigunsstab Sud* (Coast Defense Staff South). The coastal defenses of Crete were actually completed. On the Greek mainland, however, a number of small bunkers were built along the coastline and at some bases, but the coastline was not completely defended. The Aegean Islands acted as a partial shield against a major Allied invasion and that is probably why they received a higher priority. Only a few sectors of the Peloponnesus, selected positions on the Gulf of Corinth, the area around Athens, and parts of the islands of Salamis and on Euboea were fortified.

Sections of the Thracian coast and the Chalkidik peninsula that protected the port of Thessaloniki were defended. The Bulgarians, who were responsible for most of eastern Thracia, decided to build their defensive positions along the Rhodope Mountains for fear of being cut off on the coast by a large Allied airborne landing. When the Germans convinced them that the Allies would be discouraged by strong

coastal defenses, the Bulgarians resumed additional construction along the coast. By the spring of 1944, the Bulgarians had pulled back most of their troops from the
coast, leaving only eleven heavy batteries to cover over
three hundred kilometers of coast, claiming that they were
securing the routes through which reinforcements could
be sent to repel Allied landings.

With the capitulation of Italy, many Italian troops became
laborers for the German military. During 1944, the Ost
Battalions, consisting of Slavic men, were brought into the
Balkans to support German troops in security operations
since the regular divisions were needed to defend against
an Allied invasion. Many Italians who had been disarmed
and interned in 1943 were recruited to join the *Hilfswill-
lige (Hiwis),* the auxiliary labor unit of Eastern volunteers
or prisoners that worked on the coastal fortifications and
other defenses. Some joined the *Kampfwillige (Kawis),*
who were responsible for security. In 1944, there were
many desertions from the Ost Battalions and many discon-
tented members of other units had to be disarmed and im-
prisoned, placing further strain on German manpower resources.

Most of the fortifications built on the Greek mainland and
probably on the islands consisted of small bunkers and
Ringstande. Transportation and manpower were limited,
as was the availability of armor plate for the fortifications.
Cavern-type positions were popular not only because they
were easily concealed, but alsc because they required less
construction materials. They became particularly important in completing the defenses of the islands. The "Cre-
tian" construction method which was adopted to save on
materials, consisted of bunkers whose walls were made of
rubble covered with a thin layer of concrete. The aridity of
the climate on the Peloponnesus and Crete presented a
special problem, because the concrete dried too fast to be
properly cured. Special units had to maintain a constant

water supply for working with concrete, so the number of bunkers and positions in Greece was not as large as in the West. Despite the German's efforts, the Greek coast and islands could not be heavily fortified, as was demonstrated by a British commando assault that resulted in the capture of General Karl Kreipe, commander of the 22nd Airlanding Division on Crete in April 1943. The commandos passed right through the coastal defenses without being detected. Raids against other islands were equally successful. Greek guerrilla attacks on the Peloponnesus in May 1944 led to the death of the commander of the 41st Fortress Division, assaults on supply lines, and even armed vessels in the Greek harbors that were supposedly defended. Early in 1944, work on coastal positions was slowed on the Greek mainlanc because the troops needed for construction work were diverted to clearing partisans threatening vital regions and some units were sent to more critical fronts.

Notes from a February 1944 conference between Hitler and Donitz, commander in chief of the Kriegsmarine, reveal the seriousness of the situation in the Balkans. For instance, plans for a submarine base at Lemnos had to be abandoned because of inadequate transport, but plans for fortifying the island went ahead. Work on concrete construction for a submarine base at Salonika and Mudros had to be abandoned because it put too much stress on the transport available; instead plans were made to create underground galleries in Volos. In another meeting ir. May 1944, Hitler expressed concern about the possibility of an Allied operation against the Rhodes-Crete-Peloponnesus area and the adequacy of the defenses built until that time, especially in the Peloponnesus.

Late in June, General Lohr, commanding Army Group E, pulled back his bes: divisions leaving the fortress battalions to hold the coastal positions and placing the other mobile elements of other divisions in reserve. This did not bode well for the overall situation because many of the soldiers of the fortress battalions of the 41st Fortress Division were former military prisoners. Its battalions defended the coast of the Peloponnesus while the llth Luftwaffe Division was assigned tc defend Attica and Thessaly which it quickly lost to guerrillas. The coast of the mainland was thus weakly defended and depended on the 4th SS Panzer Grenadier Division, and the 104th and 117th Light Divisions to repel any invasion force. The situation was made even worse by the fact that the west coast of Greece, near the Albanian border, was held by twelve thousand men of the EDES guerrilla group of General Zervas. The British sent five thousand Greek reinforcements from units stationed in Egypt, forcing the Germans to commit the 104th Light Division and other reserve units to support the units on the beaches in a campaign against this enclave on the coast.

After Kesselring's Winter Line in central Italy collapsed and his forces withdrew northward in the summer of 1944, the position in Greece and the Aegean became precarious. It worsened when Romania began to waver and changed sides in August, and Bulgaria, which had never been at war with the Soviet Union, prepared to join the Allies when faced with a Soviet invasion in September. Tito's partisans and the Greek guerrillas left the German units in the Balkans virtually isolated and unable to continue resistance. Army Group E ordered the evacuation of its units from Greece at the end of August. The key islands of the Aegean were to be held. Over eleven thousand combat troops were flown out of Crete and Rhodes by order of General Lohr because he needed them to help support the withdrawal from the south. Another 26,500 troops were prevented from being extracted from these and other Aegean Islands by Allied air power and remained in their positions until the end of the war. As the last German troops departed Greece at the beginning of November, the British sent in an occupation force. Army Group F and the divisions of

Army Group E continued to extract themselves from Yugoslavia and take up new positions. The German troops remaining in the Balkans were of little use to the defense of the Reich after the summer of 1944.

The French Mediterranean Coast and the Riviera

After Operation Anton began (the occupation of Vichy France on November 11, 1942), the Germans began work on defenses in south France. The First Army sent three divisions from western France into neutral Vichy territory as a special two-division task force from OB West moved down the Rhone valley. The Italians sent in four divisions from their Fourth Army to occupy part of the Cote de Azur, the French Riviera, and also Corsica. The addition of a few seaports this late in the war was of little advantage. The French fleet at Toulon had been scuttled as German troops raced to reach the port on November 27 and attempted to seize the fleet. Only five submarines escaped while the two battle cruisers and a battleship were left sunk in the harbor. The German occupation force began organizing rudimentary defenses and relieving French troops from their duty at coastal batteries. They also disarmed all other Vichy troops by November 27. One heavy battery near Toulon with naval gun turrets was still intact. The OT set to work on construction of submarine pens at Marseilles in the spring of 1943. The task of controlling both the south and west coasts of France while maintaining observation of the Spanish border was too much for the First Army. In August 1943 the Nineteenth Army was formed to take control of southern France. The Allied invasion of Sicily made this move necessary since it opened the French Mediterranean coast to a future landing. During the next year OB West received Rommel's Army Group B which took control over the armies on the northern coast and construction of the Atlantic Wall from Brittany to the Netherlands. Army

Group G was formed in the spring to command the First Army on the Atlantic coast and the Nineteenth Army on the Mediterranean coast. With the surrender of Italy several months earlier, a number of Italian troops had become laborers in southern France while German units and the troops of Mussolini's new Fascist government in the north took control of the coastal batteries on the Italian Riviera up to La Spezia. Some additional Regelbau coastal artillery casemates were built on the Italian coast.

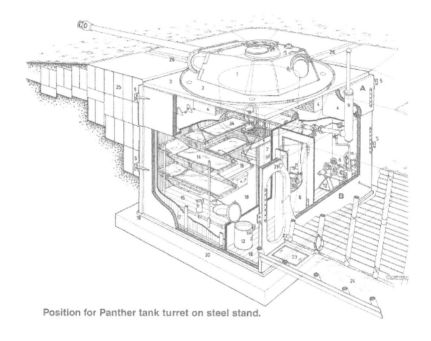

Position for Panther tank turret on steel stand.

1.Panther turret
2.Turret ring
3.Plate I
4.Ammunition
5.Cable
6.Armored door

7.Pressure door

8.Motor

9.Chimney 10. Heater

13.Toilet

14.Bunks

15.Folding table

22.Entry for power cables

24.Access trench

25.Concrete blocks

Serious work on the fortifications did not begin until the summer of 1943 at about the time the Nineteenth Army was created. By the summer of 1944 about five hundred concrete positions had been built on the French Mediterranean coast. These included about sixty single and double troop shelters of Regelbau 621, 656. 502, and 622, over seventy Regelbau 66 small six-man bunkers, about twenty munitions bunkers of various types, and eight command posts for field units (regiments or battalions). For coastal artillery less than fifteen command posts and fire-control bunkers were built. For defending the coast just over one hundred small Regelbau 670 and 671 casemates were built which had a central pivot for a gun along with sixteen larger naval M-272 gun casemates. A small number of various Regelbau for machine guns and antitank weapons were built. The largest number of antitank gun casemates included about ninety for 75-mm and 88-mm Pak, Regelbau 680, 677, and 703. Almost 120 Regelbau 612 casemates for assault guns were used. These accounted for most of the bunkers built, although there were a few other types which completed the total of about five hundred. In some places beach obstacles were placed, but nothing to the extent found in the north. Minefields were laid, but the coast was not heavily defended.

The heavy artillery batteries were mainly east of the Rhone, but a few were to the west of the river. In the vicinity of Sete there were several medium batteries and a heavy battery of 150-mm and 155-mm guns of a railway unit, Battery 611 E. Most of the batteries west of the Rhone were medium of about 105-mm caliber. East of the Rhone the area around Marseilles was well-protected, but mostly by medium batteries. The only heavy batteries included two of 220-mm guns and another of 240-mm guns which were French weapons. Actually over half the batteries of medium and heavy guns were French and Russian pieces. In the region of Toulon the situation was the same. The heaviest guns were two turrets of French twin 340-mm naval guns of Battery Cepet. The area around Nice was defended by only eight batteries of medium artillery.

The coast was divided into coast defense sectors, KVA. These began on the Spanish border with KVA A and extended to the Italian border with KVA G. West of the Rhone KVA C was the most heavily defended with Strongpoint Group Agde located around the town of Agde and occupying the cape of the same name and the bar leading to the port of Sete. At the opposite end of the bar was Sete with its own strongpoint group. In KVA D at the mouth of the Rhone was a strongpoint group of the same name. To the west of it was Strongpoint Group Port-de-Bouc and Strongpoint Group West Coast. In KVA E, Marseilles was designated as the *Verteidigungsbereich* of Marseilles. In KVA F was the *Verteidigungsbereich* of Toulon. From Toulon east into KVA G there were no other large groups of fortifications. This Mediterranean line of coastal defenses was known as the Süid Wall.

The Northern Front

In the far north, the Germans complemented their defenses with those of their ally Finland, which had joined the Axis reluctantly and attempted to extract itself from the war without success. After the Winter War of 1939-1940, the Finns lost their Mannerheim Line and most of the Karelian Isthmus to the Soviets and had to build a new defensive position to replace it. Work on the new defenses began in the summer of 1940 and consisted of several lines that were given the name of the Salpa Line—"The Lock of Finland"—by Marshal Mannerheim on July 10, 1944. These lines of defenses began on the coast and moved north into the lake region to Joensuu, where the line of concrete bunkers came to an end. Further north the defenses were lighter and combined with the natural features of the Finnish "wilderness."

In 1940 only about five thousand men worked on the Salpa Line, but that number had increased to thirty thousand by the spring of 1941. The second phase of construction began after the German invasion of the U.S.S.R. in June 1941 and lasted until September 1944. During this time the line was moved northward and expanded in the direction of Joensuu. Most of the work was done between the coast and Lake Saimaa. When the Salpa Line was completed, it numbered about three thousand positions, only 802 of which were of a permanent character. The permanent positions included 295 machine-gun positions and 254 "Ball" bunkers, a new type of bunker that was built by pouring concrete over a large rubber ball that served as a form. The resultant bunker had a spherical interior. In addition, there were fifty-two antitank gun positions and sixteen artillery positions. Some of the machine-gun bunkers included an observation cloche and an "L" type entrance similar to the Germans's. In general, the bunkers of the Salpa Line were smaller than those of the Mannerheim Line. The machine-gun bunkers were designed for flanking positions.

The field positions included forty-nine Russian tank turrets armed with machine guns, 1,250 covered machine-gun positions, 720 troop shelters, 500 artillery positions, and 400 observation positions. There were also a large number of wooden bunkers called *korsu*, which were more practical to build in areas where it was too arduous to haul heavy equipment and materials for mixing and pouring concrete. The Finns also built antitank obstacles consisting of large boulders placed in four rows covering two hundred kilometers. In addition fields of antitank and antipersonnel mines were laid in 1941, but they were removed during the summer. However, no mines were laid in 1944 because the engineer units were committed to the defense of the front lines.

The Germans were also involved in the defense of Finland because they needed to protect the valuable nickel mines at Petsamo. They created a defensive system to protect Petsamo and the approaches to occupied Norway. The troops of the 2nd and 3rd Mountain Divisions setup defensive positions along the Litsa front in the tundra of Lapland with picks and jackhammers. The German forces spent the remainder of the campaign protecting the mining operations at the Petsamo nickel mines and the Norwegian iron-ore mines near Kirkenes. The XIX Mountain Corps had five fortress battalions placed at five small Norwegian harbors flanking the Varanger Fjord, but beyond support of each other. The mountain troops established strongpoints in three lines along the Litsa River front. The defenses had to be placed on hilltops because the surrounding tundra offered little vegetation cover and turned into swamp when the frozen ground thawed down to the permafrost layer. The terrain was so difficult that it was not until the summer of 1944 that the concrete positions could be completed. The strongpoints consisted of standard concrete bunkers and were set up for all-around defense and spaced at intervals of two to five kilometers for a short distance south of the Litsa front. The spacing increased to fifteen kilometers or more up to the town of Ivalo. This heavily forested region was relatively isolated, and like the tundra region to the north presented many advantages to the defender.

The standard positions included bunkers for machine guns, mortars, antitank guns, shelters, observation, and command posts. They varied in size to accommodate units as large as reinforced companies or as small as platoons. The strong-points also included a trench system and were surrounded by obstacles, but the tundra made it difficult to maintain minefields. The second line was on the west bank of the Titovka River about ten kilometers to the rear with a third line abou: twenty or more kilometers back on the west side of the Petsamo River.

The second and third German lines were not fully occupied, but they were ready for use if the first line became untenable. Other strongpoints were built tc protect ore mines, ports, and airfields. The troops were housed in huts behind the line while a skeleton force maintained the forward line until attack was imminent. Hitler, consumed with the importance of the nickel mines, ordered all installations for the mines and processing plants to be placed either underground or in concrete bunkers as soon as possible. Some of the strongest flak defenses on the Eastern Front were established in this region and a full infantry regiment was charged with guarding the mines. In late 1943 plans were made for Operation Birke which involved the creation of a defensive bastion in the Far North if Finland should defect. Hitler was determined to protect the Petsamo mines and *Reichsstrasse 50,* a new road that constituted the direct supply line out of the Arctic area. When Finland finally signed an armistice in September 1944, the two German mountain corps south of the XIX Mountain Corps began to withdraw across Finland to the planned defensive positions as part of Operation Birke. The Soviets launched attacks and limited amphibious operations against the XIX Mountain Corps in October 1944. By October 13 they managed to push the Germans out of the fortified positions they had occupied since 1941 to Petsamo. By October 19 the Germans retreated to the Finnish

Arctic Ocean Highway, and by October 25 the 210th Division lost Kirkenes.

The Eastern Front

Hitler's solution for most defensive problems, which he had adopted during the first winter in Russia, was to hold to the last and declare a position a fortress. The precedent was set in February 1942 when Soviet offensive operations shattered the southern flank of Army Group North where it met Army Group Center. As ; result, six divisions were trapped in a large pocket around Demyansk in the Valda: Hills southwest of Lake Illmen. Another division was encircled at Kholm, which was then designated a fortress even though it contained no fortifications. The pocket at Demyansk was held and supplied by the Luftwaffe until a combat group from Starya Russa was able to break through and open a supply corridor, allowing the position to be held and reinforced for months. Part of the reason for the success of this operation was that further south on the Lovat River the "fortress" of Kholm continued to hold out until it was relieved and the front line was restored.

On November 20, 1942, Hitler had implemented the same policy when Velikie Luki, located in the area of operations of Army Group Center near the flank with Army Group North, was surrounded by Soviet troops. He forbade his troops from withdrawing and declared the position a fortress. As a result, the 277th Grenadier Regiment and several other units were trapped at Velikie Luki. The highest ranking officer was declared the fortress commander. At the end of November, the 8th Panzer Division from Army Group North attempted to break the Soviet ring, but Army Group Center, stretched to the limits, had no formations available to help. By December, the last one thousand men continued to resist, mainly using the town's structures as their fortifications. The fortress commander surrendered

in mid-January 1943, proving that Hitler's policy of cling-
ing to unfortified fortresses was destined to fail. However,
despite this resounding failure, Hitler continued to
implement this policy time and again. Excluding headquarters sites, no major fortifications were built on the
Russian front by the Germans between 1941 and the
summer of 1943. However, towns with permanent structures were frequently used as such.

In the summer of 1943, after the great battle of Kursk, the
situation became desperate for the Germans, whose resources were stretched to the breaking point. Although
some of his generals urged him to establish defensive positions that would allow them to shorten the front and build
up reserves, Hitler objected strenuously.

As the battle of Kursk drew to a close in mid-August, the
Second Panzer and Ninth Armies of Army Group Center
pulled out of the Orel salient to a position known as the
Hagen Line at the base of the salient. The withdrawal was
executed as slowly as possible to give civilian laborers time
to build field fortifications for the new position. However,
when a number of divisions were siphoned off and sent to
the Ukraine to bolster the defenses of Army Group South,
the commander of Army Group Center informed OKW
that the Hagen Line and the remainder of his front could
not be held much longer under the existing conditions. Finally, as the Eastern Front teetered on the verge of collapse, Hitler allowed his generals to create a fortified position to hold the front. It has been called the Eastern Ram-
part or East Wall, but New East Wall is a better term to
avoid confusion with the German border fortifications of
1939. In the sectors along the front of Army Group North
and Army Group Center this line was given the name of
the Panther Line.

Work on the Panther Line began in September 1943. The
construction force consisted of fifty thousand men, even
though the engineers had determined that at least seventy

thousand men were actually needed. According to some estimates, it would have taken about 400,000 men to do the work on all fronts. However, it is doubtful that the combined work forces available to all four army groups totaled more than 200,000. Despite the shortage of labor, three thousand to six thousand bunkers were built in the area of Army Group North. Most of these bunkers were made of logs instead of concrete and were small in size, but a number of them had turrets. However, it is not clear how many turrets were of the mobile type or old tank turrets. It is a fact, however, that a number of small mobile turrets were delivered to the army groups and installed. Many included their own internal heating units.

According to a secret report of Army Group Center dated August 27, 1943 Reconnaissance and Construction Groups I-IV were assigned ten to fifteen sections each, numbered 1-50. Each of these groups operated under one of the areas assigned to an army of Army Group Center. The OT was assigned the mission of preparing the sites, building concrete bunkers, and emplacing steel cloches. (It is not clear if any cloches were actually installed.) *Einsatz Wedekind* and *Einsatz Helfmann* were transferred from OT *Einsatzguppe Russland-Mitte* to *Ausbaugruppe III* under the Fourth Army which worked on sectors 26 to 36, spanning the area east of Mogilev, northward to the land bridge and the main east-west road. This area was considered the most critical on the front of Army Group Center, and needed to be fortified as strongly as possible.

According to a report of August 1943 from Army Group Center, some of the main focal points were the sectors where the roads or railroads ran in an east-west direction. *Ausbaugruppe* II (Construction Group II) was ordered to setup the Gomel Bridgehead. *Ausbaugruppen* III and IV were responsible for creating the defenses of the land bridge between the Dnieper and Dvina (Düna) Rivers. *Ausbaugruppen* I and IV had the responsibility of securing the links between Army Group North and Army Group South. The sections with the focal points were to have antitank and anti-infantry defenses by November 1, 1943. The defenses included barbed wire, trenches, antitank ditches, and other types of antitank obstacles. Double apron wire seems to have been favored in the Army Group North sector. The Panther Line was to consist mainly of field works with strongpoints at key locations, which were to include individual concrete bunkers and reinforced concrete Ringstande.

Sichelschnitt

The World War II German invasion plan of 1940 (*Sichelschnitt*) was designed to deal with the line. A decoy force sat opposite the line while a second Army Group cut through the Low Countries of Belgium and the Netherlands, as well as through the Ardennes Forest, which lay north of the main French defences. Thus the Germans were able to avoid a direct assault on the Maginot Line by violating the neutrality of Belgium, Luxembourg and the Netherlands. Attacking on 10 May, German forces were well into France within five days and they continued to advance until 24 May, when they stopped near Dunkirk.

During the advance to the English Channel, the Germans overran France's border defence with Belgium and several Maginot Forts in the Maubeuge area, whilst the Luftwaffe simply flew over it. On 19 May, the German 16th Army successfully captured the isolated petit ouvrage La Ferté (southeast of Sedan) after conducting a deliberate assault by combat engineers backed up by heavy artillery. The entire French crew of 107 soldiers was killed during the action. On 14 June 1940, the day Paris fell, the German 1st Army went over to the offensive in "Operation Tiger" and attacked the Maginot Line between St. Avold and Saarbrücken. The Germans then broke through the fortification line as defending French forces retreated southward. In the following days, infantry divisions of the 1st Army attacked fortifications on each side of the penetration; successfully capturing four petits ouvrages. The 1st Army also conducted two attacks against the Maginot Line further to the east in northern Alsace. One attack successfully broke through a weak section of the line in the Vosges Mountains, but a second attack was stopped by the French defenders near Wissembourg. On 15 June, infantry divisions of the German 7th Army attacked across the Rhine River in Operation "Small Bear", penetrating the defences deep and capturing the cities of Colmar and Strasbourg.

By early June the German forces had cut off the line from the rest of France and the French government was making overtures for an armistice, which was signed on 22 June in Compiègne. As the line was surrounded, the German Army attacked a few ouvrages from the rear, but were unsuccessful in capturing any significant fortifications. The main fortifications of the line were still mostly intact, a number of commanders were prepared to hold out, and the Italian advance had been successfully contained. Nevertheless, Maxime Weygand signed the surrender instrument and the army was ordered out of their fortifications, to be taken to POW camps.

When the Allied forces invaded in June 1944, the line, now held by German defenders, was again largely bypassed; fighting touched only portions of the fortifications near Metz and in northern Alsace towards the end of 1944. During the German offensive "Operation Nordwind" in January 1945, Maginot Line casemates and fortifications were utilized by Allied forces, especially in the region of Hatten-Rittershoffen, and some German units had been supplemented with flamethrower tanks in anticipation of this possibility.

Campaigns

Operation Fall Weiss September 1 1939

In Operation 'White', Hitler commits the German Army and Luftwaffe to the invasion of Poland. When two Army Groups, North and South, strike concentrically at a weak opponent - mostly infantry divisions deployed within fifty miles of the frontier, Polish forces are encircled and within seventeen days the campaign is virtually at an end. Warsaw, unsuited to armoured attack, continues to resist until 27 September. German double encirclement strategy and previous experience gained from Condor Legion operations in Spain prove decisive.

Hoth and Hoepner (Third and Fourth Panzer Armies) 1 September 1939. The main weight of Panzer assault lies with the three motorized corps, XIV, XV and XVI, spearheading German Tenth Army (von Reichenau).

Von Kleist and Guderian (First and Second Panzer Armies) 1 September 1939, also deployed in conjunction with infantry armies, operate on the wings of the offensive.

Operations are led by six panzer divisions, including a 'mixed' division (Kempf), four light divisions, and four motorized divisions. Included in the invasion force are SS Regiments: Adolf Hitler (SSLAH), Deutschland and Germania.

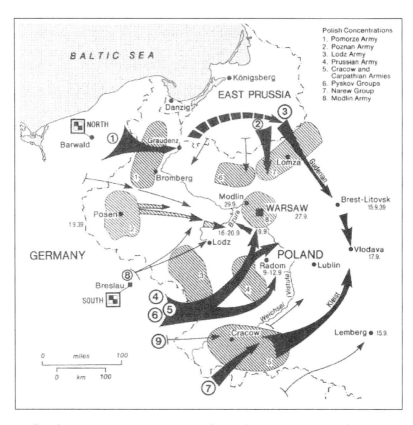

Guderian (1) XIX MotK: 2nd, 20th MotDivs; 3rd PzDiv

Kempf (2) PzDiv Kempf: 7th PzRegt, SS Regt Deutsch-land, etc.

Guderian (3) Redeployed XIX MotK: After 7 September includes 10th PzDiv

Von Wietersheim (4) XIV MotK: 1st LtDiv, 13th, 29th MotDivs; and later 5th Pz Div

Hoepner (5) XVI MotK: 1st, 4th PzDivs; two InfDivs

Hoth (6) XV MotK: 2nd, 3rd LtDivs; 25th PzRegt

Von Kleist (7) XXII MotK: 2nd PzDiv; 4th LtDiv

(8) **(Eighth Army)** XIII AK includes SS Regt Leibstandarte Adolf Hitler before transfer to Tenth Army

(9) **(Fourteenth Army)** VIII AK includes SS Regt Ger-

mania

A Gr North/South von Bock/von Runstedt; 37 infantry, three mountain, fifteen mobile divs, 3,195 tanks

Polish Army 38 infantry divisions, eleven cavalry, two motorized brigades, 600-700 light tanks (500 battle-fit)

Luftwaffe Kesselring 1st Air Fleet-A Gr North; Lohr 4th Air

Fleet-A Gr South, 1,550 aircraft

Polish Air Force 750 aircraft (500 battle-fit)

Operation Fall Gelb May 10 1940

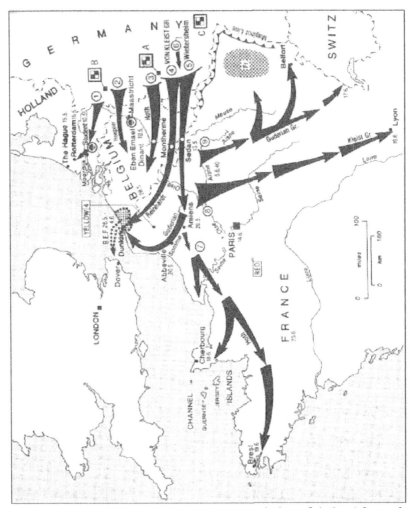

In Operation 'Yellow', Army Groups 'A' and 'B' with Luft-waffe support, smash across the Meuse and in ten days outmanoeuvre the Western Allies whose armies, including a British Expeditionary Force of nine divisions, serve a French commander-in-chief - General Gamelin, replaced 19 May 1940 by General Weygand.

Schmidt and Hoepner (Fourth Panzer Army) 10 May with

two panzer corps (1) and (2) allotted to Army Group 'B', lead a decoy offensive into Holland and Belgium where airborne operations under General Kurt Student aim to reduce key defences astride the Army Group axis of advance. Von Kleist and subordinate Guderian (First and Second Panzer Armies) 13 May attack west across the Meuse at Sedan-Montherme (4), (5), (6) initiating the main armoured movement of Operation 'Yellow' - a westward thrust by two panzer and one motorized infantry corps under Panzer Croup von Kleist (K) - the vanguard of Army Croup 'A'. See also Panzer break-through, France.

Von Kleist leads German Twelfth Army (List), but under pressure from superior headquarters, limits subordinates to a narrow range of action. Despite this, the panzer group pushes ahead until Hitler's nervousness at the danger to the resulting panzer 'corridor' and technical considerations finally halts the armour.

Hoth (Third Panzer Army) 13 May starting from a Meuse crossing at Dinant - (3) - also strikes west, reinforcing von Kleist.

A total of ten panzer divisions, six and two-thirds motorized infantry divisions support Army Groups 'A' and 'B'. The panzer force is swiftly regrouped for phase two of the battle - Operation 'Red'* commencing 5 June 1940.

Schmidt (1) XXXIX PzK: 9th PzDiv; SS Verfugungs Div; After 13 May LSSAH

Hoepner(2) XVI PzK: 3rd, 4th PzDivs; 20th InfDivMot; SS Totenkopf

Hoth (3) XV PzK: 5th PzDiv; 7th PzDiv

(K) Reinhardt (4) XXXXI PzK: 6th PzDiv; 8th PzDiv

(K) Guderian (5) XIX PzK: 1st PzDiv; 2nd PzDiv; 10th PzDiv; Inf Regt Mot-Gross Deutschland

(K) Von Wietersheim (6) XIV MotK: 2nd, 13th, 29th InfDivs Mot

***Hoth** (7) XV PzK: 5th, 7th PzDivs; 2nd InfDiv Mot

"Von Kleist Gr (8) XIV PzK von Wietersheim: 9th, 10th

PzDivs; 13th Inf Div Mot, SS Verfugungs Div, InfReg Mot-Gross Deutschland. After 12 June SS Totenkopf Div XVI PzK Hoepner: 3rd, 4th PzDivs; Reserve LSSAH

*__Guderian Gr__ (9) XXXIX PzK Schmidt: 1st, 2nd PzDivs; 29th InfDiv Mot XXXXI PzK Reinhardt: 6th, 8th PzDivs; 20th InfDiv Mot

German Army Von Brauchitsch: 120 infantry divs, 16% mobile divs, 2,574 tanks

A Grs 'A', 'B' Von Runstedt 45 1/3 divisions; von Bock 29Vi divisions

Luftwaffe Kesselring 2nd Air Fleet-A Gr 'B'; Sperrle 3rd Air Fleet-A Gr 'A': 2,750 aircraft

Western Allies Gamelin; 10 Dutch, 22 Belgian, 9 British (plus 1 Inf Tank Bde), 77 French infantry divs, 6 (Fr) mobile divs, 3,600 tanks

Allied Air Forces 2,372 aircraft ind 1,151 fighters.

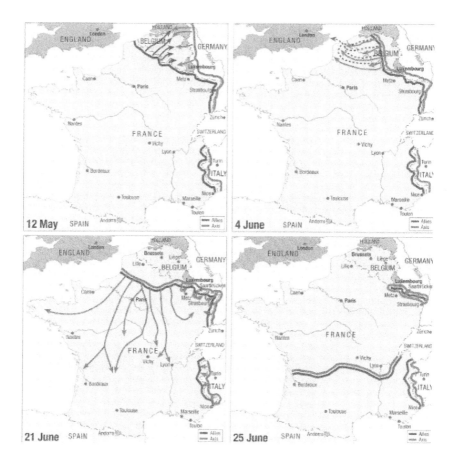

Panzer break-through: France, 1940

Striking west across the Meuse at Sedan and Montherme, Panzer Group von Kleist (K) - two panzer and a motorized corps - is responsible for the main armoured movement of Operation 'Yellow'. Weak opposition is concentrated in French Second and Ninth Armies deployed along the west bank of the river.

Orders issued to the leading divisions, especially 1st Panzer Division at Sedan, illustrate the high level of air support required to give effect to *Blitzkrieg;* Panzer Group von Kleist (First Panzer Army) leads the offensive commencing 0530 hours 10 May 1940, when five panzer, three and a half motorized divisions strike through the Ardennes to the east bank of the Meuse, ready to smash all opposition and establish a west bank bridgehead.

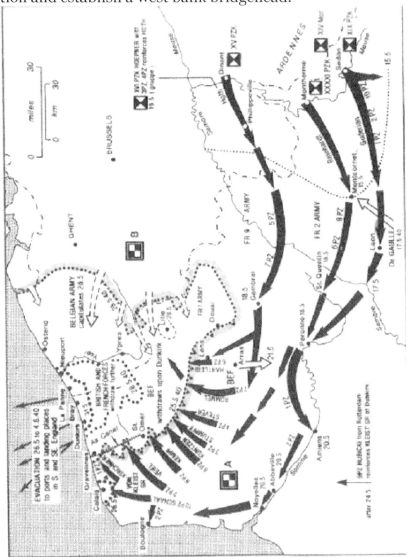

Guderian (Second Panzer Army) 13 May 1940. Arriving at

Sedan with *three panzer divisions* XIX Panzer Corps leads von Kleist across the Meuse in mid-afternoon; timed for 1600 hours, the assault is initiated by panzer grenadier/ engineer battle groups of 1st Panzer Division. Simultaneously downstream at Montherme, Reinhardt's XXXXI Panzer Corps, attacking westwards with *two panzer divisions,* also secured a foothold on the west bank, while von Wietersheim's XIV Motorized Corps waits in reserve to follow through when called.

Hoth (Third Panzer Army) 13 May precedes the main effort by von Kleist at Sedan with XV Panzer Corps providing flank protection at Dinant. Hoth wins a Meuse crossing with *two panzer divisions* on the morning of the same day and prepares to drive west; Rommel (7th Panzer Division) in the lead.

Hoepner (Fourth Panzer Army) 19 May. XVI Panzer Corps redeployed from Army Group 'B' with *two panzer divisions* joins Hoth to form a Gruppe reinforcing the main armoured effort. N.B. On 24 May, *9th Panzer Division* joins Kleistgruppe from Rotterdam.

Allied counter-attacks - 17 May. A French armoured contingent under General de Gaulle pushes north-east from Laon. On the 21st, a scratch British armoured force led by General le Q. Mattel strikes south around Arras. These attacks create concern in higher German headquarters, but do little to stem the tide of armour which on reaching the coast at Abbeville 20 May, swings north-west and by the 24th, co-operating with Army Group 'B' closing on Ypres, is shepherding the BEF and other Allied troops into a coastal pocket around Dunkirk.

But Hitler's nervousness puts a brake on operations; the thought of danger to an over-extended panzer force operating in unsuitable terrain and the need to conserve armour for the next phase of the offensive-Operation 'Red' - is enough to halt armoured progress at the Aa canal. Slow-moving infantry catch up in forced marches while the

Luftwaffe unsuccessfully attempts to finish off defenders besieged in Dunkirk. 330,000 British and French troops evacuated from Dunkirk port and beaches by an armada of small ships, escape to England in Operation 'Dynamo'.

Conflict in the Balkans, 1941

In the aftermath of victory over Western Allies in May 1940 (map 3), a prime German concern is to safeguard Roumanian oil supplies and deter Turkish intervention in the Balkans. The German Army and Luftwaffe are consequently filtered as 'training' units into friendly Roumania and Bulgaria. But Hitler is faced with an unexpected military situation when Axis partner Mussolini, invading Greece from Albania (28 October 1940), fails against the Greek Army and a British expeditionary force lands in Greece in November.

Instructing German Twelfth Army (List) to invade Greece ('Marita') and eliminate opposition to the Italians in Albania ('Alpine Violet'), Hitler also thereby expects to counter British intervention in the region. But anti-German moves in Yugoslavia complicate the issue and Hitler deploys German Second Army (von Weichs) in Austria and Hungary for Operation '25' - the subjugation of Yugoslavia - in which Twelfth Army, invading the southern part of the country, will also participate.

Kleistgruppe (First Pz-Army) 8 April 1941 joins the German offensive. Striking at largely immobile opponents, military operations are concluded in twenty days. The British Expeditionary Force, including a tank brigade deployed in northern Greece, is outmanoeuvred by XXXX PzKorps and withdraws south - escaping mainly to Crete; 5th Panzer reaches Kalamata 28 April 1941.

The Luftwaffe then takes control of the offensive, improvising Operation 'Mercury' at short notice. Enlarging upon the paratroop and glider assault tactics that had taken the west by surprise in May 1940, XI Air Corps (Student) with the assistance of 5th Mountain Division (Ringel) and a panzer detachment, landed late in the campaign, captures the island in twelve days; VIII Air Corps (von Richthofen) in support.

Six panzer divisions, three and two-thirds motorized divisions including SS Das Reich and LSSAH lead the Balkans offensive.

Kuebler (1) XXXXIX Mtn K; LI AK six infantry inc. 1st MtnDiv

Vietinghoff (2)XXXXVI PzK: 8th, 14th PzDivs; 16th InfDiv Mot

Von Kleistgruppe (3) Von Wietersheim XIV PzK: 5th, llth PzDivs; 60th InfDiv Mot; Reinhardt XXXXI PzK: SS Das Reich Div, Regt Gross Deutschland, Regt General Goering XI AK: 294th InfDiv, 4th MtnDiv

Stumme (4) XXXX PzK: 9th PzDiv; SS InfBde Mot Leibstandarte AH and after 12 April, 5th PzDiv

Boehme(5) XVIII AK: 2nd PzDiv; 5th MtnDiv; 6th MtnDiv; XXX AK: three InfDivs

OKH uncommitted Reserve: 4th, 12th, 19th PzDivs, three InfDivs. Twelfth Army reserve, 16th PzDiv (frontier security Bulgaria-Turkey)

German Second, Twelfth Army von Brauchitsch: 23 Infantry, 9 2/3 mobile divisions, 1,200 tanks

Luftwaffe Lohr 4th Air Fleet, 800 Aircraft (400 Stukas, 210 fighters)

Yugoslav Army/YAF 28 inf divs, three cav divs, 400 aircraft

Greek Army/GAF 20 inf divs, one motorized division. 80 aircraft

BritExp. Force Greece: 1 Tank Bde, 2-3 inf (Brit. NZ, Aust) divisions, Crete: 2-3 inf (Brit. NZ, Aust, Greek) divisions. No air support

Italian Ninth, Eleventh Armies in Albania: 38 divs (two armd) 320 aircraft.

'Mercury' Student XI Air Corps: 1st Para Div, 1st Assault (glider) Regt, 5th Mtn Div; part 5/31st Pz Regt landed 29 March 1941. 530 Ju 52 transports. Von **Richthofen VIII Air Corps** 150 Stukas, 180 fighters, 320 other aircraft.

Operation Barbarossa June 1941

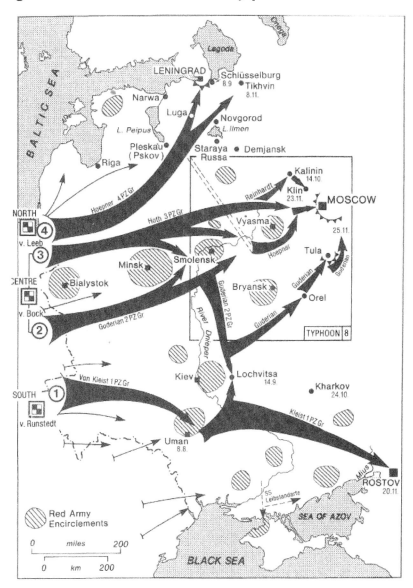

In Operation 'Barbarossa', Army Groups North, Centre and South with powerful Luftwaffe support strike in three directions: Leningrad, Moscow and Kiev-Rostov.

Encirclements of the Red Army are a triumphant feature of the early days, but military operations fanning out over a vast and often trackless interior are soon brought to a standstill. Halted by difficult terrain, bad weather, inadequate supplies and exhausted by an unyielding defence, the panzer divisions after capturing Kiev are driven to unrewarding battles for Leningrad and Moscow.

Hoepner (Fourth Pz-Army) 22 June leads Army Group North (von Leeb) to Leningrad. Guderian and Hoth (Second and Third Pz-Armies) 22 June responsible for the main German effort, lead Army Group Centre (von Bock) in the Moscow direction. Von Kleist (First Pz Army) 22 June leads Army Group South (von Runstedt) to Kiev and Rostov.

The outstanding panzer success of the early weeks is an envelopment of five Russian armies east of Kiev resulting in 600,000 prisoners for which von Kleist and Guderian are responsible. In the course of a subsequent operation, 'Typhoon' 2 October 1941, convergent action by Guderian, Reinhardt and Hoepner encircling Bryansk and Vyasma proves equally rewarding.

Seventeen panzer divisions, thirteen and a half motorized divisions lead 'Barbarossa' - but despite optimistic predictions of a three-week campaign, operations are destined to last four years. Expanded and re-equipped, in later campaigns the panzer force will nevertheless fail to match Russian numbers or strategy. Divisions are switched between theatres, fronts, and controlling corps. Four years later on the Central Front in January 1945, when the Red Army pushes across the Vistula, only four panzer divisions supporting indifferently equipped infantry divisions face 163 Russian divisions. At the conclusion of hostilities the panzer force is totally burned out and only weak battle groups remain at the Army's disposal.

Hoepner (4) PzGr 4: XXXXI PzK Reinhardt, LVI von

Manstein: three PzDivs 1st, 6th, 8th: three MotDivs 3rd, 36th and SS Totenkopf (later trapped with SS 'Polizei', 'Danemark' and others at Demjansk).

Hoth (3) PzGrS: XXXIX PzK Schmidt, LVII PzK Kuntzen: four PzDivs 7th, 12th, 19th, 20th: three MotDivs 14th, 18th, 20th: No SS formations

Guderian (2) PzGr 2: XXIV PzK Geyr, XXXXVI PzK Vietinghoff XXXXVII PzK Lemelsen, five PzDivs 3rd, 4th, 10th, 17th, 18th: 3 1/2 Mot Divs 10th, 29th, SS Das Reich (later switched to Hoepner for attack on Moscow) and Regiment 'Gross Deutschland'

Von Kleist (1) PzGr 1: III PzK von Mackensen; XIV PzK von Wietersheim; XXXXVIII PzK Kempf; five PzDivs 9th, 11th, 13th, 14th, 16th; four MotDivs 16th, 25th, SS 'Wiking', SS (Brigade) 'Leibstandarte' AH, Regt Gen Goering. OKH Reserve 2nd, 5th PzDivs: 60th MotDiv

German Army von Brauchitsch 153 divisions (seventeen Pz, + two reserve, 134 mot divs) 3,417 tanks

Luftwaffe Keller, 1st Air Fleet; I Air Corps/A Gr North; Kesselring 2 Air Fleet, II, VIII Air Corps/A Gr Centre; Lohr 4th Air Fleet, IV, V Air Corps/A Gr South; - 3,800 aircraft

Red Army/Air Force 150-180 divs, 20,000 tanks, but only 1,000 T34s and 500 KVs, 10,000 aircraft (2,750 modem types).

Citadel 1943

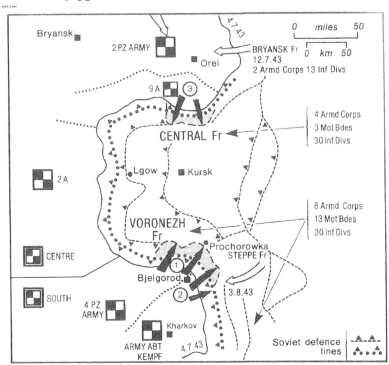

After suffering two disastrous winters in the east, a revitalized panzer force enjoying new weapons and equipment - Tigers, Panthers and Ferdinands - is assembled on sectors north and south of a huge and strongly defended Red Army salient centred on Kursk. Operation 'Citadel' involving Army Croups Centre and South will strike concentrically to eliminate the salient.

Hoth Fourth Pz-Army 5 July 1943 responsible to Army Group South will carry the main weight of the offensive; SS PzKorps (Hausser) providing the cutting edge; Army Abteilung (AA) Kempf in support.

Model Ninth Army responsible to Army Group Centre will co-operate in attacks from the north. But 'Citadel' is not a success.

Losing more than half its armoured strength, 'Citadel' fails to break the deeply echeloned Russian defence and after seven days' fighting when the offensive coincides with 'Husky', the Allied invasion of Sicily, Hitler calls it off. (Panzer Action in Italy, page 201.)

Critically drained of resources, the German Army will never recover the strategic initiative. Fourth Pz-Army, failing to reach Kursk and link up with Ninth Army, is shattered in the attempt; the decimated panzer divisions lose their power and German domination of European Russia is permanently broken.

Twenty panzer/panzer grenadier divisions (including OKH reserve) plus infantry and Army troops assemble for 'Citadel' led by Hoth and Kempf (Army Group South) and Model (Army Group Centre).

Hoth (1) Fourth Pz-Army, II SS PzK Hausser: 1st SS PzDiv, 2nd SS PzDiv, 3 SS PzDiv: XXXXVIII PzK von Knobelsdorff; 3rd, llth PzDivs, Gross Deutschland, 167th Inf Div, 10 Pz (Panther) Bde Decker, III AK Ott, two Inf divs.

Kempf (2) Army Abteilung, 111 PzK Breith: 6th, 7th, 19th PzDivs, 168 Inf Div, 503 (Tiger) Bn; XI AK Raus, three Inf divs: XXXXII AK three Inf divs.

Model (3) Ninth Army, XXXXVII PzK Lemelsen: 2nd, 4th, 9th, 20th PzDivs, 505 Hvy (Tiger) PzBn, 6th Inf Div, XXXXI PzK Harpe: 18th PzDiv, 10th PzGrDiv, 653, 654 Pzjaeger (Ferdinand) Bns; XXXXVI PzK Zorn: Five infantry divisions and Gruppe von Manteuffel: XX and XXIII AK with seven infantry divs.

A Gr South Reserve (uncommitted) XXIV PzK Nehring: 5th SS 'Wiking', 17th PzDiv.

OKH/A Gr Centre Reserve 5th PzDiv (OKH) switched to Second Pz-Army, 12th PzDiv, 36th I.D. Mot.

A Gr Centre Von Kluge; 21 divs inc 6 PzDivs, 2 Pzgr, 700-800 tanks (45 Tigers), 350 assault guns.

A Gr South Von Manstein; 22 divs inc 11 PzDivs, 1 Pz bde, 1,300 tanks (101 Tigers), 250 assault guns. (Total 2,700 tanks/assault guns, inc. 146 Tigers).

Luftwaffe (1) (2) Dessloch, 4th Air Fleet, Seidemann VIII Air Corps - 1st, 4th Air Divs. 1,100 airc. © Greim, 6th Air Fleet, Deichmann 1 Air Corps - 700 aircraft (Total 1,800 aircraft).

Red Army/Air Force Rokossovsky Central Fr; Vatutin Voronezh Fr; Konev Steppe Fr (from 18 July). 100 divs inc five tank armies, 3,306 tanks and assault guns, 2,650 aircraft.

Bibliography

Allcorn, William. *The Maginot Line 1928–45*. Oxford: Osprey Publishing, 2003. ISBN 1-84176-646-1

Kaufmann, J.E. and Kaufmann, H.W. *Fortress France: The Maginot Line and French Defenses in World War II*, Stackpole Books, 2006. ISBN 0-275-98345-5

Kaufmann, J.E., Kaufmann, H.W., Jancovič-Potočnik, A. and Lang, P. *The Maginot Line: History and Guide*, Pen and Sword, 2011. ISBN 978-1-84884-068-3

Mary, Jean-Yves; Hohnadel, Alain; Sicard, Jacques. *Hommes et Ouvrages de la Ligne Maginot, Tome 1*. Paris, Histoire & Collections, 2001. ISBN 2-908182-88-2 (French)

Mary, Jean-Yves; Hohnadel, Alain; Sicard, Jacques. *Hommes et Ouvrages de la Ligne Maginot, Tome 2*. Paris, Histoire & Collections, 2003. ISBN 2-908182-97-1 (French)

Mary, Jean-Yves; Hohnadel, Alain; Sicard, Jacques. *Hommes et Ouvrages de la Ligne Maginot, Tome 3*. Paris, Histoire & Collections, 2003. ISBN 2-913903-88-6 (French)

Mary, Jean-Yves; Hohnadel, Alain; Sicard, Jacques. *Hommes et Ouvrages de la Ligne Maginot, Tome 4 – La fortification alpine*. Paris, Histoire & Collections, 2009. ISBN 978-2-915239-46-1 (French)

Mary, Jean-Yves; Hohnadel, Alain; Sicard, Jacques. *Hommes et Ouvrages de la Ligne Maginot, Tome 5*. Paris, Histoire & Collections, 2009. ISBN 978-2-35250-127-5 (French)

Romanych, Marc; Rupp, Martin. *Maginot Line 1940: Battles on the French Frontier*. Oxford: Osprey Publishing, 2010. ISBN 1-84176-646-1

Mary, Jean-Yves; Hohnadel, Alain; Sicard, Jacques. *Hommes et Ouvrages de la Ligne Maginot, Tome 2*. Paris, Histoire & Collections, 2001. ISBN 2-908182-97-1

Julian Jackson, *The Fall of France: The Nazi Invasion of 1940* (New York: Oxford University Press, 2003), p.30.

Karl-Heinz Frieser, *Blitzkrieg-Legende*, p. 81

Diary (1946) Vol. 2, 9 September 1942: *La Vittoria trova cento padri, e nessuno vuole riconoscere l'insuccesso*

Karl-Heinz Frieser, *Blitzkrieg-Legende* p. 92

Franz Halder, *Hitler als Feldherr*, 1949, p.28

Maurice Vaïsse e.a., *Mai-juin 1940, Défaite française, Victoire allemande - Sous l'oeil des historiens étrangers* Autrement - Mémoires 2000

Alexander, Martin. *After Dunkirk: The French Army's Performance Against 'Case Red', 25 May to 25 June 1940*. War in History, Volume 14, pp. 219–264

Belgium, Ministère des Affaires Étrangères. *Belgium: The Official Account of What Happened 1939–1940*. London : Published for the Belgian Ministry of Foreign Affairs by Evans Brothers, Limited, 1941. Library of Congress Control Number 42016037

Belgian American Educational Foundation. *The Belgian Campaign and the Surrender of the Belgian Army, 10–28 May 1940*, Third edition. Belgian American educational foundation, 1941, University of Michigan.

Blatt (editor), Joel (1998). *The French Defeat of 1940: Reassessments*. Breghahn Books. ISBN -57181-109-5.

Bond, Brian (1990). *Britain, France and Belgium, 1939–1940*. London: Brassy's. ISBN 0-08-037700-9.

Buckley, John (1998). *Air Power in the Age of Total War*. UCL Press. ISBN 1-85728-589-1.

Chappel, Mike. *The Canadian Army at War*. Men at Arms. Osprey, Oxford. 1985. ISBN 978-0-85045-600-4

Citino, Robert Michael. *The Path to Blitzkrieg: Doctrine and Training in the German Army, 1920–1939*. Boulder: Lynne Rienner Publishers. 1999. ISBN 1-55587-714-1.

Citino, Robert M. *The German Way of War: From the Thirty Years' War to the Third Reich*. Lawrence: University Press of Kansas. 2005. ISBN 978-0-7006-1624-4

Citino, Robert Michael. *Quest for Decisive Victory: From Stalemate to Blitzkrieg in Europe, 1899–1940*, Modern War Studies. Lawrence: University Press of Kansas. 2002.

ISBN 0-7006-1176-2

Churchill, Winston S. *The Second World War: Their Finest Hour (Volume 2)*. Houghton Mifflin Company, Cambridge, 1949.

Durand, Yves. *La Captivite, Histoire des prisonniers de guerre francais 1939–1945*, Paris, 1981. Best available study of French prisoners of war in German captivity.

Corum, James. 'The Luftwaffe's Army Support Doctrine, 1918-1941' in *The Journal of Military History*, Vol. 59, No. 1 (Jan. 1995), pp. 53–76

Corum, James. *The Roots of Blitzkrieg: Hans von Seeckt and German Military Reform*. Modern War Studies. Lawrence: University Press of Kansas. 1992. ISBN 0-7006-0541-X.

Corum, James. *The Luftwaffe: Creating the Operational Air War, 1918-1940*. Lawrence: University Press of Kansas. 1997. ISBN 978-0-7006-0836-2

Dear, Ian and Foot, M. *The Oxford Companion to World War II*. Oxford Oxfordshire: Oxford University Press. 2001. ISBN 0-19-860446-7

DiNardo R. L. and Bay, Austin. 'Horse-Drawn Transport in the German Army'. *Journal of Contemporary History*, Vol. 23, No. 1 (Jan. 1988), pp. 129–142

Dunstan, Simon. *Fort Eben Emael: The Key to Hitler's victory in the West*. Osprey, Oxford. 2005. ISBN 1-84176-821-9

Durand, Yves. *La Captivité : 1939-1945*. F.N.C.P.G.-C.A.T.M.; Édition : 2e éd. 1981. ASIN: B0014L7NF4

Ellis, John. *The World War II Data Book*, Aurum Press Ltd. 1993. ISBN 978-1-85410-254-6

Ellis, Major L.F. (2004) [1st. pub. HMSO 1954]. Butler, J.R.M. ed. *The War in France and Flanders 1939–1940*. History of the Second World War United Kingdom Military Series. Naval & Military Press. ISBN 978-1-84574-056-6.

Evans, Martin Marix. *The Fall of France: Act of Daring*. Osprey Publishing, Oxford. 2000. ISBN 1-85532-969-7

Frans De Waal. *Peacemaking Among Primates*, Harvard University Press. 1990. ISBN 0-674-65921-X

French, David. *Raising Churchill's army: the British Army and the war against Germany, 1919-1945*. Oxford University Press. 2001. ISBN 978-0-19-924630-4

Frieser, Karl-Heinz. *Blitzkrieg-Legende: Der Westfeldzug 1940, Operationen des Zweiten Weltkrieges*. München: R. Oldenbourg. 1995. ISBN 3-486-56124-3.

Frieser, Karl-Heinz. *The Blitzkrieg Legend*. Naval Institute Press. 2005. ISBN 978-1-59114-294-2

Gardner, W.J.R. *The evacuation from Dunkirk: Operation Dynamo, 26 May-4 June 1940*. Routledge, London. 2000. ISBN 978-0-7146-8150-4

Gunsburg, Jeffrey A., 'The Battle of the Belgian Plain, 12–14 May 1940: The First Great Tank Battle', *The Journal of Military History*, Vol. 56, No. 2. (April 1992), pp. 207–244

Gunsburg, Jeffery A. 'The Battle of Gembloux, 14–15 May 1940: The "Blitzkrieg" Checked'. *The Journal of Military History*, Vol. 64, No. 1 (Jan. 2000), pp. 97–140

Harman, Nicholas. *Dunkirk; the necessary myth*. London: Hodder and Stoughton. 1980. ISBN 0-340-24299-X.

Harvey, D. *The French Armee de l'Air in May–June 1940: A Failure of Conception*. Journal of Contemporary History, Vol. 25, No. 4 (Oct. 1990), pp. 447–465

Healy, Mark, Ed. Prigent, John &. *Panzerwaffe: The Campaigns in the West 1940*. Vol. 1. London. Ian Allan Publishing. 2008 ISBN 978-0-7110-3240-8

Hooton, E.R.. *Luftwaffe at War; Blitzkrieg in the West*. London: Chervron/Ian Allen. 2007 ISBN 978-1-85780-272-6.

Hooton, E.R. *Phoenix Triumphant: The Rise and Rise of the Luftwaffe*. Brockhampton Press, London. 1994. ISBN 1-86019-964-X

Jackson, Robert. *Air War Over France, 1939-1940*. Ian

Allen, London. 1974. ISBN 0-7110-0510-9

Jackson, Julian T.. *The Fall of France: The Nazi Invasion of 1940*. Oxford UP, 2003.

Jowett, Philip S. *The Italian Army 1940-45 (1): Europe 1940-1943*. Osprey, Oxford - New York, 2000 ISBN 978-1-85532-864-8

Kershaw, Ian. *Fateful Choices: Ten Decisions That Changed the World, 1940–1941*. London: Penguin Books, 2008. ISBN 978-0-14-101418-0

Krause, M. and Phillips, C. *Historical Perspectives of Operational Art*. Center of Military History Publication. 2006. ISBN 978-0-16-072564-7

de La Gorce, Paul-Marie. *L'aventure coloniale de la France - L'Empire écartelé, 1936-1946*, Denoël. 1988. ISBN 978-2-207-23520-1

Longden, Sean. *Dunkirk: The Men They Left Behind*. Constable Puplishing. 2008. ISBN 978-1-84529-520-2

Maier, Klaus and Falla,P.S. *Germany and the Second World War: Volume 2: Germany's Initial Conquests in Europe*. Oxford University Press. 1991. ISBN 0-19-822885-6

Mansoor, Peter R. 'The Second Battle of Sedan, May 1940', in the *Military Review*. Number 68 (June 1988), pp. 64–75

Melvin, Mungo. *Manstein: Hitler's Most Controversial General* W&N Publishing. 2010. ISBN 978-0-297-84561-4

Murray, Williamson. *Strategy for Defeat: The Luftwaffe 1933–1945*. United States Government Printing. ISBN 978-1-4294-9235-5

Neave, Airey. *The Flames of Calais: A Soldiers Battle 1940*. Pen & Sword, 2003. ISBN 978-0-85052-997-5

Romanych, M. and Rupp, M. *Maginot Line 1940: Battles on the French Frontier*. Osprey, Oxford. 2010. ISBN 978-1-84603-499-2

Sheppard, Alan. *France, 1940: Blitzkrieg in the West*. Osprey, Oxford. 1990. ISBN 978-0-85045-958-6

Shirer, William L.. *The Rise and Fall of the Third Reich: A History of Nazi Germany*. Simon and Schuster. 1990. ISBN 0-671-72868-7

Sebag-Montefiore, Hugh. *Dunkirk: Fight to the Last Man*. New York: Viking. 2006. ISBN 978-0-670-91082-3

Strawson, John. *Hitler as Military Commander*. Pen & Sword Military Classics.2003 ISBN 978-0-85052-956-2

Taylor, A.J.P. and Mayer, S.L., eds. *A History Of World War Two*. London: Octopus Books, 1974. ISBN 0-7064-0399-1.

Weal, John. *Junkers Ju 87* Stukageschwader *1937–41. Oxford: Osprey. 1997. ISBN 1-85532-636-1.*

Weinberg, Gerhard. *A World at Arms: A Global History of World War II*. Cambridge University Press, 1994. ISBN 978-0-521-44317-3

Martin, J. and Martin, P. *Ils étaient là: l'armée de l'Air septembre 39 – juin 40*. Aero-Editions, 2001. ISBN 2-9514567-2-7.

Winchester, Charles. *Ostfront : Hitler's war on Russia 1941–45*. Osprey Publishing. 1998. ISBN 978-1-84176-066-7

Tooze, Adam. *The Wages of Destruction: The Making and Breaking of the Nazi Economy*. Allen Lane, 2006. ISBN 0-7139-9566-1.

Bjorge, Gary J. *Decisiveness: The German Thrust to the English Channel, May 1940*, found in Combined Arms in Battle Since 1939. Fort Leavenworth: United States Army Command and General Staff College, 1992.

Cohen, Eliot A. and John Gooch. *Military Misfortunes: The Anatomy of Failures in* War. New York: Anchor Books, 2003.

Citino, Robert M. *Blitzkrieg to Desert Storm: The Evolution of Operational Warfare.* Kansas: University of Kansas Press, 2004

Quest for Decisive Victory: From Stalemate to Blitzkrieg in Europe, 1890-   1940. Kansas: University of Kansas

Press, 2002.

The Path to Blitzkrieg: Doctrine and Training in the Germany Army, 1920-1939.

Colorado: Lynne Rienner Publisher, Inc., 1999.

Cooper, Matthew. *The German Army 1933-1945.* Michigan: Scarborough House, 1978.

Corum, James R. *The Roots of Blitzkrieg.* Kansas: University of Kansas Press, 1992.

Deighton, Len. *Blitzkrieg: From the Rise of Hitler to the fall of Denmark.* New Jersey: Castle

Books, 2000.

Department of the Army. Field Manuel 3-0, *Operations.* Washington D.C.: U.S.

Government Printing Office, June 2001.

Dörner, Dietrich. *The Logic of Failure.* New York: Metropolitan Books, 1996.

Frieser, Karl Heinz. *Blitzkrieg-Legende: Der Westfeldzug 1940; Band 2.* München. Germany: R. Oldenburg Verlag, 1995.

Fuller, J.F.C. *Memoirs of an Unconvential Soldier,* found in *The Art of War in World History* California: University of California Press, 1994.

Geyer, Michael. *Makers of Modern Strategy from Machiavelli to the Nuclear Age.* New Jersey: Princeton University Press, 1986.

Guderian, Heinz, translated by Constantine Fitzgibbon. *Panzer Leader.* New York: Da Capo

Press, 1996.

Translated by Christopher Duffy, *Achtung Panzer! The Development of Tank Warfare.* London: Cassell Military Paperback, 1992, first published in 1937.

Habek, Mary R. *Storm of Steel: The Development of Armor Doctrine in Germany and the Soviet* Union, 1919-1939. London: Cornell University Press, 2003.

Hart, Basil Liddell. *Strategy the Indirect Approach*, found in *The Art of War in World History*

California: University of California Press, 1994.

Joint Staff. Joint Publication 1-02, *Department of Defense Dictionary of Military and Associated* Terms. Washington D.C.: U.S.Government Printing Office, November 2004.

Kesselring, Albert. *The Memoirs of Field Marshal Kesselring*. California: Presidio Press, 1989.

Lewis, Samuel J. H100 Student Text, *Reflections on German Military Reform*. Fort Leavenworth: CGSOC, U.S. Army Command and General Staff College, 2003.

Liddell Hart, Basil. *Strategy the Indirect Approach*, found in *The Art of War in World History* California: University of California Press, 1994

Menning, Bruce M. "Operational Art's Origins." *Military Review* (September-October 1997).

Mosier, John. *The Blitzkrieg Myth*. New York: Harper Collins Publisher, 2003.

Murray, Williamson. *The Dynamics of Military Revolution, 1300-2050*. Cambridge: Cambridge University Press, 2001.

Naveh, Shimon. *In Pursuit of Military Excellence: The Evolution of Operational Theory*. London: Frank Cass Publishers, 1997.

Overy, Richard. *Why the Allies Won*. New York: W.W. Norton & Company, Inc., 1995.

Posen, Barry. *The Sources of Military Doctrine: France, Britain, and Germany between the* World Wars. London: Cornell University Press, 1984.

Schneider, James R. *Vulcan's Anvil: The American Civil War and the Foundation of Operational* Art Theoretical Paper No. Four. Fort Leavenworth: United States Army Command and General Staff College, 10 May 2004.

Senge, Peter M. *The Fifth Discipline: The Art & Practice of The Learning Organization*. New York: Doubleday, 1990.

Shepard, Alan. *France 1940 Blitzkrieg in the West*. Oxford: Osprey Publishing, 1990.

Showalter, Dennis. *Blitzkrieg*. Boston: Houghton Miffen Company. Available from http://college.hmco.com/history/readerscomp/mil/html/mh_006400_blitzkrieg.htm. Internet. Accessed 13 November 2004

Trevor Roper, Hugh. *Hitler's War Directives 1939-1945.* Edinburgh, U.K.: Berlin Limited, 2004.

Van Creveld, Martin. *Fighting Power: German Military Performance 1914-1945.* Washington D.C.: Department of Defense, Office of Net Assessment, 1980.

Von Seeckt, Hans. *Gedanken eines Soldaten.* Leipzig: K.F. Koehler, 1935.

Wallach, Jehuda L. *The Dogma of the Battle of Annihilation: The Theories of Clausewitz and* Schlieffen and Their Impact on the German Conduct of Two World Wars. Connecticut: Greenwood Press, 1986.

Index

Printed in Great Britain
by Amazon